D0265582

LIFEWAYS

WORKING WITH FAMILY QUESTIONS

A PARENT'S ANTHOLOGY
edited by
Gudrun Davy & Bons Voors

Hawthorn Press

ii

Published by Hawthorn Press, 1 Berkeley Villas, Lower Street, Stroud
Gloucestershire GL15 2HU U.K.

Copyright©1983 by the individual contributors. All rights reserved.

Cover design by Charmaine Williamson

Illustrations by Gertraud Hofmann

Typesetting and layout by Soluna, Rosewood House, Lydbrook, Glos.

Printing by Wynstones Press, Brookthorpe, Gloucester.

This book is sold subject to the condition that it shall not, by way of
trade or otherwise, be lent, re-sold, hired out or otherwise circulated
without the publisher's and authors' prior consent in any form or
binding or cover other than that in which it is published and without a
similar condition including this condition being imposed on the subsequent purchase

ACKNOWLEDGEMENTS

The editors warmly thank all those who asked questions concerning
children, relationships and family life, questions which gave the impetus
for this book.

Valuable editorial assistance was given by Charles Davy, John Davy,
Signe Schaefer, Rudi Lissau, Alice Fuller, Joyce Gee and Pat Jones.
Sonja M. Bonnekamp and Barbara Lovas deserve special thanks for
their translating work, as do Margret Meyerkort, Signe Schaefer, Margli
Matthews, Stephanie Westphal and Martin Large for their encoura-
gement.

The kind permission of the editors of *Child & Man* is acknowledged for
the reproducing of 'Answering Childrens' Questions' by A.C. Harwood.

Finally, we would like to thank our children, for even though some of
us could only write in the small hours when our children were asleep,
without what they gave us when they were awake—none of our contributions would be real.

CONTENTS

iv

INTRODUCTION

John Davy

This book is about children, about family life, about being a parent. But most of all it is about freedom.

For generations, innumerable parents must have felt tensions between personal fulfilment and domestic obligation. But the search for liberaration is now more conscious and more acute—so much so that many women have come to regard their homes as prisons and their children as gaolers. Modern families are no longer naturally sustained by tradition or by their surroundings. Rapid change has set religion afloat, and leaves many personal relationships in tatters. It is possible to be very liberated and absolutely adrift. Or outwardly dutiful and inwardly in despair. But however we rearrange our lives, we are still limited by our surroundings, and more significantly, by ourselves, by those unfreedoms which we carry around with us; they are our real gaolers: disinterest habit, discouragement, suffocate the soul. But wonder, reverence, creativity can open doors. In the end, therefore, liberation must be an inner question, a search for a quality of life which cannot be arranged, but only discovered and lived.

Although freedom is our own problem and our own search, we don't have to seek it alone. This book has its origins among women (and men) who met over a period of years in a Sussex village. Some were permanent residents, others were students, or wives or husbands of students, at Emerson College nearby. The College is a training centre based on the work of Rudolf Steiner, and its courses include training for teaching in Waldorf schools (see Appendix p312)But there were many who were also seeking a renewing spirit for family life, a new vision of the tasks of mothers and fathers, a new eye for the meaning of 'home' which is not a gaol but a place which supports all those involved, children and adults, in the 'life ways'.

It was a cosmopolitan group, constantly changing. As time went on, there were new trends. Fathers, for example, were showing a growing interest; some were taking the main responsibility for children while mothers studied. Those who departed for distant regions would write letters with new questions and contributions. And many expressed the wish for written material with which to work further, and to share with others. This book is the result.

Only two of the original group were left to assemble contributions from their many friends. And they have often wondered, during the three years or so that it took, what other readers would make of it all. Would they see a disguised attempt to revitalise old fashioned motherhood? Were they simply sowing flowers over the worn out carpet of household drudgery, leaving the same well-trodden stuff underneath? Were they simply offering a way of anaesthetising drudgery by making pretty things?

Readers must judge for themselves. But at the heart of the book is a question of inner rather than outer change. Why do we clean a room? To remove the dirt—or so that something new can happen in it? Why do we educate children? So that they will fulfill our expectations—or so that they may surprise us with their own unique contributions to life? The contributions to this book have been written out of a conviction that for the awakened eye, the home may become not a dungeon but a universe; children and parents can become teachers of one another; and a year can lose its routine and become filled with wonder and mystery, a never-ending journey of adventure and discovery.

The search for liberation is at heart our search for a path. It means finding a way to go. In England, birthday children are wished "many happy returns of the day". We don't mean that they should return to exactly the same place next year. When the day returns, they will have changed—and so should we. Within the family, adults are offered by life itself a demanding but progressive schooling, a path towards freedom, if they accept the challenge and go to work.

While all the contributors have drawn some inspiration from the work of Rudolf Steiner, and from the way of "anthroposophy" which he inaugurated, they write most essentially out of their own questions and experiences. Perhaps this is above all a book of questions. Suppose that life in the family is recognised as a path, a school for the soul and the spirit? What does this bring for the individual parent, for the family, for the child?

In real life, questions often bring more light than answers. So the authors offer this book to all friends, known and unknown, who find themselves on the same quest, and who are also asking those illuminating questions which give light for the path.

I. PARENT'S WAYS

1. THE MEANING OF BEING A MOTHER TODAY

Margli Matthews

After my first child was born I was surprised to find that I was a mother. The role felt so new and strange that it was hard to wear comfortably at first. I was in a new country, newly married, with a new baby, and I suddenly felt very young and immature. Whenever I went out, which did not seem often in those early days, my attention was constantly drawn to mothers. I watched them with their children as though they were of a different species and might reveal some secret to me if I observed long enough. On the surface all mothers appeared to me to be large, mature and capable. I, on the other hand, still felt very much a girl, uncertain and as small as the baby I held in my arms. Yet, at the same time, I knew from the reality of the baby I rocked, nursed and sang to, from the deep sense of wonder, love and responsibility that she awoke in me, that I was certainly and gladly a mother. But the change in my life from one day to the next was so dramatic, so overwhelming, I did not feel particularly prepared for this enormous task that I had chosen. Although there were many aspects of mothering that I entered more or less instinctively, I experienced my new role primarily as a challenge to wake up, to bring consciousness into the nurturing of my child, into the creation of a home and family. From the beginning I did not feel that motherhood was something that I could do 'naturally' or unconsciously. I knew that it would require both outer attention and inner work.

Through my day-to-day mothering over the past fourteen years I have been growing up along with my children. Observing and caring for their development, providing a space for them to unfold, living in all the smallest and grandest aspects of being their mother—these have been my tasks and my blessings. These years have been my deepest schooling. Gradually I have worn my role as a mother more easily, with ever greater confidence and familiarity. Yet sometimes I still find that I stand outside and watch myself being a mother and feel amazed. Perhaps one of the reasons for this detachment is that as much as I know that I am a mother, I know too, that I am not completely and only a mother. I am also an independent, developing personality with tasks and interests that reach beyond the sphere of family.

When I was a new wife and mother much of my previous feeling of independence and many of my outside interests and possibilities seemed to vanish in the face of my awakening, all-consuming interest in baby, husband and home. This caused me to agonize over my identity. I wondered where *I* was in my new life and what my past education, experiences and interests had to do with my life now. Was I anything apart from my new roles of wife and mother? Could I develop myself and still care for my children and have meaningful relationships with others? I questioned my new roles and struggled against the rigid definitions and expectations that seemed inextricably bound to them. I explored my rights and, more tentatively, my responsibilities. I wanted to find a way to bring together my sense of myself as an individual, independent of roles and sex, and my sense of myself as a modern woman trying to bring a new consciousness and meaning into the traditional roles of wife and mother. And so I came to ask myself: Why am I, a woman in this situation, experiencing these particular things now? What are my possibilities, my limitations and my responsibilities? What can I develop and learn and give as a woman that I would be unable to do if I were a man?

Because I felt motherhood was a task that required my free and conscious attention and effort, I wanted to know what it meant to be a *mother*. I wanted to understand the significance of what I and millions of other women all over the world were doing. This seemed especially important to me because, although I knew deep within me that what I was doing was important, it was not always easy to remember this, living in a society which tends to value only what can be seen, measured or possessed—the functional, tangible products of the intellect and the will. When my babies were small and I was submerged in all the unseen and immeasurable details of care and survival that make up such a time, if someone asked me the inevitable "what do you do?" I often found it hard to answer with "I am a mother, I stay home and look after my children." I felt it would have been much more significant and interesting to claim to be a home decorator, or a nanny, or an ant watcher.

Ironically and unfortunately, the new and strongly growing Women's Movement at that time seemed to make it even more difficult to be proud of one's work as a mother. Some faces of the Movement underlined the dominant view that motherhood was a bind, a drudge, uncreative, unchallenging, unreal. This seemed to suggest that liberation meant liberation from the home and child-rearing. A few women even suggested that we would only truly be free when scientific and technological advances made wombs unnecessary and obsolete. Freedom, self-development, creativity and recognition were acquired in 'real' jobs in the 'real' outside world—not in the kitchen with the children. A mother, though valuable as a consumer, was somehow otherwise seen as a non-contributing, non-person, blamed for much but not expected to need any help, support or encouragement.

I stress this rather bleak view not because I was 'won over' but because it provided me with a challenge to come to a true re-evaluation of motherhood, as something important for myself and for society at large. I suspect that behind my early compulsion to observe mothers lived a desire to discover the inspiration out of which mothers can work. I wanted to find a way that, as a modern woman, I could relate to and uncover within myself the deep, collective archetype of the Mother.

Central to this search has been my involvement over the last ten years in an on-going women's group. Originally we met together to share our questions and experiences as women today, with the aim of gaining a deeper understanding of ourselves and the times in which we live. We wanted to explore the significance of the Woman's Movement for ourselves and for society as a whole. In sharing and seeking to understand our experiences, we have tried to build modern imaginations of what it means to be a woman today and of those feminine qualities that need a conscious re-awakening and development in all human beings. At the same time, we have tried to support and encourage each other's individual development, intentions and tasks. Personally I know that whatever steps I have taken towards understanding my many questions about my own identity, life and work have been with the help of this group. The others have encouraged me in my effort to value and balance the various sides of my self and my life, to bring together and harmonize my need to care for my children and my home with my need to develop a work outside the home. In all our listening and sharing, my questions became clearer. They became less like problems and more like windows to my further development and my awakening awareness and understanding of others. I also realized of course, that my questions were not uniquely mine at all but that they were shared by many women struggling for self-awareness and meaning today. [1]

This group gradually evolved into what we eventually named *Ariadne* and what has now become an international working group of women, researching questions of women's consciousness today out of the spiritual perspective offered by Anthroposophy. Founding and developing this work with others has been a central task in my life, going hand in hand with my task as a mother, and out of it many other interests and activities in my life have developed. Although it has taken me outside the home it has also fed back into my family life, into my relationship to my children and husband, as a continuing source of inspiration and support.

For me, and perhaps for all of us who were involved with building up the work of Adriadne, this work has been at once a personal quest, an inner work and an outer work. In many respects the kind of work Ariadne has been involved in also lies at the heart of the initiative which brought this book into being, in that it arises out of our desire to become more aware in whatever we do, so that we can bring new meaning and harmony into our lives. In order to appreciate the various possibilities open to us today and to make responsible choices, we seek to know our intentions *as women* and how they relate to our particular destinies and to the age in which we live.

The Growth of the Woman's Movement

The renewed growth of the Women's Movement over the last twenty years has stimulated this questioning of roles and rights and values and has encouraged women in their striving for greater consciousness and wholeness. Although a full consideration of the history of the Women's Movement is outside the scope of this book. I would like to indicate briefly one way of understanding why the question of the sexes has become such a central concern in our times.

It is possible to trace the historical development of the feminine and masculine principles and to observe how the inter-weaving of this polarity has been a vital force in the evolution of human consciousness and thus in the development of culture and society. By 'feminine' and 'masculine' I do not mean exclusive attributes of women or men, but archetypal, cosmic principles at work in all human beings (regardless of sex), in all human relationships and in society at large. It is increasingly important to be aware of this, as we strive, as women and men, to recognize and appreciate our differences and yet reach beyond separation to a true unity, to find an inner point of balance through which we can bring the feminine and masculine qualities within our soul into harmony.

Simply defined, the gesture of the feminine pole is that of a round, a circle, a vessel, encompassing, receiving, nurturing, unifying, transforming. The feminine is open and vulnerable, intuitive and rhythmic; it trusts,accepts,waits and listens; it is connected with the life of feeling and the imagination. Feminine consciousness is a diffuse, peripheral consciousness.

The gesture of the masculine pole, on the other hand, is that of an arrow, a straight line, directing, penetrating, pursuing, perceiving. It distinguishes, defines, separates, analyzes and individualizes. It is precise, clear, firm, focused, objective and rational and is connected with the intellect and the will.

Both qualities can be either positive or negative. The feminine waits, but it can also vegetate; it can protect, or smother; it may be soft, or weak, diffuse, or vague, flexible, or scatty. Masculine clarity can be cold, and directness can demolish. Separation can isolate, individuality can become selfish and objectivity may turn intellectual and abstract. The negative in either pole arises if it moves too far out of balance, for both qualities are equally valuable and ultimately dependent upon each other for any true creativity. Although the feminine and masculine are often out of balance and can even be seen as conflicting forces in individuals and throughout much of history, they move finally towards a dynamic and creative union.

Largely through recent feminist research, drawing on mythological and psychological studies and as well as archeological findings, we have become aware that our present 'patriarchal' society, and more masculine consciousness has not always been the norm. Many different studies available today suggest, in fact, that in ancient, pre-historical times (during the childhood of humanity), matriarchal societies flourished in many parts of the world. These societies were connected with the worship of the all-protecting, all-nourishing Great Mother Goddess. Motherhood was the primary mystery and the hearth was the centre of social life. In these societies women had great influence and leadership over the development of culture; they had an important role in the refinement and education of the soul-life of humanity. During this time, human beings shared what could be called a more feminine consciousness, a diffuse, dream-like, imaginative consciousness; they experienced an intimacy and union with each other, nature and the cosmos. They were naturally open to the instreaming of divine wisdom and to the spirit working within and behind the things of the world. [2]

Gradually however, as fact superseded myth and the letter replaced the picture, the masculine principle began to grow in strength and challenged the power of the feminine. In many ways the development and ascendency of the masculine force is the story of humanity waking up. As people felt themselves increasingly cut off from a divine wisdom, they became more aware of the material, sense perceptible world around them. They developed a more earthly consciousness and an interest in working with, understanding and controlling their surroundings. They experienced a growing separation from each other and from nature, but they gained a sense of their own personalities and individualities. The Greco-Roman era has been identified by many as the time when the forces of feminine and masculine battled each other for power. The older, unconscious feminine principle of wisdom and union, and the lingering and now destructive power of the matriarchy, finally yielded to the growing force of the patriarchy and to the further development of the masculine principle of individuality, discrimination and knowledge of the material world. At this time, the foundations for our modern knowledge were laid. Philosophy and science were developed. Individual thought and perception began to be valued and the powers of revelation and clairvoyance began to dim. People experienced a new clarity and independence of thought, a new objectivity and detachment; they felt the stirring of the forces of the human intellect and will.

Since that time the masculine principle has grown in power and influence. It has led us toward separation and further away from any sense of divine order. But, at the same time, it has made possible free scientific enquiry, the development of science and technology and an ever expanding knowledge and control of the material world. It has been essential to the progress towards individual consciousness, freedom, and responsibility. However, in recent history, this positive masculine development has gradually become extreme and one-sided and the feminine principle has been forgotten, undervalued and generally pushed out of life. The masculine on its own has taken us further and further into materialization, mechanization and abstraction, thereby removing us from a living connection to the spirit. Throughout this development not only the feminine but women, too, were confined and oppressed. They lost much of their previous validity and influence and many of their former roles were either taken over by men and made professional (e.g. cooks, potters, doctors) or they became ever more mechanized and impersonal.

The oppression and suffering of women and the growing restrictions on their possibilities for self-fulfillment, eventually became intolerable for many individuals. Stimulated by the French Revolution and the numerous champions of the rights and freedom of humanity at the end of the 18th century, a new consciousness began to emerge in women. What at first were somewhat isolated voices of protest, gathered strength and momentum during the 19th century and reached a kind of climax at the beginning of the 20th century in the Suffragettes' battle for women's right to vote.

The struggles of the Women's Movement in this century have taken many forms. However, underlying all the various demands for economic, political and social rights, has been a call for the recognition of the consciousness, dignity, freedom and humanity of all women. Primarily, women have demanded the right to decide what they can or cannot do according to the individual abilities, not according to what men or society dictate that they should do. The Women's Movement has therefore been a tremendous impulse for the self-realization and freedom of both women and men alike, for the recognition of the individually emerging spirit in all human beings.

Much of the effort of the renewed Women's Movement in our time has been directed towards raising women's consciousness with the aim of achieving greater rights and freedoms in the economic and political spheres. Clearly, although there is still much to be done, many restrictions and barriers have been lifted and many new possibilities of fulfillment have arisen. Women today work in a variety of fields and professions. With modern methods of birth control and greater understanding of our bodies, we are more able to choose whether or not to become mothers. We have learned to grapple with the physical, material world and have developed our intellects and wills; we can achieve and provide, control and guide. Men too have begun to free themselves from their more traditonal roles as chief breadwinners, worldly achievers and providers. Some have begun to stand back and look at their values and express their willingness to give up their single-minded pursuit of fame and worldly success for more meaningful work and a life style that will allow them to express their inner, imaginative, feeling life. They say that they do not want a heart attack for lack of a heart life. The rise in unemployment may be contributing to this shift, in that many men now question the meaning and definition of work and the sense of putting all their life into a job which offers no security and which often removes them from their families and relationships. There are a growing number of stories today of men refusing advancement, or giving up lucrative jobs, in order to cultivate their inner life and to spend more time with their wives and children. As they nurture and care for their children, men begin to uncover their capacity for co-operation, for love, intimacy and tenderness. They discover the value of household in the wider universe, and the myth of the non-nurturing male begins to break down.

Thus the questioning of roles and the experimentation with different life styles fostered by the Women's Movement have created an atmosphere of flexibility. We begin to free ourselves from rigid definitions and narrow stereotyped expectations of the other sex. We want to define ourselves more fully and to develop in ourselves what we previously left to the other sex to develop. This, of course, is not easy and our relationships often become strained. Our more traditional expectations of the other sex lie deep within us and do not easily disappear just because we become conscious of them. We sometimes flounder without the security of our old roles to fall back on. But in our efforts we have increased the range and quality of our experiences. We have become inwardly more mobile. This, then, makes possible new kinds of relationships—not relationships of mutual dependency, where we expect a certain behaviour from the other and look to them to express the unexpressed sides of ourselves, but relationships of mutual development, where we are committed to the growth and wholeness of the other, where we help each other to come to balance. As we drop our roles the possibility of real relationship begins, of one self to another. We gradually come to see that neither biology nor the role of a particular moment define the totality of our individual existence—that our true humanity lies beyond the realm of the sexes.

Behind all the questioning and shifting of roles, there lives in many individuals a deep intention for balance and a search for new warmth and wholeness in themselves and for all society. Although I believe that this impulse lies at the heart of the Women's Movement today, I also know that it has not always been immediately apparent. In the struggle for political and economic recognition, some parts of the Movement have seemed to undermine a true renewal of the feminine and of women's values that would work to bring a greater balance into our lives. At times its voice has been harsh and strident, encouraging women to take on the hard, head-orientated, materialistic values that at a deeper level it opposes, fostering the very polarization and isolation that it would remedy. By extolling competition, aggression, and material gain, and by valuing skills that lead to money, status and power, the Movement has tended to encourage women to take on a masculine cloak and call this emancipation. Besides perpetuating the very system it wants to overcome and chaining us further in the name of freedom, this stance has alienated many women and in some has called forth a defensive reaction, thereby fostering a retreat from consciousness into a kind of sentimental and instinctive femininity.

Neither extreme can truly represent what seeks to emerge today from all of our questions and strivings. It is not just an imbalance of power between women and men that we find today. It is not only that women have been kept out of life but that the feminine qualities in all of us have been sleeping. Political and economic injustices must be attended to but also our overly materialistic ways of thinking and being need to be softened and warmed. This does not mean going back to the old, unconscious feminine values of the past. Rather we can begin to use what we have gained in clarity and objectivity to awaken, strengthen and develop a now conscious feminine force that we will be able to bring together with the masculine and so create a new living consciousness that can unite us all.

This deep impulse for balance that works behind the push for women's consciousness has come more to the surface in recent years. This is, I think, a result of the growing readiness on the part of many women to consider the spiritual as well as the political dimensions of their questions, and to come to a new understanding of their own values and the contributions that they can make to society through a renewal of the feminine. I feel certain that the earlier, more aggressive and strident phase of the Movement was justifiable and necessary in order to break down old attitudes and create new possibilities, and I am grateful to all the women who fought so hard. But the lifting of the limits has not made us free. We must ask not only about our rights but also about our responsibilities. [3]

The Meaning of Being a Woman Today

For many of us it is confusing to be a woman today. We are taught and encouraged to be clear and focused and independent, yet we are still expected to be soft, nurturing and self-sacrificing. We are criticized for letting our feelings get in the way but we are still supposed to be warm and sensitive. Living in such a masculine orientated society means that often our more feminine qualities have been covered over by a masculine development and influence. I do not in any way want to suggest that we should deny the masculine in us, or the time in history in which we live. Yet there is a danger that in our fight for equality we may blur the real differences between women and men and, taking on men's values as our own, reject very essential qualities in ourselves.

So we need to understand in what ways women and men are the same and in what ways they are different, and how equality does not necessarily lead to sameness. We may ask: How can we express our individualities without denying our different bodies and psychologies and the different life experiences we meet as women or as men?

Personally I have found Rudolf Steiner's conception of the individual human ego and of karma and reincarnation helpful in finding a bridge between my sense of myself as an individual, independent of sex, and my sense of myself as a modern woman. Steiner speaks of the polarity of female-male as an outer, external polarity, a kind of garment that we put on for our earthly life but that does not define our inner essence, or individuality of being. Our ego, our individual spirit, stands above the level of the sexes and can work to bring into balance the feminine and masculine qualities that weave in the soul life in both women and men. Of course the garment we wear, the male or female body that we have, obviously affects how the spirit shines through, how we express ourselves, the kinds of experiences we meet and how we meet them. The experience of being a woman or of being a man is different and offers us different possibilities for growth. Because we need both possibilities in our evolution towards wholeness and the expression of our full humanity, Steiner speaks of how the individual ego, reincarnating throughout earthly evolution, chooses sometimes to be a woman and sometimes to be a man in order to balance and develop what was previously left unbalanced and undeveloped. [4]

This is then a picture of the human being as a spiritual being, evolving through time, bringing feminine and masculine wisdom into harmony. It expresses a deep intention for balance. Such a picture can free us, allowing us to live into our differences without feeling trapped or limited by them. But it also suggests that we can ask ourselves about our specific intentions as women. Why am I a woman? What experiences do I meet *because* I am a woman and what can I learn and develop from these experiences? What can I bring to my life and relationships and work because I am a woman? What do I want to balance that I have previously left unbalanced.

For many women there is an additional question:- Why am I a woman *now* at this time of women's consciousness? Many women share a sense of common purpose and destiny, a feeling of a collective responsibility and they ask: What do we need to do together as women? What can we help to bring to birth in the life of our times? What responsibility do we have towards the future evolution of culture and humanity?

Although the feminine principle works in both women and men, through their biological nature women embody the feminine; they have a direct and primary relationship to feminine qualities, however unknown or covered over they may be. And it is this feminine, slumbering within all human beings yet somehow more easily tapped by women, that is needed in order to bring a new, life-giving, healing force into our lives.

A woman's physical body generally is soft, round and flexible. It is open, receptive, and vulnerable, with a remarkable capacity for transformation. In pregnancy a woman's whole body becomes a veil, the developing child hidden within. A relationship can be found between female qualities and the gesture of the ear; the ovum resembles a primitive ear, travelling through darkness, waiting and listening for the right moment for conception. Thus, at a fundamental level, a woman has the qualities of the ear (listening, balancing, receiving) built into her physical body.

A woman has the capacity to receive and bear a child, to maintain and nurture, to provide a space for another developing being within herself. Because of this she can have an understanding of maturation and ripening, a readiness to wait and be patient, a capacity to give herself to the unfolding mystery and to carry an imagination of who will be born, trusting in that vision. A woman who is pregnant makes her whole being into a vessel, receptive to the secrets of the cosmos and to the creative powers of the universe. I received a picture of this once when I was pregnant when I awoke with the words humming in my head: "The sun in all its glory drops its long tentacles down upon you."

Whether or not a woman becomes a mother to her own physical child, I think she carries these mothering capacities deep within her, ready to unfold in the many situations which call for nurturing, healing energies today. Also, through her menstrual cycle a woman has such a direct relationship to rhythm that she cannot easily forget the real relation of the human being to the rhythms of nature and the cosmos. The menstrual cycle is an internalised lunar rhythm, no longer directly dependent on the changes of the moon but still bearing a relationship to those changes (the average length of the menstrual cycle is 29.5 days, the same as the period from new moon to new moon).

Recently, however, this basic, life-sustaining rhythm has been disturbed (perhaps reflecting the general a-rhythmic nature of our society). More women experience difficulties with their cycle—many even have trouble getting their periods. Over 40% of women seek help for premenstrual tension, irritability and depression. Also, girls tend to get their periods at a younger age so that primary schools must now provide facilities for them. Furthermore, the birth control pill in its various forms prevents ovulation and thus interrupts the body's natural rhythm. In recent years there have even been experiments conducted to see whether women would prefer fewer periods (perhaps 4 a year) or none at all. In fact the whole modern tendency is to regard menstruation as a curse and a nuisance, to be gladly dispensed with if this were safe. But so far it is clearly not safe. The many side effects of the contraceptive pill are now well known and they range from seemingly 'minor' problems like headaches, nausea and depression to the obviously serious ones like circulatory disease, sterility and possibly, cancer. [5]

These findings, together with the growing desire of many women to understand better and to respect their bodies, have made more of us question whether the pill is the answer to our need for contraception. This in turn has led to studies which look at the deeper meaning of menstruation [6]. These studies suggest that we are very lucky to have periods, for they keep us in touch with our bodies and with the earth. They point to menstruation as an unexplored female resource, essential to our minds as well as to our bodies, important in establishing a relationship to our deepest self. Through our cycle we remember the principles of all things, even the feminine and masculine principles; in the course of a month many women recognize a time of a more diffuse consciousness, of heightened receptivity, openess and waiting, and another time of tension, self-assertiveness, clarity and quickness. Thus, to be in tune with our cycle opens us toward our potential wholeness.

I have found a book called *"Embryology and World Evolution"* [7] by Dr Karl Konig especially relevant to the recent attempt to understand the significance of the menstrual cycle. In a series of lectures, Konig considers this cycle in relationship to the biblical story of creation and to Rudolf Steiner's ideas about cosmic and earthly evolution. He suggests that in the movement and preparation of the egg for

Errata: Lifeways - page 15

The second and third paragraphs on page 15 should read as follows:-

Thus, through her physical body, through her menstrual cycle and her capacity to conceive and bear a child, a woman maintains a close relationship to the cosmos.   Because she is less bound than a man by all that is earthly and physical, and because of her soft, pliable, form, she has a potential for a warmth and flexibility of thinking, an openness for the unusual, and a closer relationship to inspirational wisdom.   She has always been the muse to whom men, who are more closely tied to matter and further removed from their origins, appeal for wisdom.   Women have an inclination for the psychic and emotional;   they live strongly in their inner life of feeling, imagination and fantasy, and are deeply touched by events and experiences.   They often show an inner courage and resilience and a power of sacrifice and devotion in love which parallels the more physical strength and courage of men.   Women are interested in the intimate and personal details of life, in relationships, in individual people (who they are as well as what they do, what they don't say as well as what they do say).   Traditionally, women have been the guardians of the hearth and of all matters that concern the heart.

Of course these qualities apply to women in general, not necessarily to specific individuals.   But if as women we all have some relationship to these collective and archetypal qualities, however individualized or veiled they may be, perhaps they can help us to reach an understanding of what we are doing and what we can learn in a woman's body.   Can we discover not only the limitations of our biology and psychology but also the creative possibilities and responsibilities that are part of our heritage as women?

Continued on p.16

fertilization there takes place a recapitulation of the coming into being of the earth and humanity. So, a kind of cosmic memory, a record of past earth history is stored within our monthly cycle. To tamper with this rhythm may be to cut off a recollection in the physical sphere of the working of the spirit, just at a time when we are in great need of refinding a strong and clear relationship to the spirit.

All of this does not mean that we should not use birth control, but perhaps our efforts should be directed to finding methods which do not cut us off from this basic boldily rhythm. Many people today are looking for, and experimenting with, 'natural' methods of birth control. For example, in recent years there has been interest shown and research into astrological birth control, which works with the rhythms of ovulation and confirms our connection to the cosmos. It can also help people wanting to conceive as well as those wanting to prevent conception. However, like all natural birth control methods (actually all birth control) it is not 100% foolproof! Its difficult but nevertheless positive aspect is that it requires the consciousness and responsibility of both of the partners. [8]

Thus, through her physical body, through her menstrual cycle and her capacity to conceive and bear a child, a woman maintains a close relationship to the cosmos. Because she is less bound than a man by what they don't say as well as what they do say). Traditionally, women have been the guardians of the hearth and of all matters that concern the heart.

Of course these qualities apply to women in general, not necessarily to specific individuals. But if, as women we all have some relationship to these collective and archetypal qualities, however individualized or veiled they may be, perhaps they can help us to reach an understanding of what we are doing and what we can learn in a woman's all that is earthly and physical, and because of her soft, pliable form, she has a potential for a warmth and flexibility of thinking, an openess for the unusual and a closer relationship to inspirational wisdom. She has always been the muse to whom men, who are more closely tied to matter and further removed from their origins, appeal for wisdom. Many women have an inclination for the psychic and emotional; they live strongly in their inner life of feeling, imagination and fantasy, and are deeply touched by events and experiences. They often show an inner courage and resilience and a power of sacrifice and devotion in love which parallels the more physical strength and courage of men. Women are interested in the intimate and personal details of life, in relationships, in individual people (who they are as well as what they do, body. Can we discover not only the limitations of our biology and psychology but also the creative possibilities and responsibilities that are part of our heritage as women?

Obviously this again is an individual question which will be met in different ways. Many women today seem to be born with strongly developed wills and intellects. Self-conscious, self-contained and articulate, they have an ability for swift, logical argument, for clarity and analysis. Some women have expressed their suprise at finding themselves in a woman's body, a seemingly strange and unfamiliar garment, and have wondered what to do with it. Some have said that for them, being a woman was connected with their need to learn to bring rhythm and flow into their tendency to rush and hurry, to bring a grace to their gestures and a gentleness and softness to what could sometimes be an overly critical, demolishing directness. Personally, know that my family has called forth a love from me that I did not know was there. Having to respond to the needs of my children, I have experienced moments of tenderness, and self-lessness which have helped to draw me out of my self-absorption and have given me an inkling of what true selfless love might be.

Of course, as I have already mentioned, the continuing development and expression of the masculine in women is also important. It is essential to our struggle to become fuller, less one-sided human beings. Just as some women feel a need to work hard to express their more feminine qualities, many also experience the need to bring clarity to their more instinctive way of working. They want to awaken from their more dreamy state to find purpose and direction. Probably all of us need to bring more form to our feeling life and to strengthen our powers of objectivity and detachment so as to work effectively with our caring, nurturing qualities where they are most needed. We all need to work in such a way that the service we offer comes freely and surely out of a strong centre.

Finding A New Conception Of Life

This brings me again to the question of a collective task and responsibility for women today. What do we intend to awaken in this time of the advent of women? Many of the most urgent questions today are closely linked to women's consciousness and to women's role as nurturer and sustainer of life. Daily we read in the news about conception and contraception, abortion, test-tube fertilization, genetic engineering, heart transplants, death and dying and euthunasia.

Behind all of these and the many other urgent issues that we face today live the questions: What is the meaning of life? What is our conception of life today? How do we conceive the human being? What are the images that we live by?

A sense for the wholeness and purpose, meaning and mystery of life is often submerged by a literal, objective view of the world and of human possibilities. The advancement of science and technology appears to be our highest goal while conscience and imagination seem so impossssibly frail and underdeveloped. We have pushed back the mysteries of life and death and made them legal, rational concerns, and in the process we have lost a living imagination of what a human being is. Severed from the rhythms of nature and the cosmos, from the renewing and sustaining energy of the spirit, it is often hard for us to conceive that we are more than our physical bodies. We are tempted to believe that we are very elaborate computers, machines with replaceable parts to be programmed at will, and that the world too is finally just the bones and mechanics that we have reduced it to.

Both women and men often feel apologetic and embarrassed about their softer, caring, nurturing sides. We are all proud of our ability to articulate and initiate but are less sure of our imaginative life. We often ask: "Is that true or did you imagine it?" as though the imagination were not real. We are interested in behaviour but ashamed of feeling. Preoccupied with self, caught in excessive competition, manipulation and exploitation, we become locked in our separateness, and so it becomes harder for us to understand each other and to form lasting relationships. A growing number of people express their wish to remain single, unencumbered and uninvolved, for without the complexity and commitment of relationship, they feel they can be independent, productive and successful. Yet that which appears to bring freedom may only further isolation and imprisonment.

It is not hard to recognize a crisis of caring in our society. Our heart life is undernourished and underdeveloped; we have forgotten how to love, care for, and heal one another. This situation seems to be intensified as increasing numbers of women go out to work. As women move out of the home and drop their traditional roles, who will pick them up? Who will attend to the numerous small but essential details of caring that make up the fabric of life? Who will weave this network that, though unacknowledged and unseen, is so essential to the health and continuity of our human community?

Some of the many details that make up this network and that have been traditionally attended to by women at home are: bringing flowers into a room; writing to distant and otherwise forgotten relations; sending birthday cards; talking over a problem with a neighbour; helping the ill, the aged, the handicapped; relieving the loneliness of someone by a talk over coffee; making costumes for school plays; celebrating festivals; making a day memorable in a child's life. The list is as endless as life itself and encompasses life. Our survival depends upon these details of caring, they ground us in life and warm and ensoul that life. Yet less and less people find time to do them. We are in danger of creating a loveless society. There is a tremendous pressure on women to have careers and to acquire material possessions while the state takes over responsibility for our children. But who cares for them? Do we want them to pay the price of our freedom? What do we really want to do with our liberty? Can we balance our need to express and develop ourselves with our need to care for others?

There is a fine but important line between asking this question and pushing women back into the home to sleep again in their old roles. We cannot drop the thread of consciousness once we have picked it up. We can no longer rest unconsciously in our old roles or depend on an outer authority or morality, however unsure we are or however difficult it may be to come to the truth in any situation. Our questions are not easy and there are no longer any wise men to tell us the answers. We can only rely on our individual powers of understanding and judgement and find the courage to act from such understanding with conviction and compassion. But to do this we need a thinking that can lead us to wholeness. We need to stretch ourselves to develop new ways of thinking and looking, to find new ways to live and new values to live by, so that our social life comes to be valued along with our political and economic life. We need to learn to come to understanding with our heart as well as our head, with our feeling as well as our thinking, with our imagination as well as our intellect. Bringing a more peripheral awareness of the whole of life together with our knowledge of the parts, we can embrace each moment with both care and consciousness.

I see this challenge to develop a new enlivened consciousness primarily as a responsibility towards the heart and the whole middle realm of feeling. I do not mean this in any easy or sentimental way. Rather, we need to *consciously* awaken and work with the heart so that it can become a creative social force, stimulating in us a capacity for compassion and service, for love and self-lessness. To do this is to work towards what Rudolf Steiner refers to as heart consciousness, or heart thinking. It is the joining of our head wisdom with our heart, and the building of a bridge between what we think and what we can do so that we can act and think and feel out of our full humanity. [9] Then our hearts will begin to listen and respond to the real questions of our times. Obviously this is a task for both women and men alike. However, if traditionally women have been open to the heart's prompting, if we do have a deep innate connection with much that concerns the heart—with rhythm, healing, nurturing, with the life of feeling and the imagination—then perhaps we are called upon to act as midwives for this new consciousness which is wanting to be born in all of humanity today. We can make a space for its conception and hold a vision for its future unfolding; we can care for and tend its development. Uncovering and working consciously with our capacities, we can begin to revitalize the feeling life around us and bring a new warmth and flexibility to the thinking life of our time. If we truly attend to and foster our connections to each other, nature and the cosmos, we will be able to encourage an awakening towards the spirit in all human beings.

There are many places today where we can glimpse the beginning of such efforts. As women have gone out to work in increasing numbers and have gained a certain amount of influence, some changes have been noticed in the ways of working and in the atmosphere of the work place. Many women now bring into their work a new consciousness of being women and a growing confidence in their own deeper values. In order not to deny these values, women have begun to say "no" to old ways of doing things and to find the courage to do things their way. A woman journalist once wrote of how she gradually realized that her most successful articles were based on an attitude of superiority and ridicule where she had used and manipulated people in order to get a good story. She found that she could no longer continue this pattern but wanted to work in such a way as to be open to the "divinity" in the other person. [10]

It is now widely recognized that where women work the atmosphere is better and the relationships between workers are more caring and harmonious. Women allow for more honesty and directness; they say what they think and do not so easily play games. In tougher jobs such as the police force they appear to have a calming, civilising influence and can sometimes ease a potentially violent situation. Women can bring flexibility into their work situations; they demonstrate an ability to carry the whole without getting fixed in one particular aspect and they seem to be able to loosen or dissolve rigid hierarchical working orders.[11]

This is a very general indication of how women are beginning to bring something new into their working life. However, I would like to look now in more detail at the opportunities available to women who choose to be mothers to work towards the development of a more balanced, enlivened consciousness, not only for themselves and for their families, but for the whole of society.

Motherhood As A Conscious Work

In spite of the large scale rejection of the importance of motherhood and family life in recent years, more women begin to say that they choose to have children and to stay at home, to channel their energies into the care of their families. I am not speaking of a retreat from liberation, those voices of reaction and fear that would make it a moral necessity for women to stay at home. Rather, I mean a choice to be a mother which is born out of the consciousness and personhood that women have won in this century. Some women begin to call for the recognition of motherhood as a profession that needs education, training, research and support. There is a growing awareness that parenthood and the creation of a warm, imaginative family life is a vital role that makes possible the growth and self-realization of others and can also become a path of self-development (see Welmoed Tomenstras' article on women's support groups and also Gudrun Davy's article *The Journey of a Mother*).

As more women *choose* to be active mothers, they make possible a re-evaluation of the hearth, of home and child care in society as a whole. I think we are all becoming more aware that what flows from this centre, which forms us and grounds us, ultimately affects our economy, the entire earth and the universe; that household is not separate from the "real" world but is part of that world. The words "ecology" and "economy" point to this truth. "Ecology" is derived from the Greek oikos, which means house. Thus ecology is house logos, house wisdom. Similarly, "economy" (coming from *nomos,* to manage) means house management. So, contained in these words is the idea that the earth is our home and as we care for our particular, seemingly small, household we also nurture the earth and build a healthy human economy. The smallest circles need as much attention as the largest. All spheres flow into one another, and the way we care for one affects the health of the other. The following nursery rhyme captures this idea. It speaks about a true ecology, one where household is not cut off from the outside but embraces the kingdom and is in fact the key to the kingdom.

Key of the Kingdom

This is the key of the kingdom:
In that kingdom is a city,
In that city is a town,
In that town there is a street,
In that street there winds a lane
In that lane there is a yard,
In that yard there is a house,
In that house there waits a room,
In that room there is a bed,
On that bed there is a basket
A basket of flowers.

Flowers in the basket,
Basket on the bed,
Bed in the chamber,
Chamber in the house,
House in the weedy yard,
Yard in the winding lane,
Lane in the broad street,
Street in the high town,
Town in the city,
City in the kingdom:
This is the key of the kingdom.

My children have always particularly loved this rhyme for its repetition, its inward and outward movement, and because, I think, they
have instinctively known its truth as I have come to know it—that even
the smallest details of home life flow out like radiating circles into our
other interests, relationships and tasks. As householders, we often
become abstracted from the details of our lives and from a real
communion with the house. But, when done as conscious work, creating
a new home presents us with continual opportunities to become more
sensitive and careful of our surroundings. In the past, women's traditional
tasks—such as cooking, tending the fire, sewing, gathering and preparing
medicines—were sacred because it was recognized that within such

tasks there took place a transformation of the material into the spiritual. Today we need to build a bridge between spirit and matter, to refind the spirit in the things of this world. I believe that one way we can begin is by cultivating a reverence for the small, by attending to the many details of life that we are in danger of neglecting. We can try to permeate our daily, life-sustaining tasks with the purpose and meaning they have—whether we are making bread or a salad, arranging flowers, packing a lunch for a child going off to school, or sweeping in the corners of the room. We can approach such tasks negatively or frantically without care; we may find them dull, mechanical activities; or, we may get lost in the details. But I also know that a real attention to detail can be a process of transformation, creating spaces for the spirit to enter. In cleaning a room, if we are present in what we are doing, we soon realize that we are not only clearing a physical space for physical bodies but also for the human soul and spirit, for the human imagination

When I am very busy with the work that draws me outside the home, I often forget this. I ignore all the details and tear through my household in full gear with my focused consciousness, ticking off the "jobs" on my list as soon as they are done, caught in my busyness. This works for a while, but if it goes on too long I am aware that the house begins to feel empty and hollow. Sometimes the children respond by becoming ill. So I have to put away my work, slow down and catch my breath. Although when I plan my days and weeks I dread such an "interference", I am usually grateful for these times. They give me a chance to remember my priorities and to bring more balance and rhythm into my life again. They remind me to take more care in whatever I do, to pay attention to the dying flowers and the corners of the room. Most important, they are special times which allow me to nurture and deepen my relationship with the child who is ill. Once when one of my daughters was ill and I was re-making and freshening her bed, smoothing her covers, fluffing up her pillow, so that she would be more comfortable, she said to me: "Mummy, you are a real artist at making a bed." I laughed, but quietly, because, although it was funny, what she said was also serious and she meant it seriously as a compliment. Surely this points to one of our tasks today—to work creatively with matter so that every detail of our lives reveals its true relation to the spirit—to make every activity artistic, to make a home and world where what is truly human in us can be revealed.

Working With Rhythm

In order to create a healthy family life today we also need to renew our sense of rhythm (see also: John Davy, *Living In Real Time*, p136). In the past, before the industrial revolution, people lived in close connection to the earth and to the changing seasons; their lives were held and sustained by the rhythms of nature, of the moon and the stars. All human activities took place in relation to the activities of the natural world and the cosmos. People experienced a connection between the changing seasons and their own alternating states of consciousness. Their days were marked by a succession of regular activities which gave each day its uniqueness. This is expressed in the following traditional verse:

> Wash on Monday,
> Iron on Tuesday,
> Mend on Wednesday,
> Churn on Thursday,
> Clean on Friday,
> Bake on Saturday,
> Rest on Sunday.

This regular ordering of their days, and also of their months and years, gave people energy; they gained a sense of security and continuity and a feeling for their place in the flow of time. Today we have freed ourselves from external dependency on the rhythms of nature. To a large extent, we have lost a real living sense of time. We no longer experience a connection with nature and the cosmos. We cannot, nor would we want to return to the past. To impose the old rhythms would be artificial and would deny our freedom. Yet our very a-rhythmic life results in stress and tension—cutting us off from each other and any sense of the wholeness of our days, weeks and years. Traditional festivals are now often fixed on seemingly convenient days without any attention to natural or cosmic rhythms. In most places in America it is possible to shop seven days a week, at any time of day or night. One advertisement I saw claimed that at 2.00 a.m. in New York you could play tennis, get a hair cut or go swimming. Life in England is more "difficult" for people used to the complexity and pace of modern urban existence, for in many places shops shut at 5.30 p.m. and often for up to two days a week!

Many of us hurry through life, always out of breath, always cramming too many things into any one moment, so that we are unable to digest what we have done or be open to what speaks to us in the present. Our sleep, rest, work and play life is erratic. Many people no longer sit together at meal times but quickly grab something to eat when they feel like it, out of the freezer or a tin if possible (see Bons Voors: *Family Mealtimes,* p154). In order to "save time" they may also read the newspaper, watch television or talk on the telephone while they eat. Weekends too are often a rush, filled with all the things (meetings, frenzied exercise, etc.) that could not be squeezed into the week. Children do not have bed times but fall asleep wherever and whenever they can, while many adults have to take sleeping pills to get to sleep. Electricity blurs our days and nights, central heating and all the other trappings of modern life tend to cut us off from seasonal changes so that we no longer feel the correspondence between our lives and the activity in nature. Such things as cars, airplanes, television and video games, instill the rhythms of the machine into our waking and sleeping life.

Having a family made me conscious for the first time of how necessary rhythm is if we are to bring health and sanity to our lives and warmth and security to our children. It is modern to be impulsive and chaotic but after a while we all suffer. The growing interest in ecology today reflects our awareness of the need to nurture and care for the wholeness of the earth and to pay attention to the changing seasons and the movement of the stars. Similarly, in order to renew the values of the hearth and to build a new family culture, we need to imbue our lives with rhythm—not now instinctively or through an imposed rigidity but out of our full individuality. We need to consciously regulate our lives by working with both form and chaos, slowly finding the balance between them. Then, through a conscious relationship to rhythm, rather than an external dependency on it, we can bring new meaning and direction to our lives; we can awaken to mystery and ceremony and to the creative interaction between work and play, spontaneity and form, movement and rest. Bringing rhythm into our lives draws us out of our isolation and strengthens our bonds with others, with the earth and with the universe.

Because as women we have a strong experience of rhythm from within, through our menstrual cycles, perhaps we have an opportunity and challenge to work consciously with rhythm—to discover meaning in our monthly rhythms and also to develop a new awareness of the many rhythms in and around us. We may then begin to awaken in ourselves and others a sense of the spiritual dimension of our lives.

For me, working with rhythm has much to do with developing a sense for ritual and ceremony, creating celebrations which raise the daily and momentary to the universal and eternal. Our children will help us in this work. They want all of life, every moment to be a festival, alive with meaning. Dead animals need to be mourned and buried. A new broom or duster, a mended doll or the discovery of a lost thimble can be just as much the stimulus for a party as someone's birthday. Meal times, bedtimes, arrivals and departures, weekends, the beginning and the end of holidays, as well as the traditional festivals, are all potential celebrations.

If we listen, children ask us to help them to discover balance and meaning. They ask: What are we doing today? When are we going shopping? What will we do on Monday? What comes after Wednesday? What happens after Christmas? Is my birthday in the summer? They want to know the order of the events in their lives—changes in the seasons, whose birthday comes after whose, how mother and father were little once and how they grew up. They love the expectation and anticipation of what is to come. One of my children always began to ask the day after her birthday how many days, weeks, months there were before her next birthday and what all the special days were in between.

Our children and the reality of family life may then call us to work more consciously for an enlivened sense of time. Of course how we actually take up this task is an individual question, and in this book there are many different suggestions of ways to work with rhythm in our lives. Perhaps we can try to pay more attention to the changing moments of our days, the transition moments, and mark them. Meal times are such moments. Can we make them festivals of meeting and gathering—by putting flowers and a candle on the table, by saying a grace, by giving them a real beginning and ending, by creating a space for relaxed conversation, by making a nutritious and visually appealing meal? Can we also find ways that are right for us as individuals and for our family, to greet the day and welcome the evening?

In our family our evening rituals are very special and warmly antici-pated by all of us. First, after supper, I tell or read the children a story before taking them to bed; then we say prayers and, when they were younger, we would sing a song or two. Now, as they are older, I find that we have some of our deepest talks at this time, in the quiet of the evenings, when the bustle of the day is over. Both girls have also had particular rituals, regular "things" to be said before I turn out the light and they cross the threshold into sleep. For my ten year old this evening rhythm is still important and expected. However, for the last few years, it has no longer been appropriate for my eldest daughter, now 13. When she started to go to bed later and no longer wanted to be read to, I found that we were in between rhythms and had to work to find new, creative ways to be with each other in that space before bedtime.

Another moment in the day that I have found important to be aware of is the time when the children come home from school. I have tried not just to carry on with whatever I am doing but to stop, prepare a drink and a snack for us all, and make a space in which we can all share what our day has been like.

Mothers can also try to develop a sense for the different moods and qualities of each day of the week and work with them (see Gudrun Davy's article *The Journey of a Mother*) by planning special activities for the different days—perhaps a particularly nice meal on Friday as the end of the working week, a special breakfast or a family outing on Sunday, or going to the library with father on Saturday. Of course everyone must find their own way in this. I once decided that every Sunday we would have pancakes for breakfast because it seemed to work so well for another family that I knew. However, for us it was a disaster—it just felt like we were eating and washing dishes all day—so we soon had to give it up to save our Sundays. But out of this attempt we evolved the custom of having pancakes or waffles for breakfast on festivals and birthdays. My children have helped to awaken my understanding of the wholeness of a week. When my daughter first went to school she asked every morning for months, "What day is today? What lessons do I have today? What are we doing when I get home?" Every morning I would tell her. So she learned the days of the week through the expectation of certain regular activities that she could count on.

The months of the year also have their own particular qualities which are also connected with the shifting seasons and the yearly festivals that mark those changes. A good calendar often captures the tone of each month through different pictures. Children can learn to know the progression of the months and seasons by making their own calendars with a special drawing for each month. January might be a snowy picture with snowdrops bravely flowering, children sledging or a birthday party if there is a birthday in the family in January. February may be a Valentine's Day picture with hearts and nesting birds; April can be bright and busy with Easter eggs, rabbits, daffodils, primroses, and new leaves on bare branches; August may suggest sea and sunshine and a campsite; October, pumpkins, apples and witches; December, the festivals of Advent and Christmas. My children have often made such calendars, for themselves or as gifts for others. Sometimes they ask: "What happens in June or May or September"? and I try to remember with them as many happenings as we can. Then their imaginations are fired and they can carry on.

In the past, the yearly festivals—Michaelmas, Advent, Christmas, Easter, Whitsun, Midsummer and others—marked like conscious pauses the passage of the year and the changing seasons—the life, death and rebirth of nature. However, for most of us today, these festivals have been forgotten or have been cast aside as meaningless or "religious". Or they have become habits, materialistic events which are hollow and empty of real meaning and feeling. If we celebrate them at all, we often do not know why we do so—we no longer sense the correspondence between our lives and these eternal rhythms. Yet they speak, if we would listen, to our essential humanity. As we refind a relation to these moments in the year, we re-kindle our imaginations and open ourselves again to the universe and to the spirit working there.

As mothers, we have a unique opportunity to work consciously with the rhythm of the year through the festivals that chart its movement. Children love these events and eagerly anticipate them, knowing the mystery and meaning at work within and behind them. Having to respond to their expectations and questions, can stimulate us to deepen our own experience of the festivals by bringing new content and understanding to what may have become old and dead forms. Our children's desire that the year be one grand round of praise and thanksgiving may also lead us to explore and find a relation to festivals which may be new to us, such as Michaelmas or Whitsun; their changing needs, questions and attitudes as they grow up ensure that we constantly expand our understanding and find new ways to celebrate the festivals for what may be appropriate for a four-year old may not work for a twelve-year old.

The whole experience of a festival is enriched if the inner and outer preparation as well as the celebration itself is shared in a group or community. Creating the festivals with my family over the years, I have become convinced of their deep and lasting value for all of us. They confirm the family's connection to the wider sphere of community, earth and universe and foster our human relationships; they awaken our imaginations and bring meaning, purpose, devotion and wonder into our lives; they teach us to breathe. I know that, whatever challenges the children may meet in the future, these celebrations will remain a true light for them, giving them certainty and trust in the enduring human spirit and the courage to meet whatever they have come to meet.

The Challenge To Love

Just as rhythm is an experience of the middle realm of the heart, so there is another experience that flows from the heart and that has always been a priority for women: love. Many women speak of waking up to their capacity for a truly nourishing, encompassing, sustaining maternal love through having children. The purity of love that a mother can sometimes feel for her children is a gift that allows us to imagine what a true selfless love may be. Of course, it is not always easy to get up in the night to feed or comfort a crying baby who may scream for hours on end; we may feel far from selfless at three o'clock in the morning; we may be exhausted, worried or even resentful of the disturbance to our sleep. Yet in having to put aside our own needs and to respond to what our baby wants, we may sometimes experience something of what it is to offer love as a free gift, expecting nothing in return.

However, although at first a woman may feel a strong "instinctive" love for her child, gradually this love must become a more conscious carrying of the evolving being of the child, free from possessiveness and exclusiveness, if it is not to smother what it once nurtured. We meet this challenge more and more as our children grow up. Can we leave them free to make their own friends and values and mistakes? We need to become friends and guides to our children, offering them love and protection but leaving them free to go their own way, trusting in their destiny and carrying true pictures in our hearts of their unfolding capacities and tasks.

Of course it is not just with our children but with all of our relationships that we need to practice and encourage this activity of love today. Within as well as outside their own families, people often feel like strangers and find it difficult to understand others or to feel understood. Increasingly the bonds that united people in the past are falling away and we need to replace this more instinctive love for one another, which was often based on ties of blood, with a more conscious carrying of one individual by another. Perhaps an image of such an attempt which arises out of the breakdown of all the old forms and ways of relationship, is the new kind of extended family that has appeared as a result of the high rate of divorce and remarriage. Often a couple which marries for the second time brings together many unrelated people who must try to build a shared life together. They may be hurt, confused and in need of love. To create a warm and caring family life in this situation, to embrace and love one's step-daughter as one's daughter, requires a high degree of sensitivity, clarity and commitment.

Of course we do not necessarily need to be mothers in order to develop our nourishing, maternal qualities, and it is certainly not hard to see the need for these qualities in all realms of our society. Just as more women today can and do choose to have children, many also decide to channel their energies into another task to which they feel more suited. But the capacity for maternal love still lives within them and, if they tap its source, it can work as a creative force in whatever they do.

The Search For Balance

Balance is another aspect of the healing realm of the heart that calls for our conscious attention today. The Women's Movement has encouraged both women and men to strive for inner balance, to bring together both feminine and masculine qualities within through the strength of their individual ego. Because society has accepted and fostered the expression of the masculine in women, while our strong and more feminine connection to reality cannot easily be denied, perhaps women especially have both the challenge and the opportunity to work consciously for a new and living balance, whatever their task or situation in life. There are many women today beginning to live this balance. An example that comes to mind at the moment is the women at Greenham Common, protesting against the nuclear arms build up by weaving pictures of life around the military base, by joining hands in responsibility and love for life and embracing the serpent. Their protest is at once peaceful and imaginative and clear, firm and courageous.

One place where most women struggle to find and express their balance is in their work in the family. Many women today want to find a way to have and care for their children and still maintain their other interests, develop a career and participate actively in the outer affairs of the world. They seek to find a way to do both together, to combine a creativity in the home with a creativity in the world. The growing number of single parent families and the current financial situation means that many women have no choice but to make this struggle. But I think that the reasons for women's search to bring together their interest in home and the world go beyond the economic. Our growing consciousness of self and the world means that many of us not only feel a calling and responsibility towards our children and families but also towards the larger world. And this need to find a wider role in the work of the world, and to bring something new into this work, is important not only for our individual development but also for the destiny and evolution of culture and society.

In the early years when the children are small and in need of so much care and attention I wonder how it may be possible to fruitfully integrate homemaking with a career, nurturing with achieving. Also, of course, when children "grow up" and go to school and seem to become more independent their needs for nurturing, protection and guidance change but do not diminish. On afternoons which are filled with taking to and collecting from various ever-increasing after-school activities, helping with music practice and homework (which often stretches me to my limits, and beyond) listening to and smoothing over the trials and troubles of the day, I wonder what I did with all my free time when the children were small. Even teenagers who may often seem burdened by your presence, want you to be around for long, impromptu hours of discussion when they feel like it. The time and space you can offer at these times is vital if the relationship is to stay open and develop. Still, as children grow up mothers do become freer to take up other interests and tasks and it is important to the children's own growth that they experience the growth and expansion of their parents and realize that they have interests and commitments outside the family.

Even though it may be impossible to find a healthy, all satisfying balance between work in the home and some outside work in the years when the children are small, I also know that many women cannot help but attempt it. From the efforts and sacrifices of a growing number of women to care for their families, maintain their interest in school and community activities and take on some outside work, new social situations may begin to arise. As women demand jobs near their homes and working hours that allow for family life, the 40-hour week and the relationship of work to home and community comes into question. Job sharing between husbands and wives may become more possible, and more employers now offer longer maternity and paternity leaves. Experiments allowing more flexible time-schedules have resulted in increased production and improved morale among workers, as well as a reduction in absenteeism, lateness and job turnover. Working women, calling on fathers and other members of the community to help with the children and the various domestic tasks, have also created new supporting networks that may begin to help overcome the loneliness so many people experience, and the separation of young from old, work from home, men from women.

It is hard to say how the rise in unemployment will affect these possibilities. It could give reign to the forces of reaction in society that would insist that women stay home and leave all the available jobs for men, thereby reversing any changes that have been brought about by the increased number of working women. But it could also underline and support the need for a re-evaluation of the relation of work to family and community life.

Many fathers today are willing and wanting to participate in the care of the children and the home. Where there are two parents or adults concerned with the upbringing of the children and the creation of family life there are many different possible arrangements that can be and are being made to ensure that there is harmony in the home life as well as the opportunity for each partner to fulfill the different sides of her or his self. The traditional situation where the mother stays home and the father goes out to work may be reversed—the father may choose to stay home and the mother may choose to go out to work. Or, both partners may work part time and share the child care. Another common arrangement is that the father works full time but arranges his work in such a way that he can *actively* support the mother's part-time work.

However, whatever the arrangement, essential to any and all situations is the need for consciousness on the part of the adults concerned—consciousness and honesty about their own needs, their balances and imbalances, about their partner's needs and about the needs of the children and the life of the family. A sharing schedule may sound good in theory but the couple may be passing each other by, without ever having time to see each other; the household may function but may grow to feel like an empty shell; and the children may be looked after but still miss the real substance of care. Harmony cannot develop in such conditions. So, it is important in sharing and experimenting with roles to try to be clear, and to be flexible enough to change the situation and one's ideas if necessary. It is also helpful to remember that *there is time* to do the many different things we want to do and feel called to do. We do not need to do everything at once. If we can try to awaken to what is needed and asked of us in the present and can respond with love for what we do, we may then be ready to meet the next moment and be open to what comes towards us out of the future.

So I want to stress that if we choose to stay home we do not stop developing; we do not always need to go out to work to balance ourselves. Anyone who has been a "full-time" parent knows that all one's qualities and capacities are constantly called upon. To be able to cook a meal, talk to a friend, help an older child with homework and soothe a crying baby, remaining present for all, is not easy; yet some such combination of activities is usually part of a typical day at home. In order to meet such situations creatively we must continually balance efficiency, precision, order and form with flexibility, spontaneity, chaos and openness. One moment we may need to be tender and affectionate caring and nurturing with our children, the next second, firm and controlling. It requires tremendous inner strength and calm to be able to move quickly from playing a game with a child, to taking responsibility for discipline, to judging a quarrel that has flared up, to protecting and comforting a hurt child. Every day, every moment with children our fullest resources are called upon. If we can respond and bring consciousness into what we do, we will grow with our children.

I think that if we choose to be mothers today we are aware that we can only truly serve if our centre is strong—if we pay attention to our inner development (see Gudrun Davy's article *The Journey Of A Mother*). We want to find ways within the daily caring and serving to take time and space for ourselves. This is not always easy. If we have a moment we are often too exhausted to do anything except read the newspaper. Also, children sometimes uncannily sense the slightest movement of their mother's energy away from them and are often quick to respond by demanding, crying, or just wanting to take part in whatever she is doing. I knew a woman artist who tried to paint at night when the children were asleep—but they always woke up. When my daughter was small if I wanted to read a book I went into the kitchen. Because I was there, I think she assumed that I was about "useful" business and so would continue to play happily where she was. But if I wanted to take a few quiet moments alone in my room, or even if I tried to talk to a friend, she seemed to sense something exciting going on that she did not want to miss. However, although finding and taking time and space for ourselves is often difficult when our children are small, the attempt is important—not only for us but also for our children, for our inner work can only enrich and strengthen the quality of the nurturing that we can offer. Women can help each other in this aspect of their work by *actively* encouraging each other's inner development. This is one of the important possibilities of women's support groups; I have experienced such support and I know what a gift it has been in my life.

Service and self development are not separate; they belong together and enhance each other. As women, caring for our children and creating spaces in which others find themselves, we have the opportunity to understand and experience this. Through all the daily challenges of living together with others and attempting to love, through the moments of crisis and failure as well as moments of joy and satisfaction, our capacity to give and to grow, to love and to find an inner balance, expands. No one would pretend that this work and the continual need to move beyond ourselves and our limits is easy or painless. But where people strive within the "small" circle of their household for balance, for love, for a new quality of heart-filled consciousness, their efforts radiate far beyond their intimate circle bringing healing forces and a renewed imagination of the human being into the life of our times.

2.   THE JOURNEY OF A MOTHER

Gudrun Davy

When I look back on twenty years of being a mother and living with four exuberant children as they grew up, I ask myself what the journey meant. What have I learned? What help did I get, and where did it come from? What obstacles did I meet, and how might I have done better?

Reflecting on these questions, I realise that my deepest support has come from the sense of being on a significant journey, a path I had chosen myself but one where my "gurus" were my own children. Whatever I have been for them, they have been as much and more for me. This conviction carried me along, and made it obviously senseless to try to get off the path when the going was rough—as it often was.

It gradually became clear to me that I was being offered a schooling from two directions. The first came from the changing needs of the children as they grew up. The challenge here was to open my eyes and see the depth and interest of what was right in front of me. I was being offered a task, a work, which I could reject as an enslavement, or recognise as a career of profound interest. I could take myself seriously in this career and see myself as a scholar in this new discipline of learning. This itself brought a sense of being on a new footing alongside my husband. We were both at work—he at his office and I at home. Why sitting in an office from nine to five should ever have been regarded as more of a real job than caring for another human being around the clock is baffling. Perhaps many more fathers feel this nowadays, and take a share when at home.

The second kind of schooling, which I had to seek out more consciously, was an inner practice, a set of meditative exercises for the days of the week. These gave me a basis for a rhythm of inner work to accompany my outer work. I will describe them later.

First, I will try to indicate how the developing work of being a mother, which comes naturally from life itself, can be recognised as an opportunity to develop and practise capacities which most people would recognise as desirable for all human beings. At the same time, it is only by struggling to find these capacities in oneself that one can bring to the children what they need.

It seems to me now that the journey has three main stages. The first, from birth until the children begin school, is like a voyage over water in a small boat. The second, until the children reach adolescence, is like a journey through a rich countryside of trees, rivers, forests, villages and cities. The last, when the children are teenagers, is a climb into high mountains, full of challenge and risk, but also of the excitement of entering a wider world.

Of course it is not as simple as this. There were times when I seemed to be struggling in water, on land and in the air at the same time. But perhaps my map, as it now looks to me in retrospect, can be of value to others seeking to get their bearings for their own journeys. So I will describe a few aspects of each phase, and the different kinds of schooling each bring.

Journey In A Small Boat

Already in pregnancy, women often realise they are embarking on a quite new journey, without any idea of what it will really bring. The past begins to dissolve as an unknown future announces itself. Physically, this often shows first in the face. Features become softer, and contours dissolve, as though immersed in a more watery moonlike realm. The inward changes often take us by surprise as well. I have often heard women say: "Nobody told me that I would suddenly lose all interest in study, would want to dream more, that my whole temperament would change." Familiar ground dissolves beneath the feet. Not many women can really imagine beforehand what it is really like to expect and then to live with a child. One woman who had been involved for years in responsible professional work, wrote to us while this book was in preparation, describing her astonishment at the sudden and total commitment demanded of her when the child arrived; neither the days nor the nights were any longer her own.

So with the baby's arrival, mothers find themselves as it were in a small boat, floating away from the familiar shore, totally involved in a new small world, almost alone. Husbands, friends, doctors, may sometimes wave across the water. Occasionally you may land temporarily—somebody looks after the child, you manage a holiday. You often look back on this time with amazement: How could I have put up with having so little time to myself, so little sleep? How was I able to go on and on? But in sailing the boat, you can gradually become a helmswoman. A new stamina and new inner capacities grow.

Nowadays, many women find themselves steering an erratic course between two extremes. The modern world offers technology—during pregnancy, at birth, during infancy, by way of labour-saving inventions to minimise "drudgery". There are disposable nappies, plastic underwear, convenience foods, electronic baby-minders. Mothers are tempted by brisk, no-nonsense advice that babies are quite tough, and don't need too much coddling. It is more important that mothers should enjoy themselves and "have a good time". The swing of the pendulum then carries many "New Age" mothers to an opposite extreme—births by candlelight, breastfeeding for several years, a conviction that the infant's instincts will show the way and that everything "natural" is desirable.

Perhaps the uniting theme for all the contributors to this book is their search for a middle way, not a grey compromise, but an *art* of mothering, of being a parent, of making a home. Art lies *between* nature and technology, and is where we can seek to discover ourselves and our children neither as animals nor as machines, but as truly human. It is in seeking to become artists in this sense that we can begin to recognise the value of the schooling which caring for children brings.

One of the first disciplines is to learn how to observe. And the gateway to this is wonder. A newborn baby in its cradle is an invitation to wonder: Who is this little being? From where? Promising what? When Rudolf Steiner spoke of the new-born child as "all sense-organ", all ear, all eye, the reality of what he meant begins to dawn for us when we observe with wonder. Then it is not too difficult to begin to see and feel the baby's openness, the receptivity to all that goes on around, deeper than at any time later in life when we have built so many defences, physical, emotional and intellectual.

As we become aware of this receptivity, we will begin to feel the meaning of another of Steiner's pointers to the fundamental nature of the first years. During their first seven years, he said, children learn, above all, by imitation. This imitation is not only physical. The wide eyes of little children drink in all that goes on around them. A sense for this profound openness and for the imitative nature of her baby can awaken the senses of the mother to her surroundings. Such an awakening can be the surest guide between the extremes described above. She may begin to realise a little of the baby's experience of the light, the sounds, the smells, and the textures of the world into which it is plunged as it leaves the womb. The full sun on a beach by the sea may be natural, but what is it like for a small infant? Taking a baby in a sling to a noisy adult party may be fun, but is it fun for the child? At the same time, the baby has not been born in order to be hidden away from the world. When awake, it is drinking in every sense impression, like a food woven of light. But we are responsible for the food which the baby's senses receive. Abstract precepts and commandments about child care are of little value compared to a capacity for sensitive observation.

People are often amazed at the sensitive ear a mother can develop for her baby's cries. They sound all the same to the bystander, but for the mother, one means hunger, another tiredness, a third a wet bottom, a fourth some real distress or fear. The baby's colour, movements, cries, postures, smells, warmth or cold, can all become a reliable language, pointing perhaps to a need for a better rhythm, a change of diet, or a need to call the doctor. Yet many of us have an upbringing which has never demanded any practice of careful observation, and all too often that upbringing has been without a sense of wonder. What a grace when a baby demands of us that we try to make good this loss!

As babies awaken wonder, so they can also offer an experience of peace. A small baby asleep in its cradle radiates a peace that is a blessing, bringing enrichment and joy to all who are open to it. My husband remembers a blessing which his mother used to say at his bedside when he was very small:

" And may the peace of God, which passeth all understanding,
    And which the world can neither give nor take away,
    Keep our hearts and minds in the knowledge of the love of God."

He remembers how the words were comforting and supportive, although he had no grasp of their meaning. The peace which radiates from a sleeping child is indeed something not quite of this world. But it can give something to us, to both parents, if our eyes and hearts are open to it.

A sense for this peace can make us feel that it is natural to create a suitable corner in the home for the cradle and perhaps to arrange a veil so that a gentle coloured light diffuses in. I shall never forget over-hearing our two older boys discussing the veil over the cradle of their newborn sister, and the eldest one saying: "Don't you remember, where she comes from, the light is pink" (not meaning the womb, but the Spiritual World).

But infancy is not only peace and joy. Babies get things like colic, and their distress turns the whole house upside down. When we first meet such situations, we seem to have no ground under our feet. I had a baby whose digestive system was thrown into acute disorder by some wonder drugs given for an infection (which may nevertheless have saved his life). During his first weeks, he would often cry for six hours at a stretch, and those cries were ones of real distress. My husband would hear them still ringing in his ears while riding in the underground train to work. At the time, I was so distraught and involved in the child's misery that I believed I would never smile again. (Incidentally, I now know that many colicky breastfed babies improve if their mothers give up eating dairy products for a time and bottlefed colicky babies improve if switched to goat's milk.)

In such experiences, there is a schooling too. A baby in turmoil has such power that it can rob us of sleep and drive distraught mothers into post-natal depressions, breakdowns and even baby-battering. Yet if we take the challenge seriously, as an opportunity to learn how to take the helm of our small boat, and to practise the art of keeping our balance and hanging on to our identity, then a new courage for the voyage may be found. Each mother's voyage is unique. But to understand its challenges is the first step in meeting them. And perhaps all will meet in one way or another these questions I have tried to describe—the need to re-form our identities, and to find a centre of balance and peace.

In the second year, life becomes very different. The child no longer spends much of the day in the cradle, but begins to sit up, stand up and take the first walking steps. Soon afterwards the first words begin to come.

At this time, there has to be added to observation a good deal of presence of mind. Active infants, given half a chance, are on the move for much of their waking life. I found myself resorting, for part of the day, to a traditional item of nursery technology, the playpen. There is a middle way here, too. Many modern parents see the playpen as a prison and give the infant the run of the house all day. I know one mother who used to get into the playpen herself, with her sewing, in order to get some work done while her child roamed the room!

Some children if let loose like this, begin to run wild and tyrannise their mothers and indeed the whole household. Their mothers in turn begin to feel increasingly distracted, scattered, on the verge of disintegration, as they have to attend hour after hour to the intense explorations of their restless child. I found the playpen a blessing for both of us for a limited part of the day, as part of the daily rhythm. I would start before they began to walk, or even crawl, and give them a basket of favourite toys. During this playpen playtime I could get on with other things, but for most of the time would try to be in the same room, or be visible to the child through an open door.

Far from being a cage, it seemed to me that my children experienced the pen as a safe and familiar haven, where they could unpack cotton reels, manipulate soft toys and rattles, and practise pulling themselves upright. We had to tie the pen to the sofa so that it didn't get pushed all round the room. As a stable space, it could then become perhaps a small house, a home, or a secure arena in which to practise a few first steps. I remember watching in amazement how one of our otherwise very restless little boys would settle down to a spell of standing practice, letting go of the pen first with one hand and then the other. The idea that he needed to spend all day exploring stairs and cupboards, pulling things off shelves, opening every box and tin, did not really come from him, but from adult ideas about not frustrating "nature". He seemed thoroughly contented and supported during that part of his daily rhythm he spent in the playpen, a time to collect himself—and a time for me to collect myself too. It makes all the difference, I believe, if the playpen time is part of a regular rhythm. If it is simply used erratically and arbitrarily for the mother's convenience, then indeed it can become a temporary prison, and will set active children tugging furiously at the bars. But as a regular oasis in the day, it worked for both of us, until the child was really walking confidently.

Such experiences point to another aspect of our schooling in this period. As we contemplate the mysterious, almost magical achievement of uprightness, and sense the immense forces of will and movement which bring it about, we need all the more to seek our own centre of balance, and of inner stillness. This centre can protect us from being torn apart by distractions, scattered to the four winds by the effort to get all the work done, while not allowing our intensely active little companion around the house to drop out of mind. It was always when

I ceased to be more or less aware of where a child was and what he was doing that some crisis would occur: I would find him about to eat a sharp knife, shuffling backwards towards steep steps, or trapped behind a door. This practice of centering, of presence of mind, of finding a rhythm, belongs with the task of shaping the day so that we do not lose ourselves completely in chasing after every impulse the child has—or, for that matter, every impulse that we ourselves might have.

Most child psychologists seem to agree that in the first two or three years, children learn more deeply and fundamentally about themselves and the world than at any later time. Of course this is a deeply practical learning, which has little to do, at that stage, with more abstract forms of understanding. But in play and other kinds of activity are laid the basis of security, of feeling at home on earth. As a mother, I felt the more challenged to re-establish my own security and to be at home with myself, for my stability was also my children's support. It is perhaps just at this time during the child's second year when women may be most in need of finding or forming mutual support groups (see *Mothers' Support Groups,* page 60). But just during the child's second year, there is a deep need for mothers to support one another, to talk over questions and problems and to exchange practical ideas, as well as to relieve loneliness and build companionship. Through this mutual support, mothers can help one another in this task of finding their own centre, an inner uprightness, the counterpart of what is being achieved by the child.

The third year brings a famous new challenge, which Dr. Benjamin Spock calls "the dreadful 'No' stage". The intense energies which were at work in achieving uprightness and establishing physical autonomy in the surrounding world now make use of the new-born faculty of speech in strongly expressed declarations of personal independence. The power of "No", often accompanied by "tantrums" reveals the amazingly rapid transformation of our helpless infant into a determined personality, practising an energetic confrontation with the surrounding world.

Whatever they may have done before, no mothers can avoid meeting at this stage some questions of discipline and authority (see *Creative Discipline* page 214).

The aspect that concerns me here is what is being asked of the mother. She is being asked at this time, or so it seems to me, whether she also has a mind of her own. What aims has *she* got? What are her plans for the day? If her only plan is to be tyranised by every whim of her three-year-old, she will rapidly lose herself. How often are mothers of children of this age to be heard consulting their infants on every issue: "Would you like a biscuit? Would you rather have honey or peanut butter? Would you like to go into the garden, the house, upstairs, downstairs, into the bath? Do you want your sweater, hat, gloves, coat, boots, on or off or both or neither? Do you want to go to sleep, wake up, get up, not get up, go back to sleep, or what?"

Such consultations are inspired by the best of intentions, that is to say, to be kind, caring, unauthoritarian, and so on. This problem is perhaps not so great for "technological" mothers, but I have seen "back-to-nature" mothers driving themselves and their children frantic with a kind of non-stop mutiple choice examination from morning to night.

If we have truly learned to observe, to empathise, and at the same time to find our own human centre, we should by this time have discovered a great deal about the real needs of our children. The "No" stage is then a challenge to us to find an inner basis for our own sound judgement. This needs much sensitivity, anticipation and clarity—but we can discover this part of our schooling as a natural continuation of the search for inner uprightness and stability.

I have found much stimulus here from what at first appears to be a strange statement by Rudolf Steiner that parents and teachers of pre-school children must learn to be "priests". [1] Priests are, or were, through custom and ritual, the guardians of the divine order as it is reflected in human life on earth. It is almost certainly a myth to imagine that earlier societies were ordered by "natural instincts". In every so-called primitive society we know today, the elders and priests are guardians of the most elaborate tribal rituals and customs, at once social and religious, into which children enter from infancy as a matter of course. The more sympathetic and perceptive studies of this century have helped many people to see an extraordinary and often beautiful wisdom in what are sometimes very complex ways of life. This wisdom is not conceived as coming from nature, but from the beings who order nature, and the priests are guardians on behalf of these beings.[1] Their authority is not a personal one, but resides in this guardianship.

So-called advanced societies have little order of this kind. They just have clocks and conventions. So we have lost much of our sense for how to be responsible for the order of a day. The contributions on family meals and sleeping and waking give some illustrations of how we can try to practise a more conscious responsibility for the daily "rituals". Observant mothers will soon see how healthy children thrive and are supported by rhythm and ritual in their lives. Perhaps children are not as remote as adults are from the heavenly order which we knew before descending to earth.

Our responsibility for a true "order" needs to extend inwards as well as outwards. Just because all that we do is imitated by small children at such a deep level, we are faced with the task of being responsible for all that goes on in the child's surroundings, for our movements and gestures, for our speech, but also for our inner feelings, thoughts and impulses which we may try to keep hidden. They are probably not as hidden from small children as we often believe, even if their experience of what is going on in us is not fully conscious.

It was at this stage that I realised most strongly the importance of looking after my own children myself as far as possible. How could I ask another to act as a "priest" in this sense on my behalf? Of course this is not always practicable, and many mothers must entrust the care of their small children to others for part of the time. But where this happens simply to pursue personal needs and interests, it seems to me that in a deeper sense both mother and child may be the losers. It may be just at this time that the child asks of the mother, not explicitly but out of its own stage of development, to seek most deeply for her own best resources. In so far as she finds inner resources out of which to order her own life and that of the home, she brings to the child what it most needs to imitate—the true "order" of the living and upright human spirit. And for the mother, whatever she can achieve in this way must surely belong more centrally than anything else to any human being's truly "personal" interests.

These reflections also relate to another of Steiner's suggestions for parents and teachers. Until they are ready for school, he once said, children particularly need to find *goodness* in their surroundings; in the first school years they need to find *beauty* and in adolescence they need above all to find *truth*.

Genesis tells of God who stood back from six days of creation and saw that what He had made was good. "Good" is the craftsman's word for what is well made, using substances which have been well made by nature. As mothers, we are largely the makers of our child's surroundings, of what meets their senses. We make their rhythms, their mealtimes, story times, bedtimes, birthdays and all festival times. When we learn to make these well, our children know "goodness". Mothers have in this period the most precious opportunity to learn how to give real substance to the American greeting, "Have a good day!"

My husband remarks how truly impoverished in this respect are the lives of very many fathers. Out there in the world of "real life" there are no rituals but only routines, no festivals but only weekends and public holidays, no craftsmanship but only manufacture. So men are deprived in the schooling that they receive from the real world and may find only with difficulty their way into the "priestly" functions of their home. But mothers who learn to shape and care for the festivals and rituals of their family can then also bring special gifts to their partners.

Journey On Dry Land

So the first years bring an intense schooling in wonder and observation, in the meaning of peace and the finding of balance, in presence of mind and finding an inner centre, in loving judgement and responsibility and in the tasks of becoming a craftswoman and bringer of goodness into the order of the family life.

When the children are ready to go to school, the "boat journey" comes to an end. By this time, many mothers feel they are standing on firmer inner ground. What does the next part of the journey bring?

From the small enclosed world of infancy, the family moves into a wider social landscape. Of course the transition is seldom a sudden one. There may be infants and new babies while the eldest are already at school. And before school, there may have been a time of playgroups, nursery class and kindergarten. But for mothers, the family's world begins to expand and to take in a rich and often bewildering wealth of activity.

This is often the time when mothers return to a previous career, or take up other work outside the home. If they have the stamina, such interests will enrich the family's life. At the same time, other demands will develop through the children, who now become more widely involved with other children, and with teachers with whom they may be making the first significant adult relationships outside the family. So mothers meet and become involved with children, teachers, parents of children in the same class, with school activities, the families of school friends, and also with neighbours through the neighbourhood groups, and the tribes and "gangs" so characteristic of this time.

These bring corresponding social demands to the mother. "Gangs" have their own social complexities. Some children are always "in" with one group or another, others are always "out", some are constantly in and out. So you have to stand by with support, comfort, and encouragement. Or your child may take up with some family nearby and almost live there for a while. You feel neglected and wonder if you are making a proper home. Is your child really welcome down the road, or is he being pushy? Alternatively, your home or garden may become the main base for one of the gangs. You are expected to provide, at a moment's notice, a tepee for Indians, a rope for Tarzan, planks, string, saucepans which can be ruined in campfires, food and drink at unorthodox times, first-aid, or perhaps emergency accommodation: "Can so-and-so stay the night?"

The rituals of bedtimes and mealtimes, so carefully established in earlier years, easily dissolve into anarchy, especially at weekends. A small war can sweep through the house just before lunch. You have to dish up, and simultaneously get the two sides to negotiate a ceasefire, wash their hands, and sit down before the soup gets cold. In late afternoon, a vast, muddy construction project begins outside, needing at least until midnight to complete. You have to get some kind of contract agreed about baths and bed.

You have to negotiate with adults, too, especially when hostilities have broken out through your children or their friends. I remember a phone call from a very angry farmer, complaining that two nine-year-old boys, one of them ours, had felled a sizeable tree on his land to make a sailing boat. Nowadays, parents will often have to cope with at least one episode of shoplifting, with the ensuing confrontations with shop-keepers and even police.

Then there is school. Some teachers may not be finding one's child all that wonderful in class. Or the child may be a darling in class and a terror at home. So mothers find themselves undergoing, along with their children, an intense new phase of social education.

These outer events have their inner counterparts. With the change of teeth around the sixth year, there awakens in the child a more conscious interior life accompanied by a wonderful flowering of fantasy and imagination. This can be easily followed by observant mothers if they are sensitive to the stories the children enjoy. The best stories for very small children are more like rituals: very simple sequences of events, whose appeal is in repetition and rhythm. As a more conscious imagination awakens, the stories begin to need drama: changing moods, moments of tension, a climax, and the right ending (see Almut Bocke-mühl, *A Key To The Images In Fairy Tales*, p231 and Margret Meyerkort, *The Hidden Treasure In Fairy Tales*, p244). This inner awakening to drama accompanies the family's fuller entry into the wider social drama of the neighbourhood.

When Rudolf Steiner said that at this time children need to meet *beauty* in their surroundings, I think it was an aphoristic way of saying that they need *art*, and not just art in terms of crayons and modelling wax, but an *art of living.* He was certainly emphatic that teachers must learn to be artists in education.

True art is also, in a deep sense, a middle way. It means creating something new out of a meeting between the personal and the universal. Shakespeare's *Hamlet* is full of great and universal themes, as ancient as they are modern. But the play itself is also uniquely Shakespeare's. So he made a work of art which remains alive through centuries.

The dramas of most families' lives, luckily, are not as fraught as Hamlet's. But the family play is real life. Mothers find themselves centrally responsible for directing a large and fairly complex drama, with an extensive and varied cast, and an elaborate plot unfolding from day to day.

This points to a central task of mothers in this period of time in the child's life. Mothers are challenged to become family and social *artists.* This applies in both small and large matters. Thus I gradually realised there is a real art in helping children achieve what is often quite a demanding transition—the return from school each day. I learned not to meet them with a stream of questions such as "What did you do today? Did you like French? Were you in trouble again in handwork?" and so on. It was better simply to be around, doing something, but available for talk, support, comfort, or a sharing of adventure as needed. On some days, and with some children more than others, the events of the day are poured out immediately. Sometimes one hears of crucial events only much later. It was also vital to make some time available for each child separately every day. The art is to steer between disinterest and excessive attention, to avoid favouritism and to help the children breathe freely between home and school and among themselves.

In learning these arts, there are two trials which are often repeated, and where I felt frequently tested. Both concern conflict. The first trial comes to every mother whether she likes it or not. For she will have to learn to deal with *disputes,* and to be a judge, conciliator and arbitrator in many different situations. The second trial comes particularly to parents whose values and customs are in one way or another different or at odds with those of their surrounding culture. I will return to this later.

The first trial concerns judgement. In learning the art of judgement, the main quality expected of us by children is, that we be *fair.* It is worth remembering that the word "fair" also means beautiful. The children are really looking to us for true social imagination, a way between two extremes. One extreme is the rigid application of rules, used as a technology, imprisoning life. At the other extreme is anarchy, where life is made chaotic and arbitrary by the momentary whims of children or adults, a life without structure or rhythm which can gradually confuse and exhaust all concerned. Between clock-bound mechanics and anarchy is the quality which people are often seeking when they talk about "spontaneity". True spontaneity is the art of living creatively in the moment between the tensions of order and chaos. You have to seek, sometimes desperately, for a special kind of creativity when confronted by two children, or two groups of children, bringing you an apparently irreconcilable dispute for a "fair" resolution: "He's been a robber all afternoon, and now he says he's going home for tea and I haven't had a turn yet." It is easy to respond mechanically: "Well, it's tea-time for all of you so you must stop now anyway." Or you can risk anarchy and back off: "Well you must sort it out among yourselves, musn't you?" These are understandable makeshifts, but we lose an opportunity for an imaginative and creative response—and the children lose, too. For when they bring their disputes to us to resolve, they are seeking an experience of fairness, like the sunlight which shines from the wise king who knows how to bring order and justice to the conclusion of a fairy story; "And they all lived happily ever after"— at least until after tea.

The second, and related trial, arising from conflicts of values, are also tests for both parents and children. It is in the nature of the first seven years to create a shelter, a protected environment, for the gradual journey from infancy to the start of school. I don't think it harms children during this time to live absolutely within the world determined by the parents, assuming, of course, that this has some qualities of "goodness" as described earlier. But it is neither possible nor appropriate to sustain this shelter in the same way once the children need to socialise more widely and meet the worlds of school and other families.

A focus of increasingly painful dilemmas for many parents is television. Quite apart from the content of the programmes, the actual activity of watching (or, better said, the *in*activity of watching) is quite foreign to the real needs of infancy. During the first years, we tried to avoid any viewing at all and we made it much easier for ourselves by not having a set in the house.[2] But what is to happen when the children begin to watch in other people's houses, or accept less easily the viewing rules imposed at home? If "all the other children in my class are allowed to watch Starsky and Hutch", is it "fair" that one's own children are deprived? Similar dilemmas can arise over food, clothing, comic books and other reading matter, toys, outings, pocket money, all kinds of social questions, medical issues, and of course religious practices and beliefs.

There are no ready-made answers to these problems, as every family's situation is different. But just as the children are learning to "breathe" at this time, so are mothers. "When do I stand absolutely by my own convictions? Where do I compromise? Where have I become fixed and should learn from others?" There can be no real communication and development between families who take their stand on rigid opinions and doctrinaire beliefs. But social imagination, and a readiness to examine one's own values and enter with real interest into the lives of others, brings movement and growth.

I am labouring this point a little, because among the readers of this book will be those who already know something of the depth and richness of the educational and other work founded by Rudolf Steiner. The Waldorf schools and kindergartens all over the world now have more than half a century of experience behind them, and growing numbers of parents find their own deepest intuitions confirmed and practised in the work of this movement. At the same time, as in all substitutes, the Waldorf "culture" can also become doctrinaire and routine. When this happens, it easily isolates and makes a family or a group of families into a "sect". This is our fault, not Steiner's. "I don't want to be believed, I want to be understood", he said. When we understand something deeply and imaginatively, we are given the freedom of the thing we understand. It becomes our own and we can breathe more easily both with ourselves and with the world. Our precious opinions, and those "values" which are really set habits, can dissolve and become transparent for real meaning. Then there can be movement and growth.

These challenges also prepare us, as we shall see, for the demands of adolescents. But in this "heart of childhood" the children do not yet demand freedom. They look naturally to adults as the makers and upholders of the order in which they live. They expect "rules", as long as these are fair, and fairly administered. So they seldom resent it when parents take an absolute stand on some questions, especially when this is part of the deep support that both parents give in helping to create a living and artistic form to their children's lives. But the children will begin to suffer if they feel the family rules are cutting them off from all breathing with their surroundings.

A wonderful and much-neglected sphere of practice in the art of living at this time lies in festivals such as birthdays, family festivals, and seasonal festivals.

Birthdays can easily go to extremes, from disappointing dullness because the parents "couldn't be bothered", to monstrous spectaculars that are no more than displays of parental ambition, and which leave everyone ill and exhausted. Somewhere in between lie those parties which come alive as works of art, having balance and rhythm, and above all some unifying quality of imagination. I remember one party where each child had a fairy-tale task to perform, according to ability— finding a golden hair, solving a riddle, overcoming a dragon guarding a bridge. So they won their way through to gain a magic ring. At another party there was a magic wood where food hung from all the trees: silver bananas, golden apples, a bun tree. There was a lemonade well nearby. Another party centred on a street of small shops, with children dressed appropriately and serving each other. Yet another centred on a fairy tale performed with puppets.

Parties, conceived not as a duty, nor as an occasion for excesses of excitement and stimulation but as little "plays" imbued with the fresh-ness of play, can nourish the art of living in a special way.

Then there is the art of living with the rhythms of the day and the year, and with whatever religious festivals belong to the family's culture. Other contributors to this book have more to say about the meaning of festivals for children, and possibilities for creating them. But the care and development of these festivals nearly always rests mainly with mothers. It is of course a great support to be linked with a school where festivals are taken seriously and are woven into the school year. But the family festivals are just as significant for the children. Mothers who share common ideals can support one another a great deal in this sphere, wherever they live. For example, the festivals can be the basis for a year long shared study and creative work, as *Mothers' Support Groups* suggests (p 60).

Festivals have always been deeply linked with art, as they also unite the personal with the universal. They are moments that mark where we are in our own lives in relation to the life of nature. They help us to accompany the outbreathing of spring and summer and the inbreathing of autumn and winter. They help us to live into the secret victory of light over darkness at midwinter, of life over death in spring, and the turning point at midsummer when fruit and seed must set if there is to be a harvest in the future. We can try to live these festivals in the family, with appropriate stories, gathering materials from nature, making things, decorating the house, festive meals, and so on. Such a family culture can be created anywhere, given a touch of imagination and artistry and a sense for what belongs rightly to the place and to the moment. Perhaps more than anything else this Family Culture can bring "beauty" into children's lives. I also believe that it builds a strong and secure capacity for living socially in the profoundest sense of the word and that the effect of this can last for the whole of our children's lives. In this way, the "heart of childhood", with its rich landscape, brings to mothers a precious time to discover and develop new capacities as "social artists".

Journey Through The Mountains

As adolescence approaches, the landscape becomes hilly, the going more strenuous, and there are daunting mountains in sight. Soon, a steep and often dramatic climb begins. Whenever you seem to have conquered one peak, another higher one looms up ahead. There are clouds and storms, but also moments of brilliant sunshine. You can't afford to put a foot wrong, but when you do look up, you have glimpses of a high and ideal world—a world of eternal truths towards which you struggle with your children through hours of jagged discussions and snowdrifts of debate and argument.

Adolescence is a significant step for children and it is clearly a major challenge for parents. But it is less often seen as a new opportunity. No doubt this is because it often first presents itself in a quite painful form as far as mothers are concerned: suddenly, they have to meet direct and often devastating criticism.

Adults are normally quite kind and polite to one another. They have also been used to telling children to do things: brush your hair; wear this or that; don't be rude; your bed-time is such and such. This comfortable way of life is abruptly challenged. Your darling little girl now starts to tell you how awful you look in that dress, that you exaggerate, that you judge others by appearances. Having been trying to learn to be a good judge, you are all at once one of the accused.

This can be quite traumatic in itself. The worst of it is that there is often a lot of truth in what one is being told. Polite society easily lulls us into a good many illusions about ourselves. At the same time, many mothers are often beginning to meet their own mid-life crises and to ask the same questions that the adolescent is in fact also asking—"Who am I really?" [3] This is the inner aspect of the adolescent's deep hunger and search for truth. Its counterpart is an eagle eye and a bloodhound's nose for what is true and what is bogus in adults, particularly in teachers and parents.

It is not surprising therefore if mothers react to their children's onslaughts by rejecting both the criticisms and the critic. This leads to anger and the well-known breakdown in communication: "You are always criticising me, but you refuse to listen when I tell you something. So I won't tell you anything from now on." The door slams and is locked from inside.

It was an enormous help to me when I realised that I could try to turn this experience completely around, and see the possibility of having some fellow-feeling, and a genuine sympathy for the often erratic search of this young apprentice adult for an identity. I had better re-examine my own values, try to be truthful with myself and with my children, and see that while the adolescent is struggling at a different level, the search for truth is shared.

We are also challenged in our conventionality. My children would turn up with unlikely associates, "not our kind of people". They would dress and behave in peculiar ways, and their tastes in many things were quite foreign to ours and also remote from what I thought had been so carefully instilled during their upbringing. So it is easy to feel rejected, and to feel that one is suddenly running a rather ramshackle hotel for strangers.

But these experiences can be turned around too. I learned to appreciate some of the values of adolescent life, notably the impatience with surface appearances; such impatience is an important partner to the search for an essential reality. Teachers and parents who can see no further than the length of someone's hair or the scruffiness of their jeans are perhaps rightly met with a formidable contempt. I sometimes think that adolescent scruffiness is a way of presenting an inner but not a fully conscious experience. The heart of childhood is a kind of paradise, a time of relative harmony, compared with what comes next. Adolescents are expelled from paradise quite abruptly, and, like Adam and Eve, go from riches to rags, from innocence to painful self-consciousness, from a supportive surrounding order to a desperate struggle to make sense of things. Perhaps they are simply making an inner landscape visible in their outer appearance. But if we can look behind the appearances, we can sometimes give a hand in the struggle, and establish real communication at the right moments.

Having come to terms with the ordeal by criticism, and attempted to clear the mists of convention and prejudice from our perceptions, we are led by our children towards the central test for parents of adolescents—the issue of freedom. In theory, parents may have known that their children were not personal possessions, and would in due course belong to the world and not to them. But now theory must gradually become practice—only not all at once. How far do you let them go, and when, and where, and how? Earlier kinds of authority no longer work. Childhood rituals long ago lost their power, and the rules accepted so naturally until recently, as long as they were fairly administered, become the focus of endless and exasperating arguments. Yet it often seemed to me that for all the rebellion, the children were in a curious way supported when I exerted some degree of resistance and took a stand now and again. Such resistance is, after all, a token of your real concern and interest. It is also an assurance that the adolescent is being perceived as a human being who really exists and is of significance, even if the price is a fuss every time there is a request to come back late from a party, or more commonly perhaps, a row about coming back late without having asked anyway. Teenagers who are already mentally abandoned by their parents can be sad and forlorn in a hidden way. Yet possessiveness is destructive too. I felt at this time that I was constantly teetering insecurely along a narrow ridge, trying to avoid the steep slope on either side.

In seeking to find themselves, adolescents also have an overpowering need to find out about the world. It is an unhappy commentary on the state of our civilsation that many parents, far from enjoying the prospect of their offspring discovering the wonders of adult life, are far more often anxiously preoccupied with wondering how they will deal with its various horrors. Bizarre situations can arise. Looking back with one of my older teenagers, on adolescent parties, I heard belatedly about some of the things that went on. I asked naively, "But why didn't you ever tell me about that?" The response was touching, "Well, I knew you would be worried if I had told you, and I was quite able to look after myself." Who, I had to ask myself, was looking after whom?

But can they really look after themselves? They often seemed to me to be sleepwalking towards various disasters. Yet they would come out more or less unscathed as though accompanied by some invisible protection. I have met several parents who say that at this time they learned to pray again! I gradually realised that these experiences are a fundamental test of *faith*—not of religious faith in the usual sense, but of faith in another human being.

As the outer work diminishes, so the inner work of seeing the true, and ideal being in the adolescent who was once one's baby becomes I believe, of ever greater importance. However stormy are the experiences of these years, most mothers will have had a glimpse of the "pearl", the true potential, the real human being, still not fully born and often quite deeply hidden. Perhaps the greatest service parents can render to their children in these years is to keep faith with them, to hold to a picture of their ideal being through thick and thin.

This faith is a kind of answering work to the struggle for one's own centre which came with the unfamiliar demands of caring for our children when they were infants. Now the mother, who has had the most opportunity to sense what truly lives as potential in a young person, can carry a banner of belief upright through the adolescent storms, when the true being is so easily submerged in various kinds of teenage turmoil. Such belief is at the heart of friendship, and is a faculty of the heart. Adolescents need friends, and they can recognise heartfelt friendship in their parents if it is truly present.

This faith is of course, constantly tested, right into the adult lives of our children. Yet it is the basis for one of the most difficult tasks which is to allow one's children to make their own mistakes, even fairly disastrous ones of which we ourselves might have had past experience. It is the basis for "letting go" without "writing off".

When Steiner spoke of the adolescent's need and search for "truth", he meant both the truth in themselves, their ideal, and the truths to be found in the world:—"To see the Idea in reality is the true communion of the human being", he once wrote.[4] I can see that my sense of my journey as a mother cannot be separated from a sense of the journey of my children. And just as I resent being explained away as only a product of genetics and heredity, so I know this is not the explanation of the real identities of my children. Our journeys come from before birth, and in childhood we are still being born. Indeed, as I hope this contribution indicates, we go on being born all through our lives if we remain open to change. As parents, we have not created the beings for whom we care, but only enabled nature to provide the vehicles which will bear them through life. We are responsible for the healthy development of these 'chariots', and our mistakes can put obstacles in the way of the charioteer who gradually takes charge. But we don't make the charioteer—that is to say, the being who is the meaning of each journey. These beings gradually emerge, and in adolescence are just beginning to grope for the reins. And in so far as we have seen and acknowledged their presence, their reality, have had trust in them, kept faith with them, then we are linked with their journeys into the future, however outwardly distant and different their lives may become.

The Eightfold Path

I have been trying to describe my experiences with my family as a journey, a path, and as a schooling brought by the children and by the world. It is a path which we tread to some degree whether we like it or not. I want to conclude by describing a counterpart, an inner practice which is not demanded by life, but which anyone can take up freely if they so choose. It is only one among many possibilities of a meditative nature, but it is one which I found especially helpful as a mother caring for children.

The very fact of making a personal decision to take up a regular practice of this kind can bring strength and a confirmation of our inner freedom. People often ask how they can put such a decision into practice. For example, they ask, "How can I make a quiet time for myself when the children are always clamouring for something?".

The first essential, of course, is one's own conviction that such a practice is as necessary as food and drink. It need not involve much time. One friend told me that when her children were toddlers, she would hang a picture of an angel outside her door for a few minutes. The children accepted that 'mother is talking to the angel' and would only disturb her in real emergencies. Five or ten minutes taken near the beginning of the day helps to remind us of where we are and what we are doing, so that we can get on with our work with a little more focus.

Among many suggestions Rudolf Steiner made for meditative practice, he several times described a group of eight exercises which are easily recognised as a version of the Bhudda's "Eightfold Path". One can also see that they are not bound into a particular religion, but are quite universal in their meaning. Steiner's particular contribution was to suggest that these exercises can be linked to the days of the week in an organic way.

Children and many adults will often tell you that the days of the week have different 'colours' or qualities. But we seldom see this as having any practical significance. Yet the rhythm of the week is one of the most fundamental in our lives, particularly for families. The "weekend" still stands out, but the qualities of the different days have unfortunately faded. Any day is washing-machine day, and the supermarket is always there. Yet the days of the week also have the names of the planets, thus linking the small rhythms of our lives with the great rhythms of the universe. Steiner's suggestion leads us to bring together the traditional "planetary" qualities which sound in the days of the week with the eight exercises originally formulated by Gautama Bhudda

Bhudda as a "middle way" and as a path towards compassion and peace. The exercises, in Steiner's formulation, are:

> Saturday *(Saturn day)* **Right Conception**
> Sunday *(Sun day):* **Right Resolve**
> Monday *(Moon day)* **Right Word**
> Tuesday *(Mars day):* **Right Action**
> Wednesday *(Mercury day)* **Right Livelihood**
> Thursday *Jupiter day)* **Right Endeavour**
> Friday *(Venus day)* **Right Recollection**

The eighth exercise, '*Right Contemplation*', embraces all the others, and is not linked to a particular day; but it belongs naturally, perhaps, to the weekend.

Steiner describes each exercise in more detail (refs..), but I will try here to describe each one briefly in my own way and to connect it with family life. [5]

Saturday—Right Conception

On this day I might find it helpful to ask: 'How am I *thinking* about my children, my husband, my friends, and about human beings in general? Am I thinking of them as objects and as mere creatures, or as beings endowed with intelligence, language, morality, and creative spirit? Am I thinking of my children as 'mine', or as free beings entrusted to my care while they grow up? Am I listening truly to my family and friends, or only hearing what confirms my own prejudices or wishes?'

These may be obvious questions which many people ask themselves often. Yet such questions are easily swept away in the rush of events; they gain much greater strength, if they are consciously given a little space at a regular time each week. Saturday also seems a good time to remember friends and relatives who have died: How am I thinking of them—as simply vanished, or as active in a different way?

Sunday—Right Resolve

Sunday is a challenge for many modern families, especially where there is no religious practice, or only one which survives as habit, tradition, or convention. Do we just drift into this day and 'relax', which of course may often be very necessary? Or do we try to include some kind of festive element or ritual? It may mean giving special attention to a meal, or inviting someone not usually present. It may mean a special walk or a special story. It is a great help to take a moment at the beginning of the day to seek a 'right resolve'. to feel one's way towards what a 'sunday' could be in the future, and to find something which can bring a moment of warmth and light into the family's day. Younger children have a natural sense of occasion, and usually respond with enthusiasm. For adolescents, who are often burdened with the after effects of Saturday night's 'Saturnalia', Sunday can be a black and difficult time. This makes it the more rewarding to find a 'resolve' which can light the mood.

Monday—Right Word

We can take a moment to consider how we are using language. This is the medium through which we bring to birth our inner thoughts, feelings and intentions, so that they begin to influence the world around. Our language, in its content, rhythm and qualities of sound, has deep effects, especially on small children. We can use words to wound and to comfort, to deceive and to speak the truth, to slander and to revere, to trivialise and to bear deeper meaning.

This exercise faced me with a question which probably meets many mothers—"Am I becoming a nagger? How can I get the children to do things every day without constant moralising and infuriating repetitions?" One day I was at my wits' end over one child's chronic untidiness with clothes. Suddenly I thought of getting the garments to speak for themselves. The child came back to find little messages pinned to various scattered and crumpled objects. A new jacket proclaimed; "I am really young and beautiful but I am condemned to live in this dusty corner. Who will rescue me?" This brought some laughter into a tense situation, and really helped for a time.

Another problem is the tendency to talk about our children while they are present, but as though they were deaf or witless. There is the story of the little girl who says to her mother; "Tell them how sweet I was the other day". If we take a few moments to reflect on how we speak to adults when our children are present, we will realise how much they take in and how deeply they are affected.

I also remember realising one Monday how, apart from nursery rhymes, family life had made me lose connection with poetry. This prompted me to rediscover poems I had loved, and to seek for new ones.

Tuesday—Right Action.

I have found this day which relates to Mars, particularly valuable for looking at things I knew I would have to do, but had been putting off or trying to not to think about—the overdue letter, the difficult phone call, and the unpleasant bit of cleaning under the stairs. To take on a few such things deliberately, having looked at them squarely in the morning, could often turn a feeling of defeat into a liberating victory.

As well as summoning strength to face things one would like to avoid, I found Tuesday a good time for trying to see clearly what my actions meant for others, independent of personal sympathies or antipathies. We all have a bit of Hamlet's indecision in us, and need to practise overcoming it, but preferably in a more constructive way than this.

Wednesday—Right Livelihood

Mercury is the messenger of the gods, and his staff is the symbol of healing. He can move freely between heaven and earth, and make whole what has fallen apart. The "eightfold path" leads gradually from the inwardness of thought to the outwardness of our tasks in the world. In fact Wednesday is the middle of the week and is the pivotal point of these exercises. Can we bring about a healing relationship between what is going on inside us and what is happening around us? "Right livelihood" may also be called "right standpoint". It is a good day to try to come to terms with our life situation, and to accept the reality rather than constantly pine for something else. This does not mean being resigned to one's lot. There is nothing wrong with wanting to change, inwardly or outwardly. But we can only change from where we are, and we won't see this if we are always dreaming about being somewhere else. It is a good day to count our blessings, both inner and outer, as well as our burdens.

Illness is a disharmony, and healing grows out of rhythm. Wednesday can therefore be a time to review the rhythms in our lives—we can ask: "Am I out of balance, ruled by the clock, or driven by my emotions?" Also, "Am I having any fun?The metal called mercury or quicksilver, is, in its way, a playful metal. It used to be found in those children's puzzle games, breaking into little drops and then re-forming into one blob, like laughter and tears.[6] If one tends to melancholy, brooding on the trials of life and seeing only a dark future, then laughter is a wonderful medicine. If one tends to be sanguine, flitting lightly from one sensation to the next and being correspondingly scatter-brained, a a moment of seriousness restores the balance. In pictures of Mercury we see that his staff is poised upright between two snakes who pull in opposite directions, up and down (or in and out). The secret of Mercury is to bring these snakes to a harmonious interplay, as we have in our heartbeat and breathing when we are in good health.

Thursday—Right Endeavour

This exercise takes the mood of Wednesday into our work towards the future. It is a good day to examine our longer term aims, to consider whether they are true and realistic, and to ask what we are doing to fulfill them. We may well ask "Do my aims have any connection with the realities of my life and the needs in my surroundings? Or am I simply wishing and dreaming?"

Jupiter is wisdom. He surveys the whole scheme of things, seeing how each human being can find a true place, neither burdened with a sense of failure, nor deluded by unreal ambitions. Teachers at Waldorf schools usually hold their meetings on Thursdays. Their work is to enable the children to realise their fullest potential, which lies in the future. It is the work of mothers, too. But "right endeavour" takes in the whole of life, marriage, family, friends, careers, and the times in which we live.

The mood of the Thursday exercise also seems to me to include *consistency*. It is no use having a different long term aim every week. It is also the mood which sustains any kind of meditative practice.

Friday—Right Recollection.

As we approach the weekend, and the exercises begin to draw inward again, we can take a little time to ask what the week has brought, and what we have learned from it. We tend to identify ourselves with our inner lives and forget how much of what we are we owe to the world. For me, a key word in this connection is "interest". Whenever we are truly interested in something, so that our heart responds to what lies outside, we also learn and are changed. It can also be instructive, and sometimes quite funny to look at what we are *not* interested in, and ask why.

There is a mood in this exercise which I have also found valuable at other times during the week especially when waiting around for buses, for trains, at airports, or for people to turn up. It is easy to fret or fall into a stupor. But there is usually a great deal going on in the immediate surroundings which becomes extremely interesting if you attend to it.

In one of his lectures, Rudolf Steiner remarked, "Progress is not achieved by merely preaching universal love, but by an ever growing interest. We shall come to do the right things through learning to be ever more interested in people with widely differing temperaments, religions and philosophies, and meeting them with understanding" [7] [4] Interest, followed up with 'right recollections', takes us beyond a purely self-centred experience of ourselves, our families, our surroundings and our times.

We tend to be rather personally entangled in our own memories, so that we are not able to exercise "right recollection". Memories are certainly our own, but we owe them to the world. On Fridays we can perhaps try to get a little beyond our personal involvement, and realise how much we owe to what life has brought to us, and this needs to be considered not sentimentally, but with sober realism. Out of such a contemplation, the word 'destiny'—a sense for the meaning within the experiences that our lives bring—may begin to have more substance.

Right Contemplation

This exercise lies, so to speak, outside time. It suggests a stock-taking, a survey of past, present and future, an effort to sort essentials from inessentials as though looking at life from a mountain top and scanning the paths below. In a way it contains all the other exercises, and is their fulfillment. Our attempts to do this exercise may from time to time bring a tiny glimpse of how we will be in a deeper sense at work in a new experience after death. It links naturally with the Saturday and Sunday exercises, which are more like a preparation for birth.

So these exercises can become a supportive rhythm, helping us to look in a quite commonsense way at things which often concern us anyway, but which we simply do not get further with if we simply fumble around with them haphazardly.

Open Secrets

I realise that a good deal of all this can seem very idealised, and that in life, there are times of physical, emotional and mental exhaustion, or a flood of events which make such demands that it seems all we can do to survive from day to day. At such times, it often seemed to me that others were all doing well, while I was a complete failure. These are lonely times, full of discouragement and even desperation. But they can also be just the times when we can discover the "open secret" which has been my main inspiration.

Our culture conditions us to expect 'happiness' or 'job satisfaction'. When we don't seem to be getting either, we become frustrated and angry. In their self-absorption, mothers may then fail to see the magic in what is actually being offered to them by their own children. This dawns in a smile, a moment of joy, a childlike question suddenly full of extraordinary depths.

In the trials of motherhood, one of its central experiences is hardly ever mentioned—the unbounded stream of warmth, radiance, trust and love which babies and young children are ready to give naturally to their parents. In this love is a power of strength and support, infinite in its possibilities. And it is in its light that one may begin to see the true potential in the life one is actually living, and to realise that the career of being a mother offers truly human riches beyond what one has ever dreamed.

In attempting to gather up my own experiences, I have looked longest at the first seven years. During this time, the responsibilities are perhaps at their greatest while at the same time we feel least equipped to carry them out properly. Both children and mothers change and develop with great intensity during this time. After a child reaches seven years old the responsibilities are more widely shared, especially with those of the school teachers. And after adolescence, the responsibilities begin to be shared with the world.

In the end, it is not the thoughts we *have* so much as the things we do, which count so far as our children are concerned— and whatever we do is shaped by what we are. Like our children, we are not complete beings, but are on a journey. This contribution is an attempt to show how much I owe to my children for that in my journey which I now really value. As a "career" it has brought both great demands and great rewards. While each mother's journey is different, I know from many conversations in groups and with individuals that my own journey has included enough universal experience to justify an attempt to map some of it in writing, in the hope that it will give support and encouragement to others.

3. MOTHERS' SUPPORT GROUPS: The How and Why

Welmoed Torenstra

Why are Mothers' Groups Helpful?

Most people who have chosen a specific profession—teachers, doctors, farmers, artists, therapists, architects, nurses, bankers—feel the need to continue developing their working skills over a period of time with other colleagues. This sense arises not only because of the daily expectations of their clients, but also through anticipating future challenges. This need is especially strong if they are trying to realise their work on an alternative basis, on a foundation which carries a new image of the human being and the world. They require contact with colleagues because their approach may rest on ideas and attitudes which are often contrary to what lives in society at large. So these people will try to find ways to exchange experiences with one another, to search for ever new sources, to try and try again to understand the true meaning of their tasks.

How do mothers develop their 'profession'? How can women, who are trying to live with and work out of an interest in Anthroposophy give shape to their mothering, especially while their children are small? I myself have felt the need for colleagues very much. I have felt a longing to exchange thoughts with other people, with other women, in a context which could encourage the conscious development of aims, tasks, and sources for our common work as mothers. This is not something you can do over a cup of coffee, nor at an afternoon visit with children playing around. Mothers have to create their own time and space to do conscious work together.

How can Mothers' Groups Come About?

I will describe a number of situations where women are working together on questions of motherhood. It is striking to see how different each group can be. In my initial enthusiasm I never expected that this would be so. I took it for granted that mothers would share the same problems and seek the same solutions. What a mistake!

A vague mood of 'we' mothers must gradually become differentiated. We must look at the individuals who exist behind 'the mothers'. Questions will arise such as: what was the life situation of each woman before she became a mother? what kind of work or study has she been doing? what kind of relationship does she have with the father of the child? how old is the woman who is now the mother? what phase of life is she in and in what phase are her children? All these aspects will influence the kind of support group a woman will need. They will influence her expectations of the group and her contributions to the group.

Here are some examples of the many different ways women's support groups can actually come about:

I. There are now many different kinds of anthroposophical institutions—schools, farms, homes for handicapped children and hospitals, where co-workers come together attracted by the work of the particular institution. Wives who have followed their husbands meet each other in these places and often may feel thrown into each other's company. I have been in this situation, in a quiet, isolated place, and I was really very glad to meet other mothers with whom I could form a women's support group. I will describe this group more fully later on. Generally speaking such a group comes together more because of the isolation than by choice.

II. It is quite different when a women's support group is brought into existence in the context of an adult education programme: an announcement is made and women may choose to participate. It is very important how the announcement is worded, The character and the approach, the aims, and the main questions should be made as explicit as possible.

III. The easiest and most common way for a support group to come about is probably through friends whom introduce other friends. It will be clear that it is quite different to work once a week with a new group of acquaintances or with friends who you see almost every day. It is important to see that each kind of group has its own possibilities and its own difficulties. In a group where members are not initially friends but meet only through a shared interest in a particular topic, you can sometimes feel more freedom to express yourself. You are not obliged to incorporate in your behaviour tomorrow what you discover today in the group. You can put a question or a difficult problem before the others without fear of being confronted with it tomorrow by your friends. This will of course be different from person to person.

IV. A fourth possibility is an initiative taken around a Waldorf school or similar meeting place. A mother can announce her wish to work together with other women in the newsletter of the school. Here again it will be helpful if she describes her expectations and the possibilities she sees for the group as clearly as possible. For mothers with babies and small children it is not always easy to meet people via the school. This is unfortunate because often women with children under six may feel particularly in need of support. It might also be possible to announce one's questions and interest in forming a group in a newsletter for those interested in Anthroposophy if such a thing exists in the area. Or an announcement could even be placed in the waiting room of the family doctor. Here, if nothing else, you will meet many women with small children.

A totally different question is how to form a support group if there seem to be no other women around who are interested in Anthroposophy or another related outlook.

A notice could be put up in a Healthfood Store or Natural Childbirth Centre or similar place where "seeking mothers" are likely to go. One could list themes for discussion or for forming "practical self-help" groups. It is surprising how often other women long for an opportunity to discuss how they feel about motherhood, how they are coping or not coping with loneliness and in which way they can also develop their own personality.

Another suggestion is to set up a serious correspondence with a good friend who lives elsewhere. I think you have to organise such an activity very strictly. Instead of going every other week to a group session you have to organise yourself behind your desk and write! I think you need a fixed day and a fixed time, otherwise the demands of daily life will easily take priority. You can start by formulating an essential question—about feeding your baby, about an illness or even more general questions like what keeps you going through the day?

What inspiring thoughts, prayers or other kinds of texts do you know of? In the next letter you get involved in your friend's question; you try to contribute to her situation. Writing can become an art and although it will never replace a group, if there is no group, such a regular correspondence can become a conscious growing process.

In an isolated situation it can also be fruitful to use the telephone more consciously. I often used to feel that I could not afford long distance phone calls, but later I reassured myself by thinking of the price of a train ticket. I remember a period when I used to prepare my phone calls in a special way. First I fixed a time which would suit both of us: a time when we would not be interrupted by children and also after a short space for relaxing from the rush of the day. This was so that we could really feel the space to come to terms with the particular point we wanted to discuss. Perhaps it sounds a little strange to be as precise as this, but I experienced that being with small children I could not otherwise really take hold of possibilities. Previously I would feel the need to talk to someone but this impulse would fail because of screaming children, burning food in the kitchen or the dangerous little hands of a toddler walking around. Such an impulse would also some- times fail in the evening time because I did not have the energy left to get myself together and formulate the question I was living with in a clear enough way so that we could work on it. Then the possibility would pass by and I would go to sleep very unsatisfied. Preparation usually gives more freedom of movement.

Support groups, support contacts, letters or phone calls all have a character of work for me—conscious work, in which the element of continuity and rhythm is essential. Support from the outside will be more effective when we support the chosen process in ourselves as well. Things do not change or grow by themselves.

One Group's Attempt

I would like to describe the development of one mothers' group with which I was involved. Four years ago I moved to the country where my husband was involved in an anthroposophical institution. I met the wives of his colleagues and soon we had a mothers' group. All of us had small children. There was no playgroup or nursery school in the surrounding area which we could feel happy with, so we started a play- group of our own. One morning a week, two of us had the responsi- bility for the play-morning.

Not all of us were very informed about children's play—about songs, stories, little jobs, seasonal festivals and so on. So we decided to come together once a week in the evening. Here we prepared the play-mornings, gathered ideas for special activities and had some singing exercises. One of us had been a Waldorf teacher previously so she could give a lot of help. We learned many things which normally are done by a professional nursery teacher, which gave us the chance to deepen our task as mothers. The ideas we exchanged and gathered together for the play-morning also had an influence on the way we lived with our children during the other days of the week. For example, to sing together became an important part of the evening. In the beginning it felt funny to sing children's songs in a group of adult women, but it was a great help to repeat, and repeat again, the melodies and words. I only knew old songs, folk songs which were very nice but often I was not sure about the words, so I had to write them down. We began looking for new songs to accompany the seasons of the year and also for pentatonic melodies for festivals and lullabys. We practised in order to present our songs the next day to our children at home; we did it so that we could support the children's efforts when they came home from the playgroup. Creating a singing culture at home is an important task of a mother, I think, and this group was a great help in doing this.

We also did observation exercises. We would choose one child in the group and spend an evening talking about him or her. We tried to build up a picture of the child, each of us trying to give some objective observations. Then we tried to add some experiences with the child and some personal thoughts about the child. We began telling each other what we had actually seen: the physical build of the child, the colouring, the movements, the voice, the patterns of communication, and so forth. It was wonderful to have an opportunity to learn to look more objectively at our own children.

We also spoke about nutrition: what do you actually feed your child? What questions arise? What is the meaning of nutrition in general? How do you give your child meals? How do you prepare them? Where do you buy the food, etc? And we spoke about clothing: what kind of materials seem preferable? Where can you get them? How warmly do you dress your children, and why?

We looked at the question of toys as well: how many? What quality? How do you handle gifts—perhaps from grandparents—sent with love but which are not what you want for your child? We also talked about children's drawings. We showed each other drawings our children had made and we tried to observe them in a conscious way. We spoke about children's games as well: what are favourite games for what ages and what temperaments? What are successful games for birthday parties? We considered birthdays: what is the meaning of celebrating a birthday? How can you build up a family tradition? How can you involve the children in this?

We also talked about our awareness of the passage of each day: when do I do what during the day? Do I ever plan the day? How do I relate to the rhythms of daily life? How flexible and how rigid am I in making plans? We went on to look at our different "going-to-sleep" rituals with our children: what pattern can you build up in bringing the children to bed? How do you guide the child from waking to sleeping?

Each area of questioning opened up ever new questions. We did some study of the temperaments, of the influence of birth order on children in a family, of the development of the child in the first three years. We also did some study of the Christian festivals throughout the year.

Weeks passed by, months passed by, and finally we had worked together for more than two years. This support group gave us much satisfaction because we became more conscious of our work, of our daily experiences living and working with our children. We got to know each other through various mother-oriented activities. Gradually some members began to feel the need to get to know the individuals, including themselves, who lived behind and through the role of mother. In talking one-to-one we had over the years exchanged some of our personal struggles with life, our difficult experiences in marriage, our problems with motherhood; but it was not possible to make this part of our joint work, part of the mothers' support group. It was not a shared aim and gradually our interests began to grow apart.

I think it is very important to accept this as a part of group development. People have different needs, feel attracted to different approaches, and live with different questions based on their different stages in life. Perhaps I can draw some general outlines about the process of development in support groups.

At first, members of the group may feel a kind of relief: "Finally I can speak with others about things which are near to my heart"; "Here I feel time and space and interest for questions I carry in myself." There is usually a real enthusiasm for each other, and an eagerness to get to know the others in a more personal way. There will be interest in the differences and excitement about the similarities. As time goes on members may become more aware of deeper expectations in themselves and of the different ones living in others. The more characteristic differences will pop up again and again. Perhaps confrontations between different approaches will occur and questions of separation may come up. If there are enough members, re-grouping can sometimes be very fruitful. Different interests can be grouped together according to common life circumstances, ages of the children, etc. But equally it may be fruitful to work through the difficulties and to find new common sources for continuing the work together. I think it is important to consider both of these as possible solutions.

Ways Of Working Together—Leadership

I would now like to give some impressions about various working styles which have evolved in different mothers' groups. Sometimes women will come together feeling a shared sense of responsibility for the group, in terms of the content as well as in relation to the group process. They may feel no need for a particular person who formulates the beginning of a session, who prepares the questions or who takes care of the continuity from previous evenings. Such a group can be very spontaneous and people can feel at ease. But I have also experienced the difficulty in such a group when everyone arrives tired from the day's work and feels the need to take in and to be received by the others instead of being able to actively contribute to a shared leadership. So a great deal of the evening may be spent nicely drinking coffee, eating delicious cakes, and talking and talking about things of the day. This is very pleasant to do and very worthwhile as well, but usually afterwards members agree that it was not the aim of the group and they feel frustrated by the lack of content. But at the time no one felt able to interrupt the flow of things. One solution to this can be to take turns preparing and guiding the evening.

A different approach can be to ask one person only to guide and prepare the evenings. This may be a person who has a certain capacity for leadership or who is in a life situation which allows her to take on this responsibility. It is very worthwhile for someone to carry the aims of the group throughout the days in between meetings. This can foster a more living process. If a foundation for adult education organises a women's support group the responsible person will as a matter of course introduce the work and offer a structure in which people can meet and grow together.

I do think it is necessary for women to take this task of preparation and leadership seriously. In coming together it is important to choose a structure for some evenings. If the structure does not meet the needs, the group can decide to try some other form, but it helps everyone to know, at least generally, how the evening will proceed.

Structure Of An Evening

Let me give one example of a supportive structure. A support group for mothers of small children can start with singing some songs related to the seasons or the festivals. Someone must prepare the song and have the courage to strike up the tune. Those who come late can easily join in. (This may often happen; there is usually someone who has to stay home a little longer because of a sad toddler, or a baby who needs an extra clean nappy, or because the babysitter is late.) The next part of the evening can be a short exchange of useful tips: a nice toy shop you have discovered, a delicious recipe, a successful way to give your children a hair cut, the name of a new and artistic picture-book for little ones, a treatment which worked with an illness of your child, and so on. If all members live during the week with this idea of exchange, they will remember useful suggestions for the benefit of the group. Sometimes it is important to give space in the beginning of the evening to a particularly urgent question or problem. Sometimes the formulation of the problem is sufficient for the time being. The group may decide to work on it further at the next meeting in order that everyone can live a bit longer with the essence of the question. Occasionally it will be clear that the problem needs to be tackled that very evening, and the group can decide to take it up. It is important to be conscious of such a decision to change plans, or frustration may be experienced later by some group members.

The middle part of the evening can be used for discussion on a chosen theme. For example: how do you celebrate birthdays of small children? How can you create a meaningful ceremony? How can you build up a tradition? And how do you prepare the birthday inwardly as well as outwardly? There are thousands of possible topics. In the beginning of the year members of the group can gather together all kinds of questions and try to make a list of priorities. In due course this list can be changed if new and more urgent questions come up. The evening can be closed off by singing again. Or, I know of another group which also finished in an artistic way: they closed with a verse, a poem, a short story or by looking at a picture together. They told me they were very happy with this, that it created a peaceful mood which could be carried away and into the following days.

Variations On A Theme—The Mother As Woman

In the above section I tried to share some thoughts about how a mothers' support group can work. The example I gave was focussed on practical questions for women needing support in the realm of everyday matters of child rearing. Many mothers of babies and toddlers feel the need to exchange as many practical problems as possible. Almost everything in daily life is a question or can become a question and needs support. But it will be clear that this is just one of the reasons to create a support group.

The aim and character of the support group will be very different according to the phase of life in which the members are, and also in relation to the ages of their children. Equally influential are the different members' previous or present outside work situations, their life-styles, and the extent to which they are conscious of their actions. All of these factors contribute to the expectations of a support group.

One can say that a mother has a relationship to four different spheres of reality: (1) her practical daily life with the children and in the home, (2) the community or communities in which she participates—marriage, friendships, or some broader community, (3) the larger society in which she lives, and (4) her relationship to herself.

There are many women today who need support in finding a relationship to themselves: who am I—as a woman, as a mother, as the wife of ...? A support group taking up this general theme will emphasise inner questions, questions of personal development and about relationships, marriage and work. In order to consciously research the question of motherhood *and* womanhood, members may feel the need to meet each other as individuals, rather than only through their roles as mothers.

I have noticed that in Holland there has been a tendency for two separate kinds of women's groups to exist. Women who feel connected to the practical questions of motherhood generally do not attend meetings on consciousness-raising. Women who feel the need to work with other women on the inner questions of motherhood often feel unhappy making dolls or Christmas decorations without the possibility of also dealing with questions like: why should *I* be making this doll? or, what does Christmas actually mean to me as an adult living in the 1980's? In Holland there is a flowering of a "family-culture movement" around Waldorf schools. Through this there are many possibilities to learn hundreds of things which really can nourish one's existence as a mother, can stimulate warmth and attention in the family, and can generally enrich the quality of one's mothering. However, I have noticed that many women miss the opportunity to relate *themselves* to all the beautiful activities. They need a group in which they can discover what kind of mother they *want* to be, and from there consider which of the many wonderful suggestions they can actually take up themselves. Many women have trouble living up to the ideal picture of what a mother can be. They feel themselves above all a person, an individual who is very willling to grow, even towards an ideal but always in connection with present, individual ways of being.

I will illustrate this dilemma with an example. In exchanging thoughts on motherhood you can come to the conclusion that how a child awakens in the morning is an important moment of the day. You can hear from others or read about the possibility of a little ritual which might accompany this moment of awakening. Perhaps you could sing a little song, or play some music, or open the curtains or light a candle. You might welcome the child by calling his or her name, or first greet the child's dolls, or do whatever you think will help the child to enter the day in a positive way. Now, the first important point is the insight that the transition from the world of sleep into the world of being awake is an important moment. The second point is: am I actually able to accompany this moment? and if so, for how many years? As the children get older they will not need such a ceremony any more. But still the atmosphere in the house is quite different if the children and the parents are both awake early so that the day starts in an active, shared way: or if the children are alone in the early morning knowing that their parents are still in bed, still tired and perhaps irritated by the children's noise.

The first kind of mothers' support group would exchange thoughts about various kinds of morning rituals; the second kind of group would try to discover how each member relates to this possible task. This second group would probably picture complications. Father wants to sleep in, mother wants to sleep in; so who is responsible for a positive guidance of the child in this situation? There might be much talk about equal rights for mother and father. The struggles can be shared. But also the group can work on questions like: did I ever consciously choose to become a mother? or, who actually feels responsible for the quality of the children's upbringing? or, who is, in a way, the pioneer of a new family culture? It can be a great help to discover in the support group that you do actually feel this responsibility, that time after time you are the "pioneer" in family educational matters. The group can help you to accept this reality and to strengthen your attitude. If you take an initiative you must also carry the consequences. If you can feel this through and through, you may then not feel you have been forced to make so many personal sacrifices.

Taking this example of the adult's wish to sleep in even further, it may help to relate this to a larger context, namely to that of our western culture. In a way this culture as a whole oversleeps the early hours of the day. Modern people find it difficult to be awake at sunrise. Only when nature is almost half-way into day-time does modern life really come into action. People tend to stumble behind the process of nature, they have trouble following consciously what occurs in the natural world. A support group can help one to become aware of the deeper meaning of questions like this, and members can stimulate each other to create a kind of counter-culture. We definitely need each other in such efforts; it is very difficult to change by oneself. A support group such as I have described can help to look seriously at a problem, in this case that of the discrepancy between one's own need for sleep as a participant of modern western culture and an insight into the deeper meaning of the early hours of the day which awakens the possible task of more consciously guiding one's child from sleeping into waking.

Other topics for this kind of group could be:

—What do you feel as basic tasks of a mother? What tasks can be taken over by another adult? What really needs the personal activity of the mother?

—How do you experience the limitations and possibilities of marriage? How can you work with these? How can we build a true and inspiring image of the meaning of marriage?

—How can we discover feminine and masculine qualities in each of us, in each human being, and how can we develop both sides of ourselves?

—How do you create a balance between the needs of your children, those of your husband, and those of yourself?

—How do you relate to your mother?

—How do you relate to your own body?

—How do you relate to men?

. . .and so on and on.

It will be clear that this kind of group asks for a personal involvement of all members. There must be a willingness to explore one's own attitudes, one's motives, one's possibilities and one's problems. And above all, it needs patience, warmth and real attention to carrying and supporting the other members.

Before finishing this article I want to mention one more possibility for a support group. At a particular time in my life I felt I did not want to talk about caring for children or household matters anymore. I was not looking any more for support in the realm of educational or social questions. But I felt a strong need to work on questions of inner development. I felt I had to build up inner strength, to work at the question: how do I become my own guide? Of course I still needed other people, and I still needed social contacts; but above all I needed contact with my inner being. If everything else should fall apart, I needed to know myself.

So a third kind of group came into existence, a group which offered support in pursuing a path of inner development. For one year I worked on this once a week for a short time in the evening with two other women. We started with a booklet by Rudolf Steiner called *"Practical Training in Thought"*. In it there are several exercises which can help one to develop one's thinking. The three of us had felt strongly the need to become more in control of our thinking activity. Like many other women, we had the experience of getting stuck in endlessly spinning thoughts. Every week we talked with each other about our struggles in doing (or not doing) the exercises. It was helpful to have this exchange with other women because we could recognise the similar circumstances in which we had to create possibilities for inner work. It was inspiring to see how others found a way to make such exercises a part of their daily lives. Together we could help each other to discover what prevented us from making improvements, but likewise we could encourage each other in our achievements. After working with this first booklet we then chose to work on the eight-fold path as described in *Knowledge of the Higher Worlds*. Each day of the week we tried to concentrate on one of the exercises. For instance on Monday we tried to understand what it means to use the "right word". For a whole day we would try to live with questions like: how do I use words? what do they mean to me? how do I listen to the words of others? On Tuesday we concentrated on the quality of the "right deed". on Wednesday "right balance". and so on throughout the week. We experienced these as very appropriate exercises in our daily lives as housewives. We could always come back to such exercises without needing to completely withdraw. We experienced this work as a support in our efforts to become more independent, to learn to take a little more distance from daily life.

I want to mention some other themes which can be treated in this kind of group. Rudolf Steiner gave verses for every week of the year, published as *"The Calendar of the Soul"*. These can provide a very

inspiring starting point. Group members can help each other to consciously live with these verses during the week. Members can consider:
what quality do they offer to the week? what can I recognise as connected to my own life experiences during this week? Or another question
for the group can be: how do I relate to prayer? what are my needs and
possibilities for prayers? Many women experience their soul life as a
flowering but also a turbulent realm. How can we become peaceful
gardeners of our souls? The exchange of experiences with praying or
with meditating can be a very important work for a women's support
group. And further there is the question of one's attitude during the
day. How do I walk? How do I stand upright? How do I move my
arms? How do I use my voice and how do I use my eyes? Do I consciously observe things around me? Am I present in what I do, or is
there a separation between what I think and what I do? Sharing these
questions together group members can help each other both to grow in
self-awareness and objectivity, and also to develop real capacities for
supporting others.

My intention in this article has been to show how important it is
to take your questions as woman and as mother very seriously, and to
encourage you to find "colleagues" who want to share in the work of
finding your own solutions. I have tried to show how these questions
may belong to the realm of practical activity in caring for children
and a home, or how they may belong to the realm of social consciousness (how do I relate to my children, to my husband, to others, to
society and culture?), or how they may also belong to the realm of
spiritual development (who am I? how do I relate to life and development?). I think that all these kinds of questions will always interweave
with one another; they do not exist separately but in patterns. But I
also think that in one phase of one's life, one kind of question will be
more urgent than others, and for one person certain questions will be
more important than for someone else. But I do wish all women, all
mothers who want to work on their "professional" development, good
luck in finding a useful and appropriate form for working together in a
support group, and I wish you all strength and courage to continue
growing!

4. COPING ALONE
A Mother's Challenge

Trudy Derwig

Λ single-parent state asks for courage, ingenuity, creativity, presence of mind, ability to live in the moment, endurance, wholeness and many other things. Most of us have these qualities more or less dormant in us, but one is not prepared for the intensity with which they are needed. The circumstances which lead one into becoming a single parent are for each of us different. However, one can point to similarities of feelings such as a sense of being lost, of disorientation, inferiority, anxiety, perplexity, anger. At some point after a separation waves of emotion never experienced before are going to hit one. If the separation is through death, this starts almost immediately. In case of a divorce one is so engrossed in practical details, that this process is warded off for quite some time. What happens though when the emotions start to hit you below the belt is crucial and I would like to share some of my experiences with you and say how I dealt with them.

Witholding Blame

Unhappiness is a marriage is often expressed through *blaming*. What emotions underlie blaming? For me blaming often expresses a deep sense of my own inadequacy to deal with a situation. And as it is most discouraging to feel inadequate one externalizes the discomfort and *blames* someone else. Had I understood this principle years ago I might not be divorced now. The inner blaming takes the form of criticism. Whether the criticism is done openly or secretly our children will *know*. And right at this point the wisdom anthroposophy brings can be of great help. The child (or children) involved in a separation has *chosen* his or her parents. *Both* the parents. Out of that choice flows a deep commitment to *both* of them. Whatever the age of the child, it cannot *bear* to be disloyal to one of the parents. That these parents can no longer live together is tragic, but for a child it is much more tragic to sense the dehumanizing act of trying to destroy each other in deed or words. So the tremendous responsibility not to let this happen lies with both parents. To achieve this takes almost superhuman strength, but do live with the conviction that superhuman strength is fully available in such very stressful moments of life.

The True Mother

At this point a picture from the Bible comes to my mind: the two mothers, who both claim a baby is theirs. Solomon orders the baby to be cut in half and then the true mother shouts: "Give the baby to her". Both father and mother must strive to be the *true* mother in times of a separation.

My message is very short: Don't fight over the children! The fight is a personal, individual one and is often not even linked with the partner, let alone the children. Ensure that the children can have a sense of *respect* for you both. After the separation our three small children immediately started to weave back and forwards between us. Both my husband and I—without having talked about this together—strove to continue the feelings of high regard and respect for each other. The children sensed this and were free to *be* with either of us, without being influenced into a one-sided opinion, or having to take sides between the people they loved and love most. We kept our disappointments in each other to ourselves and tried not to share them with friends and relatives. That was not always easy, but children sense all kinds of side-taking in the adults around them and for their sake it is important that we adults do not take sides in disagreements occurring among our married friends.

Supportive Influences

This is the time to strengthen the relationships with the teachers of the children. Most helpful can be the people around us who want to help with the practical aspects of our life. To be with other couples can be quite traumatic during such a time, yet they were then my greatest comforters. It is so redeeming to sense human beings, who may be struggling, but who are still together and may always be together. And for my children it was and is blissful to play in the homes where a father and mother are laughing, caring and coping. It somehow took the sting out of their situation and enabled them to see a little beyond this moment and reach out to a goodness which existed despite the predicament we were in.

Negative effects Of Unconscious Guilt

Very much depending on the circumstances of the separation the feelings of guilt are an important issue. Guilt is a strange thing, because it rarely comes out openly or works in a straightforward way. It has many disguises and somehow we manage to push it enough out of the way not to be threatened by it, yet then it comes out crookedly and unrecognizable. In this respect children are wonderful recipients for the fruits of this emotion. I did so many silly things out of feeling guilty, which were more or less harmful to my children and I'll try to clarify this somewhat. Suppose someone cannot continue to live with his or her partner and leaves home and children. Feelings of guilt are so tremendous that they therefore need to be disguised. The cloak covering the guilt may be accusatory behaviour towards the person one has left. One might even try to convince the children of negative characteristics of the parent they are with. One may attempt to buy the children's love through expensive presents. If one lives with the children one might feel overburdened with guilt for taking a loved parent away from them. Out of that an unbalanced authority might arise. One might accept much more than one would have done if one had not deprived them of a parent. Children are very sensitive to the undermining aspects guilt brings about and will *undoubtedly* take advantage of the situation. They cannot do otherwise, but of course it is not *really* what they want.

The Right Time For A New Start

The next issue I would like to touch upon is a very delicate one, namely the question of a new partner and how one can support the children with this. Indications Rudolf Steiner gave on this confirm that in marriage one merges together on a subtle but powerful level and after a separation it takes as much as three years to become completely separated from one's partner again. One has been joined together to a far greater extent than one can envisage and in view of this a substantial interval of time between a separation and a possible remarriage should be considered. Added to this are the *feelings* of children involved, especially when they are older, loving both their parents. So two very contradictory processes are working in on us. On the one hand one needs to be loved and find a new security, on the other hand one is not free enough to love. I know for a fact, that new security can only be found in *yourself* after a separation. No one can give it to us, we need to work for it ourselves. "Time heals many wounds" is the saying. One needs time to heal, otherwise one takes all into the next relationship. A tremendous amount of undigested experiences make a deep love and commitment towards a new partner impossible. Children feel the truth of this instinctively and it is often not the new partner they resent, but they sense it is not right for their parent to be involved too soon. In fact, in this confusing time after my separation my children had often more commonsense than I, and I am grateful for the small whisperings in me, which urged me to pay attention to their wisdom. I realize that I cannot, may not, give a decree on this matter, but I urge you to be open to the challenge of living alone and aware of the strength one gathers from this period, which is considered to be a misery, yet may well hold the pearls of your life.

Dealing With "Bruised" Children

Until now I have touched upon the more general aspects of a separation. Now I would like to try and focus a little more on the children.

Although public opinion on children from "broken homes" is not always very good, I personally have tried to take this stigma as a challenge. Children living continually with parents who live in disharmony or lack of true concern and love for each other, have a great burden to carry as well. But it is a fact that one has to be more careful with children who have gone through this experience. The ice is much thinner and cracks more easily. (I could describe my children as being both more vulnerable *and* stronger.) I found myself changing and adapting to this after I started to have the full responsibility for them, realizing fully that they were bruised as well. For instance, I tried not to expose them (if possible) to unhappiness and disharmony. I avoided situations where their worries were enhanced and looked for good moments of life. Not that one should become over-anxious, but the child needs to feel *more* that one protects it, cares and is concerned. It will feel safer with that extra care in the background. It takes a tremendous inner discipline to look after one's children properly in any case and there are stages when one wants to give up completely.

I found my children responding very well when I explained to them that I was at the moment fully responsible and therefore had to be more careful than other parents maybe were at certain times. This I shared with them as early as eight years old. Children have a strong sense of being different when their parents have just separated, even if there are five more divorced parents in the class! They somehow always feel they are the only ones. Only later, when reasoning begins to come in, can they compare their situation with others. To somewhat bridge this feeling of being different I always invited lots of their friends over at the weekends to stay the night, help bake cakes and bread or go swimming with us. This helped me to make more of an effort to get a cosy mood in the house and it helped my children with their feelings of isolation (and mine!). I must say that I often did more for the children *because* there was a guest. A guest helped me strengthen my will to make the best of a not so good situation and they could playfully break through a dark cloud hanging over the family circle. These visits engendered visits to other homes, through which horizons were widened and thus my children saw that every family has struggles.

Whenever I felt a wave of misery or depression approaching I took the children out on long hikes, walking through the hills or along the beach, rain or no rain, carrying a picnic in a rucksack. Somehow being outside in nature helps to ease out these difficult moods. They did not always go away, but the quality and intensity did change. Looking back I still see myself stepping frantically through the ferns, a trail of three small children and two dogs behind me! But it worked!

Baking Away Bad Moments

On Saturdays I would avoid shopping. My children have always hated it and I found large crowds full of seemingly happy families too much to cope with. So on Saturdays we usually baked bread rolls—whatever could be made of a large ball of yeast dough. Each of the children would bake shapes of their fancy, chocolate-filled rolls, plaits, strudels, funny faces decorated with nuts, raisins and sweets, anything going. The smell of baking bread drove away all moods. I would light the open fire, burn a candle and we would eat our freshly-baked produce. In a way I could look with a certain amount of amusement at my own actions to try and avoid a depression. The actions did not always work, but more often they did! And due to our continuous baking and cooking together my three children have become great cooks. As a working mother I now reap the fruit of this! When my teenagers don't feel well now, they start to bake something together and whatever is bothering them goes.

The Healing Value Of Routine

On Sundays, often that most difficult day in the life of a single parent, I usually went to the children's service and after that we would go swimming, indoor pool in winter, outdoors in summer. These activities gave a certain shape to the day and the children having spent their energy would read round the fireplace, whilst I prepared supper. We did exactly this for years. I stress this point because I realized the value of structured weekends, with certain rhythms and a regularity to them. The details can be different for all of you, but the importance lies in the recurrence of dearly-loved activities. A certain sameness in how we spent the weekends made the children peaceful as well as myself.

Another wonderful activity is reading to children. This does not come easily to some parents, but it's worthwhile to keep trying, for the children then start to ask for particular stories and these always carry something healing for that child. For weeks running I read the same Grimm fairy tale to my seven-year-old son—at his request. Now he is sixteen and 6ft 2in tall. A few weeks ago he was feeling under the weather and I remembered that story and read it once more to him. He was overjoyed and exclaimed: "I remember that story; I used to love it". Although at some level I understood most of their requests, I have never commented on them. Good stories carry the messages themselves and we adults do better not to comment.

I hope that from reading between the lines you understand that things were not always easy or wonderful, but a long time ago my son's Waldorf School teacher said to me: "Don't count the times it has gone wrong but *know* that the children experience your struggle to improve the situation and from that they will grow in the right direction".

5. COPING ALONE
The Father as Full Parent
Steven Briault

Every child needs parental love and care: but what are the true differences between mother-love and father-love? Is the one more essential than the other—and does this depend on the age of the child? If circumstances—such as death or illness, divorce or separation—mean that one parent is absent, is it easier for the mother or the father to assume the dual "one-parent" role?

I have had to work hard with these questions, both outwardly and inwardly, during the time—about two years in all now—that I have been carrying the major parental responsibility and day-to-day care of my son Thomas, now aged five. The experience has been one of continuous and often painful learning: but the invitation to contribute to this book now raises a new and formidable challenge—for how can I express what I have learnt along a path of development which leads through such intimate emotional realms, in clear thoughts and insights, helpful or even accessible to others?

Since his quite early babyhood, Thomas and I have had a very close relationship. I think we recognised in each other a connection which went beyond the merely biological or circumstantial. I had not expected my love for him to be so compelling or immediate: it gripped me and shook me, especially during periods when we were separated. Are fathers supposed to feel like this?

This connection can now begin to express itself in a practical partnership which brings much joy—for instance when he helps me mop the floor, or we wash each other in the bath; but at the same time contains all the tension and pain of intimacy—possessiveness, dependence and over-dependence, strong wills colliding, and so on. Now we have recently been joined by my younger son, aged three. What kind of responsibility have I taken on, as a father, in this enormous and yet commonplace task of bringing up small children?

"Parenting" is a much more lengthy and complex process for human beings than in the animal kingdom. A baby reindeer may be born while the herd is on the move across the tundra: the mother pauses briefly to give birth, and within minutes the foal runs with the rest—anything else would mean mortally dangerous exposure to predators. For the human infant, however, the physical separateness achieved at birth is only a first step on a long road towards independence. During the child's first few years, its capacities develop from a state of total helplessness to the point where it can—physically—more or less fend for itself. The body seems to achieve a certain initial perfection of form and functioning—upon which formal education then builds—around the time of the change of teeth. Until this time, the child's experience, understanding and skill need to unfold largely within the security of the home—that is, the human environment provided by the parent(s). Parental love surrounds the child with a protective "cloak" of caring, on many levels including the physical, which contains elements analogous to the shelter and care given to the foetus before birth by the mother's physical organism.

This, then, was and is my task: to provide for my child the warmth and security needed to sustain him through repeated external changes and allow his own life-forces to unfold healthily. From having worked for several years with emotionally disturbed and maladjusted children, I was acutely aware of the damage which can be done to a child by the "tearing" of this cloak during the earliest years. What qualities and attitudes would I, as a man, need to develop in myself to overcome this danger?

After the birth, and the initial period when breast-feeding is possible, it is clear that the purely physical aspects of a child's care can be adequately performed by any competent adult, male or female. But the "cloak" provided before birth by the mother's body must later be woven from the parent's higher qualities, capacities and attitudes— that is, from his or her "heart and soul". These soul-qualities will have a direct effect on the child's well-being, growth and development.

What is really involved here?

A college-lecturer I once knew developed a view of human behaviour based on "placenta-functions". He was a fiery Irishman, fond of constantly inventing new theories—but this one impressed me as having quite far-reaching significance. He said that before birth, we live in a kind of womb-paradise, receiving total service from the placenta, which provides *nutrition, protection,* and *sanitation.* In later life, he went on, we continually seek these services on all levels from the world—physically, in practical arrangements for living; emotionally, in our relationships, and even spiritually in our beliefs. He went so far as to apply the idea to the Catholic Church—of which he was a member—describing it as a holy placenta-system, offering *nutrition* through the mass, *protection* through its authority, and *sanitation* through confession and absolution!

As a parent, I am clearly responsible for feeding and sheltering my child, and keeping him clean—but each of these, on a "higher" level, seems to contain both a "motherly" and a "fatherly" element. *Protection,* for instance, if it is not to become over-protection, must gradually become *mediation*—standing between the child and the world in such a way as to strengthen him in facing its joys and hardships. This will involve on the one hand, giving the security of total acceptance, unconditional warmth; and on the other, the gradual introduction of clear guidance in the form of certain demands and prohibitions, the establishment of authority and discipline.

Where these elements are strongly polarised between the parents, we may find the situation where father commands and punishes, and the child then runs to mummy to be comforted; or where mother's direct threat is "Just wait till Daddy comes home. . ."

To find the right combination of firmness and gentleness is surely a struggle for every parent. It certainly has been for me. One may *know* perfectly well the importance of providing consistent guidelines in a context of tolerance and understanding—but how often do I find myself on the one hand trying to impose discipline in a harsh, over-rigid way, and then, seeing the suffering this causes, relenting and permitting what

I had forbidden—thus giving my child two unhelpful experiences—and then feeling angry with myself and him as a result. . . Thomas and I wrestle with this daily, and sometimes I feel we make some progress. At any rate, each visit to the supermarket confirms that mothers do not necessarily find the dilemma any easier to cope with than I do.

In what ways, apart from physically, do I provide *nutrition* for my growing infant? A closer look at the nature of food suggests that physical elements and substances do not in themselves nourish us; we cannot simply eat quantities of carbon, oxygen, nitrogen, etc. Matter can only have value as food if its component parts have been combined by the natural creative forces working in the plant and animal worlds. We need to eat what has been alive, and which contains the natural wisdom of growth, in-formed by the sunlight. The laws working in these processes "make sense" of physical elements for us by combining them, as the laws of syntax make sense of words by arranging them in sentences. Digestion depends on this, as understanding does in the case of language. The wisdom of the world is what truly feeds us; it is an enlightening, informing process for the body. In this way the creative "Word" constantly builds and becomes our flesh.

Our minds, too, are nourished by the "grammar" of the world; each phenomenon, like each word, gaining significance from, and granting significance to, a number of others. Our human speech is a reflection of the world-syntax which surrounds us. Through the parent initially, the child imbibes this grammar—in learning to use and understand language, but also in forming practical, working concepts to orientate himself in space, time and relationships.

Children demand initiation into the mysteries of the world. "Daddy, why don't frogs have ears?" Thomas asked me today—really wanting to know. Did I know? Or, hearing the story of the Three Wise Men; "Did they take the camels back to the zoo afterwards?" Children *feed* on stories—and on every clue adults give them as to the way the world works. Thomas' questions are often quite profound—"Why do you have to lie still when you're dead?"—and require true, concrete answers. Intellectual explanations do not satisfy—they are "indigestible", stones instead of bread. It is a startling, humbling experience for a rather head-bound adult to be confronted with such a task—how stilted and stumbling our sentences are, after all!

The counterpart to this, perhaps rather masculine, grammatic activity, must I think lie in the realm of play, of freedom, of fun—for children feed on fun like nothing else; it is a kind of mother's milk for the soul. Fun with words, with their bodies, with things, with the whole world.

They play with its laws—laws of language, laws of movement and gravity, of the senses, of everything. The child who cannot play, will hardly be able to experience freedom in later life.

Wisdom

NUTRITION

Play

Masculine

Feminine

Thomas and I have always been able to have tremendous fun together, and this is a great blessing. Daddies often have this privilege—and yet I think it is as such a "feminine" principle—not identical with "female"! I have learnt, I think, that it is much easier (usually for fathers) to have fun with a child for short intervals after work or at weekends than for a parent (usually the mother) who has to combine the constant, every-day care with many other chores and perhaps—as in my case—full-time work or study as well. So often Thomas wants me to play when I have to work, or would like to have time to read the paper or listen to the radio. And fun is only really fun when both "players" can enjoy it. So I have consciously to make space for this in a very full daily and weekly timetable—and try at such times to shut out my awareness of everything else I "should" be doing. . .

"Sanitation", or *hygiene*, in an expanded sense, I think means caring for the "regularity" of developmental processes. This entails both a vision of the longer-term past and future, and a constant aware-ness of day-to-day rhythms. Traditionally in our civilisation, it has been the line of heredity from father to son which has preserved the family identity from the past and projected it into the future. The son carries on the family name and may also be expected to live up to certain traditions, for example in sport or profession. Or there may just be the desire that one's child is to grow up into a capable, responsible adult; some long-term orientation is nearly always present in a parent.

The opposite, more feminine aspect of this "hygiene" is the imme-diate care of the growing organism—when the child needs to eat, sleep, be toiled—and also its emotional fluctuations.

Life-goals

HYGIENE

Daily rhythms

Masculine

Feminine

In the "polarised" parental situation, father sees in his son a future university lecturer or soccer international—but mother knows why he is a bit sulky and off-colour today. . .

I do try not to project my own ambitions on to Thomas, and to remain quite open about his future: and yet I know that many of my aims and tendencies are reflected in him. I am told that he acts, quite charmingly, as a "little administrator" (my current role) in kindergarten, organising and correcting the other children. Or again, one probably cannot realistically expect a four-year-old always to be friendly to visitors, or share toys without ever quarrelling—but my own reactions in such situations continually show me that I do in fact very much want him to grow up sociable and co-operative—qualities I am concerned to try to develop in myself!

Fortunately I have always been able to live with Thomas in situations where wiser and more experienced people—women, in fact!—have been there to advise on various aspects of physical health and hygiene; and I have actually found it fairly easy to develop and carry a "background" consciousness of his daily needs. More difficult has been to integrate these with my own, and plan each day such that its structure satisfies us both. In principle I believe his needs must come first—but too great an imbalance in that direction leaves me frustrated. I need both to acknowledge and to moderate my male achievement-orientation.

These then are the qualities which I see as raying out from the common source of parental love; the masculine and feminine elements which interweave to form a garment, without which the young child is "deprived" and vulnerable:

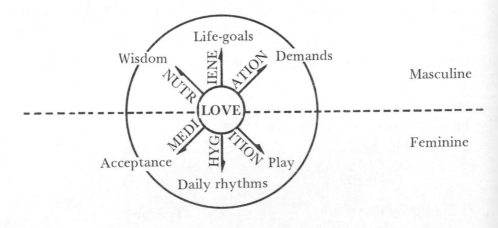

Setting them out like this shows me my strengths and my inadequacies, the directions in which I must strive to become a "full" parent
for my children.

I have been very fortunate in never really feeling alone as a "single"
parent: friends, family and colleagues have all given tremendous help
and support. If these qualities could find their proper expression and
balance in our wider communities, I believe many more children could
grow up strong and healthy in the care of their mothers *and/or* fathers.
For myself, I am learning that parenthood is a path of service and
sacrifice, but is also a powerful stimulus to one's own self-development.
It continually shatters my complacency; and for that I am continually
grateful.

6. ROLE EXCHANGE

Robert and Barbara Sim

The Father At Home

The evenings, after the children have gone to bed, have always been precious to Barbara and me; these are the only times we are able to be alone together. Last year, when I was at home with the children, I listened to her talk about her day at college (her excitement about a lecture or her struggles with a passage from Shakespeare). It was difficult for me to be enthusiastic about the price of carrots or the fact that one of the children had not eaten any lunch. At such times I wondered how it had been decided that I should stay at home while Barbara studied at college.

The decision to change roles for a year developed slowly (as with all decisions it is necessary to cast a long look back into one's biography to find its beginnings). Barbara and I grew up on different continents but at a time when social values were changing very rapidly everywhere. For myself, the rebellion against established norms first took the form of extreme left-wing political allegiance. Upon leaving home I found myself surrounded by the poverty of Liverpool. How could people live in such conditions whilst others had so much? My immediate response was to adopt a Marxist interpretation of the social structures around us.

As a student in the late 1960's I continued to revolt against the imbalances in society but less and less I felt that the answer lay in political solutions. Increasingly I saw inner development as the answer to social problems. My studies were continued in the United States where I met Barbara. It was only at this time that I was able to recognise the possibility of transforming oneself through a relationship with another person. Gradually I came to see that by giving to another person we can develop the capacity to create something new within ourself. However, for the first five years of our relationship I worked away from home whilst Barbara stayed at home caring for our family. She had little idea of what my work involved and I had little idea of what went on at home. This gulf seemed very unhealthy to us and our relationship called for more common ground between us. The care of our children and our preparation for teaching have become our common tasks.

We moved to England in 1979 with the intention that I should spend two years at college and, whilst we expected that Barbara would be involved, we had no idea of the extent of her involvement. However, not long after our arrival in England the idea began to develop in Barbara that perhaps she could study as well. She had spent nine years as a mother and felt that she wanted to teach as soon as the children were independent enough. It only took my enthusiasm for the course to convince her that she should also do it.

My initial reaction was one of resistance. I was used to being the one who was involved with the world outside the family and I did not want to give this up. My first line of defence was financial; how could we possibly afford the college fees and another year's living costs? The college countered this by offering a scholarship for Barbara to study. She grasped the potential importance of a year's study for herself, for me and for our relationship. My resistance did not disappear immediately as I struggled with the fear of leading an isolated life as a housebound housewife with all its anticipated boredom, lack of meaning and lack of public recognition. However, Barbara's determination was sufficient to overcome my struggles and I began to ask myself—"Why shouldn't I do it? What about Barbara's development, was I only concerned about my own?" Finally, I had no defence at all and I accepted the wisdom of the decision.

The first few weeks were somewhat of a novelty; I had many new experiences, for example, shopping for an entire family, meeting the children at school and battling with broken vacuum cleaners and washing machines. People admired what I was doing which was a great ego boost and a source of motivation and strength. As I settled into the routine and the novelty wore off my task became harder. I will always remember how glad I was to see Barbara upon her return home in the evening. "At last—relief." After a day serving small children I had had enough. "Take over—they're all yours." Barbara would bounce in enlivened by her contact with adults and what's more, stimulating adults who were concerned with their inner life. For me it was a round of dirty plates and dirty washing. Perhaps the darkest moment of all was when Ian (then aged 1½) tripped and bit a huge piece out of his lip. At first the blood poured out and covered him to such an extent that I couldn't see its source. At that moment of despair I felt that this would never have happened if Barbara had been there. I felt abandoned, inadequate and that it was time to cease this ridiculous experiment.

However, there was no going back and I soon realised that, if I was to survive I would have to establish a strong rhythm. I had always been used to a structured timetable; for example, as a student, the lectures and essays gave me a schedule to work within. However, in running a home there is no one to provide such a structure. I had to find my own rhythm. Of course, much of the rhythm was dictated by the children. The two eldest (plus an older girl, who, together with her mother, lived with us) were at school and therefore their timetable was established. Our youngest son had his requirements as well. In between I had to do the shopping and soon learned of the extraordinary difficulties involved in buying vegetables and fruit whilst a small child is either running out of the door (towards a main road) or taking something off a shelf or screaming because he doesn't want to keep his gloves on. In addition there were children to pick up from school at different times and laundry to do as well as basic house cleaning (never to any great depth).

Much of my day was spent preparing meals. In this respect my task was not as arduous as other housewives in that Barbara would often return home at lunch time and prepare the main course of the evening meal. My task would then be to prepare dessert, serve the food and organise the tidying up after the meal. In other respects my task was also different from that of other housewives. I was able to enjoy a change of rhythm by teaching in the evenings. This, coupled with frequent compliments such as, "I wish my husband would do that for me", or "How good of you to give Barbara this year!"—made my task much easier. The public recognition of my role contrasts directly with the lack of recognition that accompanies the tasks carried out by most women in the home. How often do women receive a compliment such as, "How good of you to give your life to your husband!"

It was in the clearing-up after meals that I saw the importance of working together within the family. By developing a strong rhythm in which the various chores were periodically rotated the children experienced what was involved in running a family. It was also a great help for all of us to work at the same time; the children could see each other working and therefore couldn't complain about any unfairness.

In reflecting upon my experience so far it would seem nothing but drudgery. However, there were many enjoyable moments. In particular the time spent with Ian our youngest son. I feel extraordinarily lucky to have spent so much time with him at a time in his life in which he grew so rapidly. The development of speech was a miracle. His courage on the swings and slides. How we would share a bag of grapes in the park every day. Once I had established my own rhythm for the day I was able to take him for long walks in the forest near our home. To be away from the contracting experience of walking near traffic with the fear of him running into the road. To see him in the woods, walking in my footsteps, swinging a stick, unaware of me. And the quiet, peaceful moments throwing twigs into a brook and watching them float downstream. Back home on my shoulders. Such a bond will be with us forever.

When thinking of what else will remain with me from my time at home I feel I have a clearer understanding of what a woman must provide in caring for her children and home. Her tasks must often be done with a small child hanging on to her leg or with other children demanding meals when she is in the middle of something else. She must be on call twenty-four hours a day without being able to separate her work and living place. What is more, she must be a teacher of aesthetics, for example, in the care she spends in setting the table beautifully or guiding the children's reading.

As I near the end of my preparation to become a teacher I am able to draw on my experience at home. Above all else when at home it is clear how we are models for the children's lives. Our weaknesses and failings, as well as our strength, reveal themselves in the children. Such a realization impelled me to be as conscious as possible in my relationship with the children. Often I fell short of my ideals but it makes a great deal of difference that I am aware of my failings.

The Mother At College

Yes, I was happy to re-establish myself as a full-time mother. But I must acknowledge that the nine months spent sharing with other adults activities, experiences and ideas such as Philosophy, Art, Projective Geometry, Medicine, Architecture, Astronomy, Drama, Literature, Ancient History, Speech and Voice Training—all these have bestowed a far deeper appreciation for the realms in which I dwelt.

Those nine months at college were marvellous. The unfamiliar situations which Robbie and I entered and the separation from our conventional roles transported us to dramatically different vantage points. Disengaged from our normal daily routines certainly brought to light how we could become more creative in relationship to the life within our home and community.

Most valuable to Robbie and me were the discoveries we made about ourselves and each other. Discoveries such as how difficult it was for me to relinquish the majority of the care for the children to someone else—even to their own father. It wasn't as though I didn't have confidence in him, quite the contrary, but the care of our children has been for me so all consuming, that had I not come home nearly every mid-day for two hours, I don't believe I would have been at ease with the change of roles.

On the other hand, to experience self-satisfaction at seeing Robbie struggle with caring for the children on a full-time basis. To hear him say to me at the end of the day, "I'm so exhausted", was absolute music to my ears. For Robbie to experience fully the myriad of details and the constancy of caring for children, spouse and home has made us much more appreciative of each other.

Then to experience the shock of realizing how intellectually lazy I had become. How I had neglected to stretch my thinking beyond the necessary daily preoccupations. Mothers must observe their children to gain insight, but most women (including myself) observe the daily happenings through an intuitive process, simply taking in everything and feeling their observations rather than a step-by-step, organized, categorized, intellectual process. Most women feel their conclusions to be true but know not why. Perhaps I must attempt to train my observational capacity by studying and observing systematically a subject for which I have little intuitive feel. As well, Robbie's awareness of this need in me has made him much more supportive and encouraging in regard to my own intellectual pursuits.

Something on the positive side and much to my surprise was the ease with which I was able to enter the classroom situation. I felt extremely uninhibited considering that for fifteen years I had had no experience of being a student. All through my previous education right into my early twenties, simply to speak, even with a small group of people, proved to be an excruciatingly painful ordeal. So this new found freedom opened me and helped me begin to express what was living in my soul.

As the college year progressed to the third and final term, I found myself disengaging more and more from our family life and allowing myself to be consumed by the various activities at college.

I decided to take on a part in the college Shakespearean production. For me this was quite a challenge. To speak in front of a small group of people was now something I could manage with relative comfort. But to have to perform before an audience was terrifying. Nevertheless, with Robbie's support and the deep love, respect and trust for the woman I would be working with, it came to be. The acting, the speech and the intensity of relationships with the other students was an experience I would open myself to again and again.

For the last eight weeks of the college year I thought almost exclusively of the play. It had been ten years since the birth of our first child and I had not had my consciousness separated from those closest to me the way most fathers, intensely involved in their task, have all the time.

By the final curtain call of the play and the end of term, I was full to the brim with thoughts, feelings and experiences and I was completely out of touch with my family. I had been stimulated to the point of diffusion and unlike the Wise Virgins in the Gospel of St. Matthew (25) my lamp was depleted of oil.

There was no harmony between work (college) and my home life. I began to come home completely preoccupied with the day experienced: there was no quiet space within me to receive, for example, a glorious sunset or a small child bursting to relate a new experience. I had to be guided out of my preoccupation and back into our family life.

Robbie and I realized that this preoccupation, this lack of centre, this inability to be in the present moment, this lack of inner quiet was something that I had complained of many times with him and now he was experiencing the same frustrations with me. Neither one of us is happy in this unbalanced state: we realize how much we depend on each other to help the other to learn how to achieve a more rhythmical lifestyle.

I was ready to come home. Now I needed to re-establish an attitude of spiritual waiting, tending and readiness for the meeting, the relationship. Through this experience of role exchange what became evident to us was the importance of attending to relationships.

I feel very strongly that my purpose here as a woman is primarily to support and nurture my children and husband. To tend the spirit with them, enrich their life of feeling and help be the midwife to their ideas and our shared ideals. Had I been a woman with burning visions of my own for humanity, most likely I would have pursued those and not had a family. But a family and relationships were and are most important to me. Then too, Robbie and I are also aware of and preparing for the time when our children are older and I may participate in a more active role in the community. This coming change of emphasis of my task in life will be embraced because our marriage is one where the harmonizing of our individual natures continuously works towards creating a balanced whole. Together we create a being consisting of our male and female qualities, which is the real parent of our children. The only way for us to bring this being into balance is to be acutely aware of each other's needs, to listen, to trust and to make possible for each other the opportunity to find the wholeness within.

7. FAMILY RELATIONSHIPS: Bearing and Being

Signe Schaefer

Ask almost anyone today what "family" means to them and you get sighs, rolled eyes, wry smiles. Everyone yearns for the connection and closeness which our imagination attributes to families of the past. Yet we live with the everyday challenges: the ups and downs brought on by increasing self-consciousness, high-mobility, consumerism and economic malaise. In all aspects of our social life we feel the need for a more living understanding of the individual and of the dynamics of human interaction. In family situations this need quite literally comes closest to home.

In this chapter I will look briefly at the enormous variety of family types today, trying to broadly define what makes a group of individuals into a family. I will suggest aspects of family interaction and development which can be observed and perhaps cared for more consciously. I will end with a look at the marriage relationship and the particular challenges which come about in a long-term commitment.

Family Bearing

In her book *The Second Stage,* Betty Friedan mentions the statistic that less than 7% of all Americans presently fulfill the long-lingering, standard definition of family as "Daddy the breadwinner, Mother the housewife, and two children (with background bark of dog and meow of cat, and station wagon parked in the ranch-house driveway)."[1] Whether one deplores the crumbling of old structures or values the variety of new possibilities, it seems clear that our definitions of family must grow to encompass many diverse groupings of people. In any residential block of any large city today we might find nuclear families, single-parent families, combined families (step-parents and step-children), extended families based on blood ties, and communal living situations where various adults and children form long-term units of choice. There are also couples without children and these people who live alone but still have ties to their childhood families or to their grown children, as well as those with broken ties to former partners and distant children.

How then can we understand this word *family*? The word itself comes from the Latin word *familia* meaning household, and this in turn is also the root for our word "familiar". It is over a period of time that bonds of familiarity are woven between people. So I would say that a family is a group of individuals who share a common living space, who spend time together, and who have a relationship of intimacy with each other. Ideally a family derives its strength from an on-going commitment and from a shared sense of responsibility for the whole.

But how can I define family without mentioning blood-ties? Such an omission I think belongs to our modern times; even one hundred years ago it would have been inconceivable. But increasingly in the 20th century the individual has emerged as more important than his or her family background. The wide-spread use of first names—even among strangers—suggests the emphasis on the individual and the diminishing importance of whether I am a "Smith" or a "MacDonald". Even a woman's marital status—so important in the past for how she related to the world—need no longer be public information with the invention of "Ms". As recently as 25 years ago for an unmarried couple to live openly together was generally considered to be living "in sin". Whatever their personal wishes, couples feared bringing shame not only to themselves but to their families. When, some years ago, my four-year-old daughter, in asking about the older children of family friends, wondered if "any of them are living with someone before they get married", I knew she had been born into quite a different world than I had been.

The bonds of blood are certainly loosening; the unconscious carrying force of family roles and responsibilities has shifted. And still individuals yearn for on-going connections: if with blood relations, then increasingly as companions on a path of mutual development, not fixed forever in hierarchical interactions; if not with blood relations, then in more consciously chosen groupings. The sudden rise of communes in the 1960's and '70's showed the desire of a new generation to try to create different foundations and varied patterns of relationship in living together as the family ties of the past began to fall apart.

Increasingly family living is a question of consciousness, of becoming more and more responsible for what goes on between family members. In families we celebrate, we grieve, we learn values, we develop traditions. Every day both children and adults learn about sharing, about forgiving, about dependence and independence, about personal responsibility and loyalty to others. Initially children become themselves through imitating other family members. They take in our gestures, our attitudes, our prejudices and fears. They experience what support is or is not, that it is possible to work things through, that mistakes can lead to development, that people can change. As adults we can grow in self-knowledge if we will also learn from our children: the little ones mirror our movements, our tones of voice, our emotional reactions; the adolescents point with scathing accuracy to our weaknesses and hypocrisy. Our children show us—if we will see them—the results of our actions. Perhaps more than anyone else they give us direct feedback about how we actually are, not how we mean to be or hope we are.

When I think of families, I think of the words "to bear", in their many levels of meaning. Essentially I see families as those who can bear each other. As parents we bring children to birth. We bear them out of the spiritual world into this life on earth, setting the stage for the unfolding of each one's particular destiny. Then we carry them along toward their own futures, hopefully developing the capacity to bear their unique individualities in our hearts—neither neglecting nor overprotecting them, nor moulding them out of our own perhaps unfulfilled wishes—but truly bearing them on toward the freedom and responsibility of their own adult selves. Furthermore, luckily, parents can usually tolerate their own children. Who has never thought when observing the behaviour of someone else's child: "I couldn't bear it if my child were like that!"? It can actually be a source of real confidence that indeed we can (with effort, of course!) stand what comes to meet us through our children. Here again is the mutuality of family relationships; our children play a central role in our being able to bring ever new elements to birth within ourselves. They help us along life's way, teaching us so much that our adult intellects could never figure out alone. And generally, with the exception of those embarrassing moments during adolescence, most children can put up with—lovingly or stoically—the idiosyncrasies of their parents.

The Multi-Levelled Household

In time every family builds a multi-levelled household. First there is the physical environment in which the family finds its protection and nurturance, and which, by its very form and structure, influences family interactions. Then there is the realm of family patterns and rhythms which reflects the daily well-being as well as making special moments in the year come alive. Furthermore there is the aspect of mood—the feeling level between family members and also what shines collectively toward the outside world. And finally there is the particular family identity which inhabits these different levels—a kind of unique family being which moves between levels, weaving them together and so growing strong, unless through finding only isolated, cold or disordered storeys it is sapped of life and so withdraws.

I would like to look briefly at each of these levels of family community. If we wish to bring ever new energy and social feeling into our family situations, we need increasing awareness of the complexities and possibilities that belong to living fruitfully and lovingly together. Through becoming more conscious of the perhaps disconnected aspects of our family lives, we may be able to discover the health-giving remedies our own family being needs.

Home Spaces

It is easy to overlook the influence of the physical spaces in which our family life unfolds. Of course we may have a sense for what kind of house we like—bungalow, colonial, cosy cottage, or split-level ranch—but often this is an almost unconscious preference, not necessarily based on family size, age or maintenance requirements. One only needs to move from one sort of house to another to discover how much room layout determines family interactions. Contact with teenagers, for example, is completely different in a six-room bungalow or a three-storey house where they have the attic rooms as their private domain. What difference does it make if the family eats in a formal dining room or in the kitchen which is also the toddler's playroom? How differently does a family inhabit an open living room-dining room combination or a separate living room which doubles as the study?

Of course most of us do not have the luxury of determining the basic architecture of our homes, but we can at least be aware of what turns a house into a home for our particular family. Again, after a move this is especially obvious; it takes time to feel that the spaces support and reflect the family reality, which is unfolding within them. If a family is constantly moving, the rootlessness, the lack of this level of support will gradually begin to be felt. It is in the painting, the decorating, the cleaning and gardening that family members become connected with the physical environment which surrounds their days. And we can ask: who does these different tasks? In what ways do different family members make connections to the spaces which encompass them?

There are many other questions we can ask in appraising our homes as life supporting spaces. How much is the house outwardly directed? Is the entrance always spotless but the bedroom a disaster area? Or does the grass grow long and weedy while we re-decorate the interior spaces? Is the size of the house appropriate to our needs or dictated by some impression we wish to make? Why do we have curtains at the windows —because they look pretty in the room and from the street, or because we need at times to close off the outside world and be alone in the family space? Is the property fenced so we can enjoy the garden in privacy or does our yard belong to the view and enjoyment of the whole neighborhood? There are not right or wrong answers to these questions but it is useful to know more clearly what matters to each of us and what is not so important.

Sometimes we may forget that the purpose of our physical homes is to protect and support life; neither a perfect show-piece house nor an unattended mess can truly do this. The rigidity of the former cramps spontaneity and lively interaction; the chaos of the latter clogs up the soul and muddies the flow between people. Local customs, temperament, personal taste and available resources will all play into any family's need for external effect and internal order, for boundaries and open spaces, for beauty and function. But growing awareness within the family context of the objective as well as the subjective factors which contribute to greater comfort and security in this sphere can only enhance a truly creative living together. When we can become clear about a discrepancy between our intentions and the real situation, we are on our way to being able to alter the situation. In this realm of our physical support structure there are often small changes we can make— a different colour for the dining room, a concerted effort to keep the mail from piling up on a counter, re-arranged furniture in the living room, flowers on the kitchen table—this attention can have noticeable effect on our family life.

Rhythms And Rituals

Now we come to a new level of what makes a household more than simply a physical shell. I think of this second aspect of family life as a kind of life-sustaining force threading our days together through time. It is composed of our habits of interaction, our patterns of daily life. This may be enforced as a rigid structure which allows little ebb and flow, or it may be so loosely attended that there is little sense of daily order or well-being.

Does the family eat meals together at regular times or is it catch-as-catch-can, each one for him or herself? Do the children have bed-times? Do the adults? Are the patterns flexible enough to accommodate special occasions? How does the family celebrate together? What rituals have been built up over the years which belong to birthdays "in our family"? What expectations belong to a cyclic celebration of the festivals? What can be relied on? And what has changed as the children have become older, as the family has evolved? Are family traditions re-created anew each year or have they become plastic festivals to be taken off the shelf?

At various times we may feel that the family is at a loose end, every-one seems disconnected. Then it can be useful to reflect on what activi-ties are shared by what combinations of family members. Have the various patterns become stale? Perhaps the habitual interactions have become so functional that there is no longer a weaving in and out between the different personalities. Have the adults neglected to be flexible enough for the changing needs of the children? The pressures of modern life can be such that we succumb to the feeling that we have "no time" and in this state we can become like strangers passing each other in our busy-ness, not stopping to share and re-create a living family community.

Here is when even one day off from the usual "work" can be so important. In the breaking of my usual routine—because of an unex-pected snowy day or even if a child is mildly ill—I find we can see each other anew; I notice suddenly that my daughter's hair is much longer, or that my son has grown up to my chin! There is a special joy for me when the ordinary lights up because an extra moment lifts me out of my daily rut.

There may be times when you notice that certain arguments have become habitual and if so, altering some factor in the patterns of interaction may be all that is needed to bring about a change. For example, in larger families there can be absolutely regular squabbles at the dinner table and often it can be noticed that these occur between those sitting directly across from each other. Re-arranging the seating at the table may be all that is necessary to allow new patterns of interaction to come alive. Or we can encourage new combinations of family members to do a chore together, to play a game, to take a walk.

This thread of shared time and activity which weaves through the family's daily life is connected with the concept of blood-ties, though the actual blood-relationship is less important today. What matters is the sense of support, of tradition, of bonding which develops between people. Children develop a sense for time, for history, as they experience their own families revolving and evolving through time. From about the age of five, my children loved to hear "tales from babyland"—stories of their early antics, of our particular family history. Here, too, grandparents have so much to offer, for their stories link the single family to a wider net of relationships and traditions. Some families will live far away from grandparents, but this is no reason not to seek out ongoing relationships across the generations. My mother has adopted (and been adopted by) several families over the years, sharing her warmth and life-experience, and enriching her own life as well. Years ago we laughed when she insisted that her first grandchild, at seven months, had named her "Gogi"; but later, while living in Africa, she discovered that this was the endearment in the local dialect for grandmother! Somehow she had known she would be a world-wide grandmother, forming lasting relationships of choice with many more than just her own small family, weaving threads of connection around the globe.

It is important to be able to feel something of an ongoing quality of support in family life. The rhythms and the bonding experienced in one's childhood family will lay a basis for future life patterns. In building new families as adults, we can let this aspect of interaction run its own way, sometimes tying us in knots, sometimes leaving us stranded; or we can bring conscious attention to how we thread our days and years together. We can try to pay attention to what rhythms foster life and well-being, to which rituals enable our particular family to know itself.

Soul Support

A further aspect of family living is the mood which permeates the interactions. This is something outsiders can often feel when entering a home: an atmosphere of warmth and openness, a cold formality, a harassed flutter. The general household mood is of course composed of the various relationships unfolding between individual family members. The home of a young couple with a new baby might have a peaceful, reverential atmosphere, while the air in a house full of teenagers seems to vibrate with electric currents.

It is the shifting quality of relationships which influences this aspect of the family's being together. What feelings exist between different family members? And how are they being expressed—violently, carefully, disrespectfully, honestly, or perhaps not at all? Is there an underlying support and care for the individual development of family members which endures through the inevitable disagreements and flare-ups? Or are the relationships only for show—"my daughter", "my husband", politely addressed and shown off in public but not really met in private? Or do some family members feel put-down, ignored, always criticized? Is there an air of hostility and distrust or a mood of acceptance and of hope? Perhaps various moods prevail at different moments.

It is not easy to relate lovingly to others, and in time this can become painfully evident in family situations. Because of course, individual family members are all changing and developing at their own pace while the outer family structure speaks of some permanence and stability. An individual's transition moments can sometimes be supported by the strength of the other family relationships, but equally there are times when various family members are so absorbed with their personal crises that little positive caring for the other gets expressed. Take for example the adolescent's need to attack the parent to find his or her own identity which so often arises just when the parent is at a low point of self-confidence, in the midst of a "mid-life crisis". Here the parent is challenged to share something of his or her own doubt and struggle instead of building a higher—and ever more precarious—wall of authority. By acknowledging this basic human striving—which the young person in his or her own way is also longing to understand—new avenues of communication can open up.

Much in our modern culture works against a healthy soul development, discourages our efforts to be open to and aware of our own inner feelings or sensitive to the real feelings of others. In the on-going rush of our family situations we can neglect to value the importance of this feeling dimension. Perhaps we fail to allow time for re-creating our relationships, or even to consider how the family seeks entertainment. Do we have times of shared enjoyment, shared reverence, shared suffering? Or does the T.V. lull us into thinking we are being together by partaking in its artificial world?

It is in the soul sphere of the family household that we can best learn to live with the seeming paradox of individual movement and family stability. In this relational dimension we can get lost in the emotional upheavals, or we can become isolated from feeling at all. But we also have the possibility of seeking ever new understanding about our human development and interactions. We can learn to respect the challenges and the difficulties of temperamental differences. We can become interested in the phases of development of the child, and of the adult. We can try to develop more insight into the working of human relationships. Then we can attempt, ever and again, to bring these various perspectives out of the ideal spheres to create together an atmosphere of active support, and heart-felt caring, and shared soul space for further growing.

Family Being

Inhabiting these three levels of a household—the physical spaces, the patterns in time, the feelings of relationship—is what I like to think of as a particular family being. This is an identity which makes every family unique, a non-physical reality like that which makes a group of individual stars come together as a constellation.

The strength and the health of any family being are dependent upon the state of the different levels of the household. In a building, if one storey is weakened—if a ceiling leaks or a wall cracks—the whole structure is in jeopardy; and so it is with a family structure. If there is no attention to the patterns of interaction, or to the physical security, it is quite possible that the family being will break down. Sometimes the weakness in one area provokes a crisis which is the beginning of renewed health—the being only needed to be remembered and attended to. But in other situations the household chaos may be so great that the family being finally seems to disappear, leaving a burned-out, lifeless rubble.

It is an ever renewing attention to the three different aspects of family life which provides the substance in which the family being grows strong. This evolving strength in turn fosters the individual development of family members and allows them to know and value their inter-connections, their mutual responsibility and indebtedness as developing human beings.

Our family being is perhaps our fundamental teacher of love, for it is in the family that we learn so much about what love is, and what it is not. We have such a tendency today to think of love as something which makes us feel good—"I love you because you make *me* happy."

This kind of love is really a taking from the other but truly loving implies giving out. Rudolf Steiner speaks of love as "the creative force in the world", which as such yields no direct benefit to the one who loves.[2] This creative activity goes out to the loved ones and into the world. Steiner connects the selfishness and lovelessness in modern society to a subconscious knowledge that there is nothing personal to be gained by our acts of love. It is as if people think, "Why should I bother to love if there is nothing in it for me?"

Amidst the isolation and loneliness which such feelings engender we can *imagine why a renewal of family life is so important today*. In our family situations we cannot so easily escape the challenges to come out of our selfishness. When a baby cries in the night, most parents respond in spite of their own desires to remain asleep. We rise above our own immediate needs. Even if we do it begrudgingly and more out of instinct than conscious choice, at some point we may "wake up" and see that this experience offers us the beginning of an idea of what selflessness might be. I know that my children have quite literally drawn love out of me. The wonder I have felt at the sound of my baby's laugh or facing a small open face saying "Look, Mommy!" has been a major power in opening me out to the world, in expanding my heart beyond its physical functioning.

In our families we can try to love one another. As adults this must be an ever more conscious effort. Luckily we get many second chances —our family being is there to help us when we stumble. And so we provide our children with their first experiences of what it is to be cared for. Within the family context they also begin to know feelings for others as they take in impressions of the possibilities of love's warmth.

A family being which comes alive and breathes through family members with a healthy sense for roots, a quality of trust over time, and a feeling for mutual support and development provides a source of love which goes out into the world. Each such family acts as a kind of leaven in our all too often hard and flat society, giving rise to renewed possibilities for real human caring and shared responsibility.

Marriage: A Path Of Partnership

I would like to look for a moment at some of the opportunities and difficulties faced by those who choose the commitment of a long-term marriage relationship. By no means are all families today held together by a marriage partnership; many derive their initial strength from the energy and dedication of a single-parent. In others divorce or death brings particular strains and challenges to the family development. Elsewhere in this book Trudy Derwig addresses the special situation of the single-parent family. Although there are increasing numbers of single-parent families, the statistics on re-marriage confirm that most adults yearn for an on-going commitment. In spite of whatever difficulties they may have encountered, most people appear to believe that a long-term relationship is possible.

When people marry today they do not necessarily expect to fulfill the traditional roles of "wife" or "husband". The old definitions are all being questioned and we are continuously being shaken, or shaking ourselves, out of a passive enactment of given relationships. Some may make "contracts" for chore division, economic support, or child-care responsibilities, reflecting how materialistic our understanding of marriage has become.

More and more we meet as distinct, self-oriented individuals and there is little in our society which encourages us to willingly bend toward one another. When faced with the inevitable difficulties of living together, we have few models of encouragement for working things through. Rather we are surrounded by a disposable culture—if something doesn't work, it probably can't be fixed and anyway there is a new, shinier model there to catch our interest. Furthermore, many people enter marriage with the proviso, stated or not, that "if things don't work out, we can always split"; and then so often that open back door makes divorce the all too logical conclusion.

Rudolf Steiner refers to the sacrament of marriage as a recognition of the couple's intention to build together a "community of life". He suggests that the commitment of marriage fulfills a spiritual intention to build this community together on the earth. Here is a background to the phrase "falling in love": the couple's pre-birth intention has come down to earth. Perhaps one of the difficulties today is that so many people marry without any idea of what building a life together on earth might entail.

Whatever the stated, outward reasons for marrying today—as the obvious next step in a couple's living arrangements, because a child is on the way, for security, or even to please the extended families— within the marriage itself there will arise, sooner or later, challenges to any permanent sense of "being in love". Because, of course, love is an activity, not an emotional state; and increasingly it must become an activity which is consciously willed. In this sense marriage can be seen as a commitment to the attempt to love one another over time.

Within this commitment must live the recognition that not only joys but also difficulties *belong* to an on-going relationship. Commitment means believing in more than just the present moment. It is knowing that we are together *because of* the growing we will be challenged to do. In their individual lives many people today will look at their physical bodies and decide they need exercise—to shape up. They will make a conscious commitment to working on this and follow through with dedication, believing that they will look and feel better at some point in the future. Yet this same dedication to an altered future within a relationship is so difficult. How can we find encouragement to stick with the heart stretching joys and sorrows, to believe that the ups and downs and turn arounds can actually strengthen healthy connections?

Through marriage two individuals share a path of mutual development. Initially the direction of this path seems to be given. Something of the pre-birth intention carries the couple forward. The openness of eye and heart which lets the partners see the positive qualities in each other at first blends peacefully with the projections on to each other of what each one's soul longs for. There is usually a common dream for the future and a sense of confidence in the strength of the relationship.

But sooner or later this idealized sense of unity begins to fade. The two evolving individuals may begin to resent the "oneness". Doubt ("if you really loved me you would understand me"), guilt ("I see I'm failing to meet your needs"), and fear ("we might *not* be able to build something together") foster the realization that the earlier dreams may have been part fantasy. With the fading of what seemed given, the question, "Now what?" must be faced.

After about six years of marriage, I can remember feeling that our relationship was like a child who was losing its baby teeth. For the child this marks the final shedding of the physical body substance it has inherited from its parents. Now the child's own life-forming forces become more fully awakened—you need only think how different a child's face suddenly looks once the second teeth have come through. Similarly in our relationship I felt like whatever we had been given as initial caring and protection was used up. I was filled with the question, "Can we now, out of our commitment and our own formative forces, build this relationship further?" I had a strong sense that we were at a new threshold of choice. If we would go on we would need to activate new qualities of caring, and relating, and supporting each other.

Times like this ask us to develop new interest in each other. Perhaps we must step back for a moment from our everyday, automatic exchanges and really look at this person we are living with. What does he actually look like now—if I would see him for the first time? Has her way of walking or talking changed without my noticing? Can I for a moment not look to the content which so often makes me irritated, but to the gesture of this person—to how he or she is standing in the world right now? Can I think my way into the other's view on some issue, not immediately bringing in my own judgment as well? Is there some activity we both enjoy but have made no time for lately? Does the other need more individual "space"—for inner or outer activity—that I could not only agree to but actually help to bring about? There are so many questions we can ask that can help us become interested in each other again, but we must first pause long enough to ask them.

Out of a renewed sense of commitment a couple can become more awake to the ways in which they are weaving a community of life together. After several years of marriage there usually comes a desire to settle down, to form roots in an area, to buy a house, and now more realistically *make plans* for the future. Perhaps there are children, and their schooling must be considered. Decisions are approached more rationally: it can be a time when the practicalities of managing everyday life become more important and, perhaps surprisingly, more interesting. I remember that a key word in this period in our relationship and among our similarly-married friends was "quality". No longer is the partner's every moment, every thought or feeling in demand; but now the times together must be meaningfully spent.

The attention and consciousness which many bring to this stage of relationship may not foster the passion or the idealism of earlier years, but there can develop a warm sense of achievement. The mutual enjoyments, the individual needs, even the themes and patterns of argument have become familiar. It is more possible to know the difference between what matters to be worked on and what is not really essential for now.

But one difficulty of this phase of married life can be that along with the growing sense of achievement there develop too set routines. Tasks may begin to be fixed into roles and partners may begin to feel taken for granted, not *really* seen. Also this can be a very family-oriented time and the needs of the marriage itself may be shelved too often in the interest of family functions and activities.

Now is a time when it is especially important to plan for some times away together as a couple—perhaps a weekend trip, but even to meet in a restaurant for lunch one day can give space to non-functional meeting. Paradoxically in this time of outer planning we may resist the need to plan for the relationship, feeling that spontaneity ought to exist between us. But the middle years of life and the responsibilities to a young family and developing careers are not always conducive to spontaneity. It may be an important step to accept the need to consciously create activities which nurture the relationship. If we only yearn for what was there in the past, we fail to notice that as individuals and as a couple we are in a completely different phase of development; and we may also then miss unimagined joys and possibilities of meeting out of who we are today.

Perhaps after ten or twelve years of marriage, having developed a seemingly solid relationship, strengthened by working together through various ups and downs, there can come a quite new state of crisis. By this time the couple may be in their middle to late thirties or early forties a time when individually there is a lot of inner turmoil. As the partners sense their own aging and become aware of new insecurities and self-doubts, they may begin to feel that the relationship is also flawed. Now the faults and inadequacies of one's partner come into clearer focus and can cause exaggerated annoyance: his or her resistance through all these years to be reformed by my wishes, the idiosyncracies which before were not offensive but now show true vanity, greed, sloth (the way she combs her hair, he slurps his coffee or shuffles across the floor).

As our own darker qualities are rising up in the soul and causing inner unrest, it is all too easy to blame what we see in the other for our unhappiness. And of course the other may be doing this to us as well. It is as if we see and relate to each other's shadow sides; we want to run from this darkness—in the other and even more in ourselves. Now more than ever a relationship with someone new offers an appealing fresh start, the chance to feel young, and worthy, and desirable again.

But it is also possible that the couple can go together through this time of trial, can help each other to face the personal struggles and so develop deeper compassion and firmer loyalty. This is a time which challenges our inner honesty and our active acceptance, both of ourselves and of the other. We must face the need to accept, and even care for, not only what we like but the unredeemed aspects as well—the insecurities, the lack of generosity, the critical tongue, the self-centredness. It is through meeting these unredeemed parts that we grow, and we are on this path of mutual development in order to help each other in our growing. The challenge is to accept where the other is starting from and still to believe in the possibility of his or her development. We need to carry in our hearts a picture of the other's potential—which is neither so far away that the other feels a continual failure, nor so close that we offer no encouragement through the self-doubts and setbacks. And of course we must each remember that the only change I can really grapple with is my own.

The different challenges which arise at different times in a marriage are not exclusive to one period or another. For example, there are seeds of the difficulties of acceptance from the very beginning, though the challenge does grow with time. Of course, people marry at many different ages, and the partners may not even be in the same phase of individual development. Nevertheless, any relationship which is alive is in a continual process of evolving. When we meet older couples who have been married for many years and still are discovering newness in each other and joy in their sharing, we can be sure they have gone through many cyclic ups and downs, crisis moments and challenges to begin again.

Every relationship builds its own particular reality and it is important to not always be comparing one's own with greener looking grass. In an article called *Reflections on Marriage,* Lee Sturgeon Day suggests a way of looking at this uniqueness within the context of basic developmental laws:

"A thought I have been carrying for a while is that of marriage— or family—having behind it a spiritual archetype, as a plant does, and yet which will manifest on the physical plane in a certain particular form, which must also continually die and be reborn. Is my marriage, for instance, a blackberry bush or a geranium? It is no good trying to shape it into a plum tree if that is the case. But I can try to nurture it so it develops into the finest of its species. This, for me, requires something of a sense of the inherent laws of growth and development—no plant will survive without water, light, earth—and I must be loyal to these. . . Then, within such a context of necessity, there are great variables. Maybe ours is a plant that only grows among rocks, under a wide sky, and flowers briefly after heavy snow. Or one that needs shade, much watering and the support of a sturdy brick wall."[3]

Extending this analogy a bit further we can see that the marriage partners are the gardeners who allow their particular relationship to root and grow on earth. The plant may only grow as far as early spring leaves, or it may come to blossom and finally to fruit. If the marriage has become a living supportive companionship built ever and again out of the choice to be together, it stands in the world bearing fruits of loyalty and confidence, shedding seeds of genuine human striving to love.

I would like to end with some words by Rudolf Steiner on faithfulness:

> Create for yourself a new, indomitable perception of faithfulness. What is usually called faithfulness passes so quickly. Let this be your faithfulness:
>
> You will experience moments—fleeting moments—with the other person. The human being will appear to you then as if filled, irradiated with the archetype of his Spirit.
>
> And then there may be—indeed, will be—other moments. Long periods of time, when human beings are darkened. But you will learn to say to yourself at such times: "The Spirit makes me strong. I remember the archetype. I saw it once. No illusion, no deception shall rob me of it."
>
> Always struggle for the image that you saw. This struggle is faithfulness. Striving thus for faithfulness, we shall be close to one another, as if endowed with the protective power of angels.

8.   WHO SHALL BE BORN?
Ernestine Ingenhousz

Your children are not your children!
They are the sons and daughters
Of life's longing for itself.
They come through you, but not
from you. And though they are with you
yet they belong not to you.

The Prophet by Kahlil Gibran

A classic film called *A Matter Of Life And Death* (1947) tells of a pilot who should have been killed when he bales out of a burning bomber. But still alive after a miraculous escape, he resists the summons of a heavenly messenger who comes to take him to his right place in the next world. His upward journey and the story of his resistance are shown through the image of an escalator. Crowds from all nations, colours and ages are carried up and stream through the gate into a big reception hall where they receive their wings, which they have to put on for themselves.

In this article, I want to deal, not with those who are on their way up, but with all the souls who are seeking to come down—those hundreds and thousands whose time in heaven is up, and who are now seeking their rightful place on earth. They, too, seem to need a "helper" to guide them into earthly existence. What will concern us here is the arrival or non-arrival of our fellow human beings on earth.

In the past, guidance in procreation was conferred by nature. Even today, among many peoples in the world, the weather, drought, or food shortages, still play a part in fertility. More recently, human institutions have intervened: the Roman Catholic Church pronounces about contraception. And in countries like China, the government makes laws allowing each couple no more than one or two children.

But very large numbers of people now expect and claim the right to "decide for themselves". With current technical innovations, both men and women can have the pleasure and intimacy of a physical dialogue without a third person—a baby—necessarily arriving in their midst. We can invite or not invite such a guest. So what are our motives and intentions? How far are conscious decisions taken?

Looking around, we appear to be able to regulate the not-having much better than the deciding-to-have. For if nature does not provide the right means, the wanting-to-have a baby can become a complicated business—hormone treatments, test-tube fertilisation and so on. It is hard for parents who plan for and want a child to accept its non-arrival. Perhaps just as hard is a consciously-taken individual decision to seek an abortion.

Many, many children are of course wholeheartedly welcomed by both parents. But some more problematic case histories can help us look at situations where things are not so straightforward:

D., aged thirty, lived with her friend for four years. Their relationship was stormy. They married. She wanted a child. He did not—or not yet. They argued. She told him that if he did not want her to be pregnant, she was going to seek another father for her child—and she did. Nevertheless, she eventually became pregnant by her own husband. After the birth of a little boy everything calmed down, until in a moment of relaxed intimacy she confessed to her husband her escapade with an outsider to get herself pregnant. This belated confession sparked off a terrible row. It led to a blood test of the child, the husband and the other man. The couple had to borrow money for the tests, and to prove the identity of the child's real father. As the mother had thought from the outset, it was shown that he was indeed her own husband. But what about the little boy? After this emotional ordeal, the father lost the paternal "bonding" with the child. He teases and punishes him continuously, and waits only for the arrival of his second child.

Another young couple, a medical doctor and a pianist, have neighbours. When the neighbours' little boy arrived, the pianist longed more and more for a child of her own. She knew that her husband was sterile. So they worked the problem out rationally and medically. After artificial insemination, a little boy arrived. But then the trouble started. The father could not accept, in his heart, the unknown contribution to the arrival of his little guest. Nor could the mother deal with her own and her husband's emotional problems involved in the role of an unknown third party in the child's conception. Of course, the mother loves her baby, but as partners, as father and mother, they are at a loss. The result is that they never show the child to anybody. If you did not know, you would never guess that there is a baby in the family. The little boy was "rationally" invited by both parents. That emotional acceptance would be hard work, after using an unknown donor for artificial insemination, was a surprise. What we think out rationally is not always easy to accompany with our hearts.

Then there is the movement of COM-mothers in the Netherlands and elsewhere—the consciously unmarried mothers. This phenomenon emerged in the 1970's. Some women want a child but not a husband. How they "get" this child is a remarkable story in itself. Some men agree to give them a child; others are tricked into it—the "aborted" person in such cases is not the baby but the father. The women have the decisive role. What the father's situation is to be is decided by the mother. Should he pay for the child? May he acknowledge it? Can he see it? Can he legally ask for his share in the child if he wants it? The law in most countries is designed to protect the unwed mother. In some countries the police can seek out fathers to make them pay.

The mother-to-be has to identify the father. But the COM-mothers reverse the situation. The law and our thinking are hardly prepared for situations where women use men, as in earlier days men used women. Our new freedoms are bringing many new questions.

An important issue now beginning to confront us forcefully is summed up in a headline in a German newspaper: "Who should be born?" Amniocentesis is a test for detecting abnormalities in the unborn child. It is used increasingly. Mothers at risk are sent to specialised clinics, to test for inherited defects. Abortion is the usual response to any abnormalities. This might seem an "objective" decision. But when Dr. Schroeder of Heidelberg's Institute of Anthropology and Genetics analysed the decisions made, he found that the psychological and social environment of the mother was the dominating factor rather than the genetic make-up of the expected child and its chances.

In the 1970's, the United States Supreme Court ruled that every woman should have the right to decide for herself whether or not she wants her child. No other factors—medical, psychological or pastoral—were to influence her. Naturally, any individual might ask for help or advice, but in her decision, each woman should stand alone.

Irrespective of whether this is put into force in all states, it indicates a move which gives great freedom, but will also face individuals with agonising decisions. We can detect not only genetic abnormalities, but the sex of an unborn child. So a woman may then be free to abort a baby girl if she is determined to have a boy.

So our society is "in labour", trying to bring to birth a new relationship to the unborn. Antonio Gramsci, in his *Prison Notebooks,* says: "The crisis consists precisely in the fact that the old is dying and the new cannot be born; in this interregnum, a great variety of morbid symptoms appear."

Our situation is complicated by the several levels of sexual life. It is a physical pleasure, a form of dialogue with a partner, and also a way to conception of a child. Nor is it something static: our physical and emotional needs change and develop through life. So do our relationships with our partners and with children (born or unborn).

Every human being in good health meets their own physically-determined sexuality and sexual needs. At this level, we are on our own. Contraception is then a matter of convenience and health. (It is striking that the pill, which alters the balance of female hormones, is being more widely experienced by women as a kind of "self-pollution", with possible long-term consequences for health.)

At the same time, the most effective methods do not necessarily put us in full control of the situation. In a university town in the United States, the current rate of abortions to births is 2:1. We demand the right to "decide for ourselves". But our bodies can still very often take us for a ride.

Nor are we usually, in reality, "on our own". The growing group of sex instructors suggests, paradoxically, that we do not touch more than the surface of our sexuality if we see it only as a matter of physical technique and personal satisfaction. We are usually in some kind of relationship with another. Here again, freedom brings responsibilities, and more complex ones (including the choice of contraceptive methods). Self knowledge is not enough. We have to try to understand our partners.

But what happens if we begin consciously to include in our freedoms and our responsibilities our relationship to our possible "guests", to souls on the descending escalator seeking hosts who will enable them to begin new lives? Perhaps women, more often than they realise, have intimations, speaking into their relationships and their sexuality, which reach beyond both of these.

Many women seem to feel the presence of a soul to come. Oriana Fallaci, the Italian writer, wrote a little book, *Letters to a Child that never was born.* Her dialogue with her unborn child is so real and the soul is so present, although in the end the child arrives prematurely and does not live. Mothers often dream about their child to come, and may already know its name. And not only mothers. A young man working hard in a profession once told me with deep earnestness of his distress that his girl friend was not yet mentally ready for child bearing, although he had a strong feeling that a child was waiting.

At the Tavistock Institute in London, research has been conducted for the last twenty years, in which students are trained to observe mothers-to-be in "dialogue" with their as-yet unborn children. After childbirth, the student then observes how the dialogue continues. The Institute does not suggest conclusions, but the students begin to recognise, through precise phenomenological observation, a definite person, the unborn child, already in relation to the mother. A unique human being with a very personal antenatal biography appears. This biography lives in the motivations of the "hosts" long before the physical embryonic stages of growth.

So when does life begin? For that matter, when does it end? Death lies ahead for everyone. We often fear it. And so it interests us intensely. "Near death experiences" attract increasing research and "reason" does not dissuade very large numbers of people from their conviction that death is somehow not a wall but a door.

Like death, sleep is mysterious. Some fear it. Vast numbers have difficulty with it. We still do not know quite what it is for. Yet we need it. At the same time, when we wake up, we do not know where we have been. We connect in memory with the previous day, but not, except in dreams, with the night. Yet we have not been in nothingness. Much has been happening. We are "reborn" physically fresh, sometimes with decisions made or problems solved. And if we have slept well, we are the more ready for a new day.

Perhaps we can learn a little from this smaller rhythm of a greater rhythm of death and rebirth. An ancient Indian text shows clearly an understanding of a rhythm of passing through death into a spiritual life, and then returning into the flesh:

> It is as when one layeth
> His worn-out robes away
> And taking new ones, sayeth:
> These will I wear today.
> So putteth by the spirit
> Lightly its garb of flesh
> And passeth to inherit
> A residence afresh.

If we can share some feeling for the truth of this, we must each of us have come to a turning point, the top of the descending escalator, when having put away our "worn out robes" we were ready to begin to take new ones, to seek a new "garb of flesh".

How and when may such resolves reach into the awareness of human partners who can provide this garb? Only human beings have the freedom to look to each other, "I" to "I", and ask consciously that they may be allowed to be "hosts" to a new "guest". There are no ready-made answers or techniques at this level. There is only a path towards a still more demanding freedom, a deeper responsibility, and a need to work for a harmony of thinking, feeling and willing so that we may learn how and when to "invite".

Such questions may also give a deeper meaning to methods of contraception based on women's rhythms. We know that these are related to moon rhythms. We are born ten moon-months after conception. But are the rhythms of the cosmos also indicators of realms which we know in the night, or before birth? Current research into an astrological approach to fertility and conception may also offer us a new freedom and a new responsibility, whereby we may open ourselves more consciously, as partners, to a soul to come.

We cannot impose these freedoms on one another. Each level brings new responsibilities and new disciplines. If we are free, we are also on a more demanding journey:

The Himalayas of the mind
Are not so easily possessed,
There's more than precipice and storm
Between you and your Everest.
C. Day Lewis.

Yet we seem to be climbing. We know deeply the need to be free. But we cannot then speak so easily of "making a child", for where, at the time of conception, is that child's freedom? As free beings, we cannot command, but only learn to invite, another being to be born through us, a being who we can help find its own path to freedom.

As the Tavistock studies indicate, our relationships with our children are already taking shape in our own intentions even before conception. So we may hope that a child freely invited will come gratefully to earth, not as our possession, but as our guest, entrusted to our care, and trusting us for our help in finding its own way into life. Children who trust their parents are also deeply forgiving of our mistakes. Perhaps their powers of forgiveness and love can tell us something of where they, and we, have come from:

Not in entire forgetfulness,
And not in utter nakedness,
But trailing clouds of glory do we come. . .

So wrote William Wordsworth, in his *Intimations of Immortality*. Perhaps in sharing such intimations, we may find a healing for the "morbid symptoms" of which Antonio Gramsci speaks, and "the new" can begin to be truly born.

9. MONEY IN THE MARRIAGE PARTNERSHIP

Joy Mansfield

Living Out Of Trust

When my husband and I were married, immediately after the last World War, we knew that our finances would be pretty tight, but we told everybody and one another that we didn't mind about this in the least. "We'll manage somehow or other!" we cheerfully proclaimed.

Looking back, I realise that we were following, if intuitively some advice given during the years of economic chaos following the 1914-18 war. The only way to keep one's courage alive, was to live out of pure trust without any kind of security. As potential mother and housewife, I had supreme confidence that I would be "supported", not by the State, as I might today, nor by my husband necessarily, nor by myself, but by forces, unseen, unknown, belonging to the future. A friend of mine has a relative who has taken this attitude to its extreme. She says she has made a contract with her own special Finance Angel to whom she appeals in times of need and who, she is convinced, will never let her down!

We had trust, but it would have been better to have had consciousness too, to have talked about the way we would finance our venture more often, reviewed the situation many times and tried harder to understand its wide implications. Then we would have avoided much difficulty and frustration particularly for me. In emphasis the difficulties have changed for a woman today, but the need for consciousness is as great or greater.

The Tester Of Relationships

Money is a great tester of human relationships; it could also be called a kind of token for them. The strains and stresses of the modern marriage will often reveal themselves in wrangles over the sharing out of however much is available. Traditional ways of setting up the financial basis cannot be relied on to work any longer and an ordinary, level headed business attitude, though helpful, doesn't meet the full needs of this special kind of partnership. Even if the family has no offspring and remains a twosome, this is so, for in the vowed attempt to share and remain loyal to one another, a mystery comes into being. Even if the marriage fails, this will haunt each separated partner to some degree. Sometimes legal battles over the financial settlements will appear to keep alive the bitterness for years. It is not really the money which is to blame, but unresolved emotional battles.

The building of a family can test a marriage to the limit, and finances are often the focus of stress and are blamed when total breakdown seems likely. Now the family unit finds itself living in two worlds, financially speaking, and one partner, usually the woman, may be more painfully torn between these than the other. Conception, pregnancy and childbirth, the rearing of the very small child, belong to a world which cannot be easily related to the everyday struggle and bustle of "earning a living", as it is called, and are removed from the stimulation and interest of this part of life. The work that is done in it is not like ordinary work; it has to be a labour of love if it is to succeed. Maybe it should be taken as a model for what *all* work should be, but that cannot but be a long way off—and the family has to exist in the ordinary world.

In my time it was very easy for the wife to suffer from feelings of inferiority coupled with guilt in the spending of money (after all she hadn't earned it!). Something of this still lives in many women, and such negative feelings can only be finally disposed of when the will to share and to understand is strong and steadfast in both partners. The traditional working class habit of the earning man handing over his wage packet to his wife at the end of each week's work, and accepting back without question what she deems right for his own spending, has something of the right mood. Only today things have to be more flexible. Sometimes the man will be earning, sometimes his wife, and both need to give freely to the needs of the family, while decisions as to spending are taken together.

Money is as complex and subtle a thing as human relationships themselves. People are often as afraid of it as they are of these! Even to speak of it seems to invite danger. Who has not observed the baleful spell it seems to cast on human undertakings, freezing one time friends into positions of wrath and antipathy, destroying frankness and sympathy. It can puff people up, removing from them the sense of reality— or achieve the same result by tucking them cosily under a woolly blanket. The lack of it can cause a sense of deprivation which will place a chip upon the shoulder for a lifetime. In every marriage it is money which has to form the connection between the web of human relationships which is being created and society as it is today, which underpins everything and without which nothing would be possible.

It is indeed sensible to try and understand money in its various workings, and you side-step financial issues at your peril. For money is like a child of obvious but unknown gifts. If left to its own devices its capacity for malicious and destructive action is immense. If understood, cared for and guided, it can do marvellous things.

Rudolf Steiner gave an inspiring picture of the workings of money, particularly in a lecture course of 1922, known as *World Economy*. His ideas have a width and grandeur which can put the claustrophobic intensity and narrowness of domesticity in true perspective. (Can we afford this or *not*?". . . " *Why* did you spend so much?". . . "What on earth are we going to do?". . . and so on. . .)

First, there was no money, only nature. There was a kind of simple economy, such as the animals and birds have today, but based entirely on the satisfaction of immediate necessities within an immediate environment, so that nothing such as money was required. But slowly human beings in their development began to feel the need for something different.

Then came barter—certain fruits of the earth exchanged for other fruits of the earth. Swopping things at school probably retains a flavour of the idiosyncratic, intensely personal delight this must have first engendered. But as soon as civilization began to become more complex with people travelling between settlement and settlement, the need for something of no intrinsic value in itself but capable of being exchanged for whatever was needed, made itself felt. So money came into being and what might be called the economic plant began to grow for the first time upon the earth.

Through the centuries, keeping pace with the development of humanity, it has developed. Now, with the whole world discovered and become, as it were, a closed economy, the economic plant is a highly complex organism. It has no actual substance, and yet it has a strange, fluid, powerful life of its own and an inherent cycle of development. In order to play a beneficial part in the life of the human beings who have created it, it needs to be allowed to develop as a plant develops, putting forth leaves and shoots, then flowers and fruit, and eventually, with the seeds ready to fall to earth to bring forth new growth, dying. At each stage of the development of this plant the money, which is its outer form, has a different quality. And at each stage this money needs to be thought of differently, and used differently.

The roots have to be in nature. It makes its first growth when human beings help themselves to what they find on or below the surface of the earth, labour upon this, move it from one place to another and make exchanges through the use of money. Stems and leaves come into being as producer and consumer evolve their elaborate web of inter-relationships.

Money Used For Purchase

Money which is used in this first basic way, to buy things or to sell them, has a special quality. When you go out with a basket on your arm to the shops or market to buy food, clothes, medicine, or maybe a theatre ticket, you feel yourself right in the present; you are a citizen of the world as it is during these final years of the twentieth century. The money you take in your bag or pocket bestows an incredible power. What can you not do with it? This is the feeling you may get anyway, though it is naive to be carried away by this as it is a pretty confined power really. Still, if you want, you can bring the whole world into your kitchen, just by the passing of a few coins over the counter. No one will blame you for taking an intense personal interest in what you purchase, whether for yourself, or friends, or for other people who have asked you to act for them, whether it is only a scarf you are buying, or a mansion. This is the joy and challenge of purchase. It depends on the simple assessment of material things. But it is a demanding activity if you are to do it well, whether in small or great things, so that the needs of whoever you buy for are met in the best way possible. And it is a highly individual matter; no two people will make the same choices. Some can: "make money go a long way"; others "let it burn a hole in their pocket". Selling is a similar if more outgoing activity. The imagination to create new things is needed or to display them well, and the courage and skill to promote them. When you buy there is, for a short while anyway, an exhilaration, as if you had actually added to your *self*. When you sell, relief comes, if tinged with regret, in having unloaded some of this.

As the economic plant establishes itself, new ways of using money develop and it transforms itself and shows two other aspects. It is loaned and borrowed; it is given and received. These uses have each a very different quality which can be experienced even in small transactions. With giving the summit of development is reached, the flower of the money plant is there. Now the seed can form and fall to earth, and the cycle of growth begin again.

Loaned Money

Money which is loaned becomes more than a symbol for the actual exchange of unrelated goods, scattered maybe over the whole face of the earth; it stands too for the relationships which grow up between people or groups of people over a period of time, a backing of initiative, a continuing interest or dependence, an exploration into trust and confidence. The process of lending or borrowing calls for quiet under-standing, careful consideration of the pros and cons, the possible effects and consequences, the possible snags. This is very different from the immediacy and quick imaginative grasp needed for buying or selling. An impulse purchase will be regretted often enough but it is not the end of the world; an impulse loan is likely to have long lasting reper-cussions. As a purchaser there will be the temptation to go the easiest way, not take sufficient trouble, to allow yourself to be influenced by advertisements without realising, to be too sluggish about it all, fall into routine, fail to complain when you should because of the fuss involved. When lending or borrowing the temptation to follow the system and take minimum trouble yourself is even greater—though at the same time hoping to benefit as much as possible! The challenge here is to be awake to what you are doing but not to push your own interests to the limit, to be aware of the needs of others, to place your loans carefully, choose who you borrow from, pay back when you should, to be conscious of the whole business of giving and taking.

Gift Money

Money that is actually *given* is again quite another thing; the element of trust is far greater and of a different quality. It is trust not so much in the activity itself which is taking place, or planned to take place, but in the person or persons themselves in their inmost core to whom you make your gift. You trust the hidden potential that is in them and you are willing to consign your money to a future which is as yet hidden and unrevealed. Gifts should be complete and unaccompanied by strings of any sort, if possible. Their purpose is to warm and encourage those in whom you have confidence, and to give them the freedom to live out fully what lies within them. And no gift is a true gift which is not freely given.

The whole subject of money is one of endless interest once you begin to ask the right questions. *World Economy*, if you can cope with it, will certainly help you do this. But it is not easy. However, even a few lines may start you in the direction that is needed so that you can find them for yourself. "Infinitely more complicated, variable and unstable", Steiner says, "are the phenomena in Economics than in nature—more fluctuating, less capable of being grasped with any defined or hard and fast concepts." And later on he stresses that: "It is essential to think in *pictures,* pictures which are endowed with life and imagination. This is the only way, indeed, to reach an understanding of the infinitely complex, ever shifting processes which lie beneath the surface of the world's finances."

Purchase, loan and gift, the three different ways in which money can act as mediator and purveyor, cannot be rigidly defined. Purchase often becomes a kind of loan; loan often shades off into purchase on the one hand and near gift on the other. The challenge is to try to be aware of what is happening both in your own affairs and in the affairs of nations. There are masks which continually build themselves up, disguising what is actually involved so that it is hard to see behind these to the true motive and intent. With lending and borrowing, giving and receiving, difficulties will be certain to arise if the motives of all parties involved are not clear at the start. There is nothing more likely to cause trouble than a supposed gift which turns out to have been thought of as a kind of loan, so that the giver expects a say in all that happens. If that was the intention this should have been made clear at the beginning, and understood and agreed by the recipient.

The money itself is only the token of the relationship between giver and receiver. Gift must involve sufficient trust to enable risk to be accepted, even total seeming loss. If there is not such trust then the relationship will remain exploratory and money is better given as a loan with certain restrictions placed upon it. This may be better for the receiver too. He or she may need to be kept up to the mark.

In this whole area what is called the "power game" is played out, in business life and also in the transactions that have to be enacted between the partners in a marriage. The control or lack of control over the money supply can arouse passionate indignation at dependence or grim feelings of loneliness at the weight of responsibility which other people do not recognise. To face these emotions calmly and to speak of them together can have a healing effect. The dependants may begin to feel that their position has been caused by their own inactivity, in part anyhow, and that in their very dependence they have exploited a kind of power. The controllers may see how they have lacked the imagination to step into the other's shoes; until they can do this they will not be able to carry their responsibilities as these should be carried.

In England, perhaps more than other countries, people are bred to a Puritanical view of life even today. This is deep in us and almost impossible to eradicate. We cannot help rather enjoying the necessity of pulling in our belts. But the virtues of plain living and sensible spending, and caution in lending and giving, though fine in themselves, are inadequate for the present time. We need to rise above the smallness of our own affairs to a bolder, less self centred handling of money, using it imaginatively so that it will benefit not only ourselves but the unknown world of the future, and being willing to shoulder risk.

Besides trying to *understand* money in its widest aspects, it is good for the partners in a marriage to dwell calmly on the feelings and emotions which steam up out of it. Many emotions arise as it passes through your fingers—(or through your mind)—but it is those which appear to "steam" which need the most investigating!

Money seems to reach deep into the heart of egotism. Why else should "people" so easily become fraught and furious over financial matters, and you yourself under certain circumstances—circumstances which, when they arise, are likely to take you by surprise and make you feel small? Shadows at least of all the negative forces which dwell in money are present in nearly everyone—of miserliness and greed, squandering and extravagance, envy and guilt which is a form of cowardice. And yet the image of how it should be, might be, is present too. It is good to feel towards this and to contemplate it.

It is an image of balance and control, of contentment with what is one's own and envy of none; of responsibility without primness; of a fine sense of value without personal grasping; of love and giving without sentimentality or self congratulation. It is an image in which spending has full blooded enjoyment; lending a quiet, responsible pleasure, giving a deep, free joy. And there is never any moaning!

Children And Money

As the marriage partnership matures and proves its capacity for endurance, there will be new challenges constantly arising. As soon as children arrive, for instance, there will come the question of how to introduce *them* to the nature and working of money and the part it plays in human life.

While they are still babies it may seem unimportant even to think about such things; all they need is to be cared for and sheltered to the best of your ability, surely? But the receptivity of babies to everything in their environment is at once subtle and complete. Everything you feel and think about money, as well as what you do with it must enter them. It is a sobering thing to bear in mind.

As they grow they are bound to acquire a lively, playful interest in these round objects you keep in your purse. They will watch your shopping activities fascinated, the passing over of money, how things are handed back in return. It is the *way* you handle the coins and the things received, the manner you finger them, which will sink deepest and stay with them until they die.

Eventually the stage will come when they like to have a little purse of their own and to keep coins in it too. Make it a pretty one and easy for them to open and shut themselves; let them see how pennies change when they are polished to brightness. Soon, perhaps, if you feel that is right for your children, give them the money to buy a specific thing and let them hand it over themselves *and* receive the big red apple or whatever to put in the shopping bag along with all the rest. Or maybe they could even have sufficient to buy what is needed for a whole meal for the family—and then help cook it and serve it up, and eat it, of course. Watch though, that the transactions are accompanied by cheerful smiles, with groans about the price of cheese and butter kept to yourself.

The next hurdle is when the demand for pocket money comes, probably sparked off by hearing their friends talk about it. There can be no rules about how best to deal with this. According to their beliefs, circumstances and the characters of the children, different people will arrange things accordingly. But it is very important that parents are genuinely interested in the whole matter. The children will be very well aware of this. If real thought has been given to it, they are likely to accept whatever regime is decided on without complaint. But parents need to steel themselves to be impervious to wheedling and cajolery, though keeping themselves open to an honest plea. It goes without saying that siblings need to be treated fairly, one with the other. The whole subject is one which makes good discussion material in parents' groups. Should children be encouraged to save, be given a piggy bank and allowed the delight of shaking it and experiencing the increasing weight—or not? Is an occasional windfall beneficial, unexpected "spending" money put into their hands to do with whatsoever they choose or not so? One thing is certain, moaning and groaning about money matters and nagging anxiety are bad. It encourages miserliness and inhibits spontaneous generosity and imaginative spending. The firm statement when necessary, however: "Sorry we can't afford it at the moment!" is healthy and sound.

During the middle years, stealing can be a problem. It often crops up in a small way, but can recur as pilfering from shop counters. The important thing in either case, is to find out what is really being stolen —for it is unlikely to be merely money or goods. Often stories, made up to fit the situation, will help more than a direct scolding. Then the person who has been stolen from might be shown grieving, and the person who has stolen making amends. The difference between mine and thine has to be learnt in an ordinary everyday sense, for without this, social peace and harmony become impossible. But it is good if children are also led, through stories, to realise that, from a wider point of view, possessions are only ours on trust and that it is our responsibility to use them well. Fairy stories and folk legends can often be helpful. *Jack and the Beanstalk,* for instance, is a wonderful story for our time, as regards the use of money. Jack, the simpleton, infuriates his worldly wise mother by exchanging the cow for a mere bag of beans. . . but he has good will, is brave and awake to intuitions which rise up in him, even if he cannot immediately understand them— otherwise, why should he have taken the beans? And how his action is vindicated when the beans start to grow and all the adventures follow!

In adolescence the problem of pocket or spending money takes on a more adult complexion. It needs to be discussed thoroughly and reassessed often so that the young people feel they have a real part in the decisions that are made. The basic question is how much they really *need,* not only physically, but socially. Whether they should be encouraged actually to *earn* themselves outside the home, or whether they should be paid by their parents for certain jobs, is another subject which it may help to discuss with other people.

Many young people as they grow up will find it helpful to be included in their parents' discussions and ponderings, both about the nature of economics and about the financial situation of their own family. It is bad that they should have to bear responsibility too soon, but to some degree they should know what is happening. Although they will be likely to demand freedom of choice when it comes to spending their own money, for a long time they will benefit from advice and protection. Their age group is scandalously exploited today. It should not be difficult to help them to see this.

Retrospect

When the children of the family have left home, the marriage partnership may, if fortunate, sail on to calmer financial waters. Then it should be possible to reflect on what has actually been achieved and distinguish the good things that were done from the not so good. If you had another chance, what would you do differently? Trust and ever increasing consciousness and awareness, nicely balanced, surely these are the two essentials for success in the partnership. The Finance Angel, if it could be contacted—assuming that it exists!—should help Trust. For the rest, there is no way but to go on trying for it.

10.　　　　　JOB SHARING

Kevin McCarthy

It's curious how our memory, or my memory, at least, seems to deliver up from the past glimpses of scenes which seem trivial, but which are, in fact, keys to whole periods of our development. For me, one such image is of a wet nappy, still inside its plastic pants, as if its owner had somehow simply de-materialised. The nappy is on the threshold of the bathroom and, in my memory, I am always skirting it, not picking it up, trying to cut it out of my attention as I rush to leave the house for some important meeting.

I often find it difficult to connect up with the person I was a number of years ago, but this incident somehow seems to encapsulate a whole period of my recent life which was particularly full of anxiety. I refer to the onset of parenthood—in my case, fatherhood—which after a few days of euphoria left me in a state of post-natal shock lasting for something over a year. I would like in this article to share with you some of the memories of that difficult period and also to look at some of the more positive directions which have emerged from it.

"The Plan" had always been that when we started a family, I would stop work and would involve myself in the raising of children. Like most plans, it was simple and grand and required no practical elabora tions of detail. I still do not know where the idea arose or why it arose: I have no memory of its gradually forming. It was a sudden, strong, unsought impulse. In fact, "The Plan" went badly awry (from which I hope we have learned something about plans!) and the arrival of our son was not the signal for a new home-centred role for me. My wife and I had been together as a couple for six or seven years and had, I suppose, built up a rather idealised picture of what family life would be like. For both of us, the reality was a shock. Thaïs, while in many ways relishing her new role as a mother, was gradually worn down by months of insufficient sleep. Also, after a while, the routine of being a housewife, the endless round of cooking and cleaning and changing and coping began to leave her unfulfilled. It was not any sense of repugnance or any feeling that the work of the home was inherently menial, simply that the jobs came round too often and unremittingly. I, meanwhile, felt left out of this tight union of mother and son. Mother and child seemed to form a self-sufficient unit and the picture needed no Daddy Joseph in the background twiddling his thumbs. Needless to say, then, I did not stop work. Quite the reverse, in fact. Instead, I thrust myself into my job; into gardening; into music-making, into anything and everything with a fanatical energy which somehow shielded me from the reality of what was changing in my life and which left my heart thudding in my head as I lay awake late at night.

Gradually it became apparent that these closely circumscribed roles: home-maker and provider, were not making either of us whole. I don't seem to learn very easily or quickly and it was almost a year before the futility of my frantic round of hyperactivity dawned on me. I was exhausted; drained, washed out. The signs were so glaring that not even I could ignore them. By now I was prepared to act to salvage the situation. Thaïs, too, felt the need for a change and, fortunately, our needs at that time were complementary. I left my full-time pastoral post and took a part-time teaching job nearer home. My unsought resolution: "I will take my share of parenting" was waiting for a response. The nappy's call was answered.

Thaïs meanwhile took to making clothes in the afternoons with a friend's small mail order business. As a result, she was able to emerge from the endless round of domestic duties and, literally, free her hands for activity outside the home. She could take on a much more creative role, working on a shared enterprise. She also had the stimulation of activity in the outside world: telephone calls, deadlines, decisions and orders. Not least, there was the satisfaction of knowing that she was no longer a dependent wife, that she was making a significnt contribution to our family income.

For me, though, the first feeling was a sense of loss. The first months going into winter are again caught in one of those frozen images. It is two o'clock. I am sitting in the kitchen, the lunch dishes unwashed, with a twelve-month old Luke. There are three and a half hours to endure until Thaïs returns. I have not much of a relationship with this little soul and I have no other company; no classes to teach, no staff-room banter. . . just the dinner to cook. An empty panic grips me.

It is still a very dim period for me, full of depression and resentment and anger. I had been quickly, if rather thoughtlessly, scaling the conventional ladder of the career-minded teacher. I had been out there in the world, being noticed, making things happen, being in charge, taking responsibility. Now? Who noticed how neatly I folded the nappies? What policies were there to formulate about cleaning the sink? Slowly, though, especially as the spring came and it was possible to be outdoors, I began to find increasing satisfaction in the domestic role. I was a competent cook and there was no special skill in the rest of the daily round. What was new, however, was to attempt these jobs with a toddler in tow. There was occasionally a tremendous sense of exhilaration which came from successfully juggling the cooking, gardening, cleaning and playing. Being at home, I discovered, could actually be creative and satisfying. It could employ—in fact, it positively required—all one's resources on every level. Ingenuity, patience, humour, intelligence, awareness: all these were necessary just to get the washing on the line. There was unlimited scope for work, in particular on my own perceptions. The success of a trip to shop was to be measured less by the speed at which it was accomplished than by the quality of the experience on the journey. Process not product. I had had that little phrase jingling around my brain for some time, had probably discussed it with my students. Now, though, I think I was beginning to live it, to take it into my whole being. This new role of part-time parent gave me ample opportunity to reflect on how success is to be measured. I had had few doubts before: it lay in making an impact, getting one's ideas accepted, changing the system. Accepting fatherhood more fully meant a change of consciousness, a deliberate fostering of inner growth.

Towards the end of the first year, it was obvious that we had certainly established a new direction, but we had not reached a final pattern. Dress-making, though interesting, was repetitive and, in the end, some-what impersonal. Part-time teachers are not well regarded in state schools and have very tenuous contracts. There came a further nudge. I have but a dim awareness of the forces which prompt such new direc-tions. Following them seems less an act of decisiveness than of obedience. We decided, or more accurately it somehow emerged, that we should share a full-time teaching post. It actually took our local authority employers over a year to formalise this arrangement. There was no precedent within the county, although other local authorities, notably the City of Sheffield had been pioneering the idea for a couple of years. With the help of a very sympathetic acting head, soon to be a mother herself, we began to familiarise ourselves with the Equal Opportunity Commission's excellent booklet *Job Sharing: A Guide for Employers*. We also made contact with the Job-Sharing Project, now re-named New Ways to Work. I even cornered the Chief Education Officer after a lecture he had given and extolled the virtues of job-sharing. In the end, it was absurdly straightforward. We simply split a single post in two parts, in our case in the ratio of about 60:40. We lost no benefits and gained job security and status of permanent full-time staff. We also, entirely incidentally, made some tax savings. We divided the weekly timetable in such a way as to avoid splitting up groups, so that the children we taught were not aversely affected. As far as I know, the local authority incurred little or no extra administrative costs. Furthermore, the new head was now able to give us a post of responsibility within the school, a scale-post in education jargon, which would not have been possible had we remained technically part-timers. We took on the remedial work in the English department and also the running of a new school library. This year, I have taught all day on Monday, Tuesday and Thursday, while Thaïs has worked on Wednesday, Thursday morning and Friday. We have almost certainly managed much more than any individual teacher could have achieved. My weekend lasts three days, Thaïs' four and somehow we seem to arrive at school re-charged after our time at home; eager, enthusiastic and energetic. We have been able to give each of our groups much more thought and attention in terms of preparation, teaching and marking. In the library, we have found a happy working arrangement with my system-making, for instance, complementing Thaïs' artistic sense.

Again though, looking back over this period, the new phase was not established without considerable difficulty. I had by now accepted and even begun to relish the new child-centred rhythm. We shared, though not equally, the cooking, cleaning, washing and tidying. When it came to sharing a teaching post, though, I was deeply resentful at first at what I felt to be a usurping of my role. The main problem this time was the difficulty I had in allowing inroads to be made into *my* sphere of activity. Secondary teaching was *my* province: I was possessive about it, tried to impose my ideas and thinking on Thaïs' approach, which undermined her confidence and made it difficult for her to establish her own style, find her own rhythm. In theory, I knew that the arrangement would make sense; that it gave us much more shared experience, greater security and so on. As so often seems to be the case for me, though, the actual experience was different and difficult. It has taken the best part of two years for me to accept that Thaïs has a separateness which I have to learn to respect.

Within our marriage, then, change has been accompanied by difficulty and conflict. It has come unbidden in an unexpected form and with an outcome that could not possibly have been predicted. We have been steadily nudged into new situations, but in the process have been tested.

Now we seem to find ourselves in calmer waters. Having just finished two years of job-sharing, we can gather some threads together. The pattern is getting clearer. It seems that we are taking part in a process which, I think, is also at work in large areas of the developed world, especially in Northern Europe and North America. The womens' movement is part of it; the Sex Discrimination Act is part of it; boys studying Child Care at school is part of it. It is possible to see the process at work in the drafts of the articles in this book. Time and time again, the various contributors have found themselves writing "The mother will cook. . .", or "The mother will make the festival. . ." and, in the light of this new impulse have obviously felt the need, in revising their articles for publication to amend "the mother" to "the parent". It is an indication that the old stereotyped roles do not necessarily seem adequate for the conditions which we find as we move towards the end of the century. Ironically, the new and unavoidable phenomenon of mass unemployment is fuelling this change, so that it is no longer evident solely amongst the "alternative" community. The popular press, too, is full of articles about "stay at home dads". We are still at the beginning of this phase. These new ideas are gaining wide theoretical acceptance in much the same way as I described my theoretical recognition of the need for change. In the next stage, we will, I feel sure, find that an increasing number of men and women begin actually to feel uncomfortable as "provider" or "home-maker". They will then seek, or perhaps be moved, to find ways of going beyond their traditional roles.

All that, however, is the tide and we find ourselves here just trying to keep on swimming in the right direction. Our task lies in trying to disentangle the web of learned responses and to take on, in freedom and without fear, the complementary characteristics of the opposite sex. I have a strong, but vague sense that humanity's future requires some such evolution and that we can begin to prepare ourselves for that future by finding a path which opens us up to new possibilities.

Neither at work nor at home, can we lean back into the old ways. For me, there is the need (and now the opportunity) to re-channel the restless male energies. Learning to be gentle; to respond; to hear and see with more sensitivity; to work unseen at unnoticed jobs—all this has required, and is therefore drawing out, a hitherto undeveloped side of my nature. Thaïs too has a new path. She has had to forego the comfortably circumscribed maternal role, the eternal province of house and hearth. She knows that its order, its pattern can no longer mirror just her personality. She has slipped free of being simply "Kevin's wife" or "Luke's mum". She is still both, of course, but the point is that she is no longer defined by those roles. The pace of school life has developed a new quickness and decisiveness in her, a greater willingness to take on responsibility, to organise and to initiate change.

What has happened means that we no longer each have our own separate zone or realm. (Call it a prison or a castle.) In going beyond the traditional roles, in taking a more or less equal share in the professional and domestic sphere we have each had to become more open. When they are deeply embedded in either their work or in the life of the home, it is very easy for men and women to sink unquestioningly and unthinkingly into patterns of activity and behaviour. We have found increasingly that with two minds focussing on any given situation, we are called to account more for our actions. For example, since we more or less have to reach agreement on all the practical domestic details, we are forced into examining even the most minute of the million daily routines. Why do we wash the clothes so often? How far should we insist on traditional table manners? How should we approach the question of tidying-up after play? In many marriages, such matters must in practice fall exclusively to one partner. The fact that we share the domestic role means that we are called to account more, to reflect more, in short, to become more conscious.

It is perhaps this last aspect that we have to keep in mind. If it is not too soon to draw out the most significant threads of this recent phase, it seems that it has made us into more thinking beings, more consciously concerned with our inner development. None of this has come at all easily for me: I have moments, days, weeks of "amnesia", when I fret and sulk because I am not on the trail to success, not running things, not being noticed. Thaïs, too, sometimes yearns to sink back into what she pictures as the unstressful simplicity of the mother's world, where the territory is well-defined, the day's rhythm uncomplicated by the multiplicity of ideas and events which seem to entangle us.

We have taken this path towards a new concept of marital roles and there seems to be no immediate likelihood of our turning back. We are particularly fortunate to have close neighbours who, in a very different way, are on a similar path. Undoubtedly there has been much to be gained by seeing parallel developments, catching familiar echoes across the garden fence. There is, I am sure, a very different quality to what we each bring to parenting. "Mother" and "Father" have a certain powerful, elemental significance which cannot be blurred or devalued by tinkering with who does what at home. It may well be, though, as we face the future as mothers and fathers, that an increasing number of parents will come to question the assumptions of the past and discover, in their exploration of new roles, a sense of excitement and a feeling that one is helping to enable a new pattern to emerge.

II. FAMILY WAYS

1.   LIVING IN REAL TIME

John Davy

I became a father at a time when young mothers were often discussing 'demand feeding'. The demands in question were the babies', not the mothers'. There had been maternity hospitals where new babies were efficiently ironed into four-hour feeding schedules during their first days of life, while mothers rested in the wards. In some places, breast-feeding was being actively discouraged. The discipline was supposed to persist when mother and child were packed off home, to the convenience of all concerned.

But liberation was in the air, along with health foods, breast milk and demand feeding. Within ten years, many progressive babies were joining adult evening occasions in carry cots, and were sucking their dinners when they felt like it, sometimes at the same time as their mothers spooned up their hosts' soup.

A similar pendulum has swung around in education. It seems a long time ago—before my time—when Dickens' Mr. Squeers was approaching education as something to be beaten into children, who were born naturally wicked. Now we live in a consumer society in which education is rather more like demand feeding. Teachers act as 'resource persons', minding supplies of paper, clay and video cassettes. The little customers are supposed to know what is right for them, and come and get it when they want it.

While my wife and I were both fervently in favour of breast feeding, I could not, as a father, contribute directly to its realisation. But I did become more immediately involved in other infant rhythms, which also play a prominent part in the lives of parents. I remember particularly the question of sleeping and waking. There hasn't been quite so much advocacy of demand sleeping or demand waking. And while disciplinarians may have rigorously woken up infants by the clock to perform some function or other, no-one has yet discovered a way of commanding a baby to sleep (except with a dose of soporifics—not unknown in some of those maternity wards determined that everyone get a good eight hours sleep at the proper time).

Our first child had, early on, a prolonged period of colics. He was a vigorous baby, and far from being exhausted by the pangs of his unquiet digestion, was stimulated by them to loud protests for large portions of the day and night. I was commuting to work at the time, and would arrive home and do my best to take on a fair share of the night shift, including chamomile teas, hot water bottles, and what seemed like hours of pacing a small prison cell, playing rock-a-bye-baby with a squalling infant in my arms. Next morning, trundling into the city in the train, I would nod off with the squalls still sounding in my ears. Sometimes, I seemed to be hearing them all day, and I wondered how my wife, who remained in direct earshot, would survive.

It was always a hopeful sign, in the small hours, when the crying began to become rhythmic. I learned to recognise it as a sign of sleep approaching, like a healing music beginning to sing in the room (I did some singing myself, and it sometimes helped).

At school, we used to laugh at a morbid joke about the visitor to a lunatic asylum who asked an inmate why he beat his head against the wall. "Because it feels so good when I leave off" was the reply. But it's true, in a way: the blissful quality of the peace which followed a stormy passage, as the squalls died into a rhythmic crying and then into the quiet breathing of sleep, is still vivid and precious.

As the child's digestive rhythms regained their balance, and we all gradually found a more regular rhythm of sleeping, waking and eating, it continued to feel extremely good. And so, with later children, we knew what we wanted to work for: Not the children making their demands on us; nor us making our demands on the children; but the art of finding the good rhythms for all our lives.

Not that we have ever fully succeeded. Most people seem to discover that technology saves us so much time that we never have enough of it. Yet when we do establish a patch of regular, unhurried life, it seems to want to drift into routine, so we develop a powerful urge to break it, and rush off somewhere in the car. All the same, we learned early on to distrust regulating life either by 'demands' or by the clock. Somewhere in between are the healing secrets of living rhythms.

Having has some academic background in biology, I knew something about this in theory. Rhythms are, in an almost literal sense, the secrets of life. Every part of a living organism—cells, tissues, organs, the body as a whole—is permeated with rhythms. Inside cells there are high speed rhythms of building up and breaking down complex substances, often several times a second. Almost within hours of the first embryonic development, there are rhythms detectable in and around the tiny embryo, forming gradually into a heart. Only some years after birth does the heartbeat settle gradually into an adult pulse. We take our first breath at birth, and breathe our last when we die. Life is sustained in between by a breathing rhythm about one fourth as fast as the pulse. The liver, the kidney, the stomach, all have their physiological rhythms too.

The wonder of these rhythms is that they are 'precise' without being 'exact' like a mechanical clock. Our breathing and heart rates change; our digestion and sleep rhythms can adapt. Like music, there can be speeding up and slowing down, different parts can move more quickly or more slowly, but the whole is harmoniously integrated.

At the same time, our biological rhythms are not regulated solely by their own 'demands'. but are constantly re-attuned to their surroundings. Much has been discovered in recent years which links living time-keeping to rhythms beyond the body itself. Volunteers have tried living in sealed-off compartments for weeks or months without clues to the passage of time outside. They often live to some kind of rhythm, but seldom a twenty-four hour one. Yet in normal life, our bodily rhythms of sleeping and waking, eating and excreting, are constantly being regulated by the rhythms of day and night. Suffering from jet lag, while our bodily rhythms readjust to a new time zone, we know directly that to be out of rhythm is to feel slightly ill. Some statesmen and jetting executives are even advised not to take important decisions until they are to some degree back in rhythm. So our 'natural' rhythms are not 'demanded' by our bodies on their own, nor are they 'imposed' by the sun and moon. Their true nature is in the dialogue between them. All this is now well-known biology.

Then we can watch children growing up. The breathing and heart rhythms of the newly born are less regular than later on. The digestive and other bodily rhythms are only gradually attuned to the surroundings, which include the rhythms we establish as parents. A sense for rhythms in language and music awakens gradually, but is in full flow in a ten-year-old. At this age, healthy children have few problems with time: they are seldom bored, or in a rush. With adolescence, and all its physiological changes, some rhythms falter again. Sleeping and waking tend to occupy hours which seem quite inappropriate to well ordered adults. Night may become day and vice versa. I learned to switch off and go to sleep, but my wife stayed awake listening for returning teenagers in the small hours. At this age, 'subjective' time is also erratic : long stretches of emptiness seem to open up when nothing happens and life is routine, then *everything* happens in a few packed minutes or hours of intense experience.

It is not too difficult to see that there is potential for illness in these extremes, although most adolescents survive their turmoils. But vast numbers of adults struggle for regular sleep, and find a solution only in pills. And they struggle with subjective time, too, seeking a balance between empty time—monotony, routine, boredom—and compressed time—frenetic rush, the rat race. Drugs may seem to help to speed up or slow down, but in the end the pendulum swings more wildly unless rhythm is found in other ways.

These disorders of rhythm underline the value of caring for rhythms in the lives of our children, of seeking a healthy way between a dead monotony and a haphazard servitude to individual whims. In the animal kingdom, the rhythms of life are constantly regulated by the rhythms of day and night and of the seasons—"precise", but not "exact". They live neither by "demand" nor by an external clock but in a balance between the two, and their lives are neither boring nor hectic.

We are different. We can step out of time, so to speak. We can change our meal times and our bedtimes. Inwardly, we can look back on our past, and make plans for the future. Here we find freedom both from nature and nurture. (If you could ask a cow in a field what it plans to do tomorrow, I suspect it would reply "I shall continue to be a cow". You would not catch it dreaming of being a sheep, or deciding to eat mice for a change.)

Because we can step out of time, and yet, as living beings, are also part of nature, it becomes both our freedom and our responsibility to relate ourselves in a healthy way to time. We do not do this by relying on the "demands" of our bodies, nor by being governed by a mechanical substitute for the sun and moon, a rigidly ticking clock. We can only try to live our way into time as a relationship between ourselves and our surroundings, a relationship which is neither chaotic nor regimented, but musical, an art of living in time like a dance.

Many people nowadays concerned with our time-illnesses seek ways of learning to live "in the present". But where is the present? We have seen that it does not lie in the spontaneous promptings of our organism. Nor is it to be found in clocks: for a scientific clock-consciousness, intent on exact measurement, the present more or less vanishes into an infinitesimal splinter of time squeezed between past and future. No wonder we feel squeezed by the clock. But once we see that by "living in the present" we really mean "living in rhythm", the rhythms of real time, we can breathe again.

The Gautama Buddha, born as a young prince into the luxury of his palace, was encouraged to live by the "demands" of his body. Every satisfaction was available instantly, at his beck and call. But he rebelled, and went to join the ascetics, who punished their bodies day and night. Yet inwardly, he became the more frantic (as we do when punished by clocks). Out of these extremes, he found a "middle way", an ordering of life which is healing, and allows a true present to live between past and future.

Elsewhere in this book are many practical suggestions for ordering the day, the week, the year by such a "middle way", an art of living between mechanical routine and erratic whim. Gudrun Davy explores the rhythms of a week into which the qualities of the Buddha's Eightfold Path are taken up, as Rudolf Steiner has suggested. Margret Meyerkort speaks of the transformation of mealtimes, bed times, seasonal times, from routines into little festivals, works of art. And I look back on our own family life with special gratitude to my wife, who developed and fostered our rhythms of life to a much greater degree than I (bound as I was to the timetables of trains and offices, rather than children, for much of the week).

It looks as though we shall have to work harder still to rescue living time, to develop a dancing rhythm of life. Now we have the digital clock, which dismembers time into electronic flicks from one number to the next. (At least the traditional clock dial reminds us dimly of the circling rhythms of the sun and moon which guide nature's dance.) Then there is fast food, instant satisfaction of the stomach's demands, but no time for grace before meals, or beauty during them.

These are symptoms, but the causes are in ourselves. And in ourselves, too, we shall have to seek the powers of healing. When my small colicky son began to quieten, at unpredictable times in the small hours of the night, I could see his breathing become rhythmic He was no longer "crying his heart out". The wonderful dance of the heart and lung reaching deep into the body through the blood, and far out into the world through the breath, came into balance and harmony. They were wonderful moments, and showed me where there is centred that part of ourselves which lives in real times, the rhythms of heart and lung which are the living clocks of our lifetimes on earth.

2. SLEEPING AND WAKING

Margret Meyerkort

Important Moments

It is seldom realised that morning and evening are among the two most important times of the day, especially the periods of waking up and going to sleep. We tend to take such times for granted. In any case, there is often far too much rush in the morning to be bothered about its quality. By the time we have got through to the evening, we are perhaps pleased to put up our feet and let the remainder of the day take care of itself.

Yet when we think a little further, we all know that the quality of our sleep life deeply affects our waking life—a disturbed night often leads to bad tempers the next day—and if we have had a fulfilling day we tend to sleep the more contentedly. Perhaps less well-known, however, are the facts surrounding the threshold of waking up and going to sleep, that is to say, how we spend the thirty or so minutes before we lie down to sleep and the time onward to the moment of falling asleep, and how we spend the period from the moment of waking up and the first half hour of the day.

Each morning and evening it is as if we stand before a doorway and hold two parts of our lives in balance. When we wake up in the morning, our soul, as it were, through the senses meets the earth and its surroundings. In the evening when we lie down to sleep we turn away from the earth, our sense organs do not react any more, and our nerves rest from their task of communicating sense impressions. It is then that our soul turns inward towards the spiritual world. So, in fact, we could think of morning and evening as highlights of our day, for they are thresholds that separate two opposite conditions of our lives—our sleep life and our waking life.

It is possible that a generation or two ago, more people than today had a better instinctive understanding of how to prepare for the dream and sleep life of the night. The evening was like a pause. It contained within it an end of the day and a beginning of the night, and it held possibilities of healing, of making whole, of regeneration, and of mending differences. People tended to gather around the hearth, and we like to think that perhaps there was peace in the house and within the people themselves. Certainly there was more story telling and singing, and families probably talked to each other more than they do now about the day's events. Such activities helped to call up the faculties of imagination.

Today, probably the greatest enemy of the evening and its qualities is the television. There is the rush to start viewing the T.V. as soon as possible and there is the temptation to continue viewing until the end of the programmes. The day becomes drawn out until midnight; sleep becomes merely a consequence of the day. The evening loses its inherent dignity and its unique character and meaning. As a consequence, there is a tendency only to regard as important the material experiences of the day while the spiritual and cultural life is disregarded.

In fact, it matters a lot how we stand before these doors or thresholds to the day or night, for, not only do they affect the subsequent quality of our sleep and waking life, but if we are sensitive to their mystery, they can hold keys to hints and questions about ourselves and our lives. Above all, by becoming more aware of these thresholds and their rhythmic quality, we can help both ourselves and our children to pass through them more adequately and in this way, we also help our family's physical and spiritual well-being.

In writing about the importance of morning and evening time, I have drawn upon the experiences of many parents who, according to their personalities, circumstances and particular needs of their children, have varied the ways in which they have dealt with these transition periods. So let us explore further and begin with the evening time and its rituals.

Bedtime

Evening begins with tidying away the toys. As many of us have experienced, this requires tact and patience on the mother's part (presuming that it is the mother who is putting the children to bed) if the next hours are to be harmonious and not leave the mother exhausted. It is always worth it if the mother can gather her strength together and help the young child to tidy up, especially if she can do this with care and interest in the child's play and toys. She may say, "The cows go into the stable, and tomorrow morning we'll get them out again." And if she sets the example and puts one toy animal into the stable, then she has set the mood for the evening. True, she will have to do this evening after evening until it has become a habit for the child. But this is part of laying a foundation for the growth of a caring attitude and for self-discipline.

Good digestion helps the night's sleep. So, as Dr.W.zur Linden points out in his book *A Child is Born,* it is not wise for the child to eat heavy food such as potatoes or fried food for his tea or supper, and, of course a child who finds it difficult to be dry during the night should not be given anything to drink or anything salty after 5 p.m.[1] Since physical activity before sleep aids the digestion during the early part of the night, it is a good idea for tea or supper to be early enough to allow time for playing before going to bed. Other activities might be to help with the washing-up or to assist in preparing a meal for mother or father who might be home late from work.

Some activities are more than just chores. For example, cleaning shoes. If we can imagine along with our children, how the shoes take the wear and tear of carrying us from place to place, we realise that we need to look after them well, and that we should care for everything else that helps us to walk through our lives with uprightness and health.

As we all know, some evenings the child can be in a bad mood. Mother (or father) can often change this for the better by making-up a game on the way to the bed room. If there are stairs, for example, both she and her child can walk up them on hands and feet, or on hands and knees, singing the child's favourite song, or perhaps reciting the nursery rhyme "Jack and Jill went up the hill. . ."

If the child is still in a bad mood when they arrive in the child's bedroom, or is particularly tired or unwell, it may help if the mother puts him on a chair and says, "There—now you may watch me get the room ready for you." Of course, he can be awkward and want to stand or creep under the table. If at all possible, the mother can ignore this and hum or sing an evening song, moving about her task in a way that is not too fast or jarring.

In the lighter time of the year, it is good to draw the curtains first so that, for a little while, the child gets a true feeling for the time of day, and then to turn on the electric light. There are further things that can be done to help the child to prepare for sleep. The bed covers can be opened up in a way that makes the bed inviting. In cold weather, the nightgown can be warmed, and in some countries such as Britain, it can be a custom to warm the bed with a hot-water bottle: a warm bed gives a sense of protectiveness. In addition to put a potty under the bed can give a child an extra sense of security. For the child to see mother put the book from which she is going to read on to the bedside table along with the bed-time candle, can also give a sense of the time of day.

And still the child might be uncooperative. To avoid a confrontation which could result in bad dreams during the night or in showing resentment the next day, the mother can help herself and the child by continuing to sing the evening song while she undresses the child. Or she may again try with humour to blow the clouds away by reciting, say, *Diddle diddle dumpling, my son John* or some other such nursery rhyme.

Just as order was important with the child's toys, so order is now important with the child's clothes. Mother can fold them and put them on the chair so that they, too, go to sleep, and she can put the shoes into their "house" under the chair.

For most children, the bathroom is a happy place for this is where there is water—water is so very, very special. Children often enjoy turning on the tap and brushing their teeth. This requires supervision and help from the mother, while at the same time she can assure herself of the healthy growth of the teeth, making sure that there are no sore lips or spots inside the mouth or at the corners: this could be a sign of indigestion.

On bath night, many mothers allow at least ten minues for play in the bath. Sometimes a doll is also given a bath or perhaps a wooden train is scrubbed, or the doll's clothes are washed. One mother's way of washing her five-year old was enjoyed by both mother and child every time. The child stood in the bath, the mother took a face-flannel and accompanied her activity with the words, "We wash the face—and wash—and wash—as far as possible." She then took another flannel and proceeded to wash the feet, saying, "We wash the feet—and wash—and wash—as far as possible. And now we wash possible" (the bottom). After a bath children of the age of six may still need help with drying.

For the younger child, there is the nursery rhyme *Rub-a-dub-dub* to accompany the drying. When it is not bath night, children can enjoy a refreshing warm wash of the face, hands, feet and bottom.

While the younger child sits for a moment on the chair in the bathroom, or an older child puts on his pyjamas, the mother can go into the child's bedroom, light the candle on the bedside table, turn off the electric light, and return to fetch the child. Where it is not possible to have a candle burning for the bedtime story and the good-night ceremony, a thin piece of bluish-red material over the bedside lamp gives a feeling of quiet light. To increase the mood of intimacy even more, many mothers speak softly, even whisper, when they carry the child or walk with him into his bedroom. The mother's movements, too, become different between now and leaving the child alone for the night: steps become slower and gestures smaller.

Telling the bedtime story, or part of it, rather than reading it, can be difficult for some mothers, but once the mother has found time and energy during the day to prepare the story, both she and the child will increasingly reap the benefit. With no book between them, the mother and child can look directly at each other. This can increase the child's feeling of confidence within the aura of his mother's love, and this, in turn, can confirm the mother in her relationship with her child.

The evening is the time when the child needs to turn his inner eye toward the ever-active and ever-moving spiritual world. In my experience, picture books tend to discourage or disturb this inner turning. This is because pictures have a way of fixing the imagination of the onlooker. A particular artist's interpretation of a subject is one in a million and may be less truthful to and less artistic than the child's own inner imaginative picture. Further, if a child gets into the habit of looking at pictures that are hard and crude in content colour and line before he goes to sleep, then these pictures will tend to overlay the child's own inner activity of picture-creating and picture-beholding. Such pictures tie the soul to the squareness and immobility of the physical world and may result in poor sleep. A mother who finds that she has to read a picture book because she has had no time to prepare a story for telling, can say to the child who wants to see the pictures, "Tonight it is Mummy's turn to look into the book. Tomorrow morning after breakfast it will be your turn." Again, the mother may have to repeat this sentence gently on several evenings.

The under-four-year old who has older siblings can have his five minutes of being told a story immediately before tea or supper time. Brothers and sisters are old enough to understand that it is the little one's turn to have mother to himself. In summer when the evenings are light, the curtains can be drawn to make it darker—the child might like to do this himself—and the candle can be lit. In winter, the mother and the little one on her knee can sit by the window and, if there is a garden, they can look out into the growing shadows and the darkening sky both before and after the story. After supper, when the older ones have their story, the little one can, as it were, water himself into dreamland by kneeling on a stool in front of the bathroom basin, ladling water into and out of the tooth mug.

There are five- and six-year old children who go to sleep more quickly when they have their bedtime story before supper. These are children whose inner picture-world is already rich for they play imaginatively rather than imitate adult activities. The pictures which the evening story creates would keep these children inwardly too active, if the story were told immediately before going to bed.

When the younger child is already in bed, the mother can have a short, quiet conversation with her six-year old about one or two happy encounters or activities which have been experienced during the previous hours. Thereby the day is drawn to a close a little more consciously for the older child. Some parents like to take their children's hands into their own while together they speak an evening verse.

Some unaccompanied music such as an evening song, lullaby or melody helps to lift and dissolve the weight of the physical experiences of the day. Until the child is about five years old, he will not notice if mother or father can sing only a few notes. What rightly matters to the young child is the endeavour and joy in singing. If the child becomes aware that the mother cannot hold a tune, for instance, and says, "That's not how it goes", mother can quietly say, "Today this is my way of singing".

The physical touch of the mother stroking the child's head, or stroking over the eyes to close them, gives the child a feeling of being acknowledged, especially if the day has been one of obstinate feelings, breakages, tempers and so on. The child can think, "She forgives me and I'll do better tomorrow." In fact, physical affection such as cradling in babyhood and cuddling as the child grows older is an important part of building the child's confidence in the parents' love and this helps the child to relax into a health-giving sleep.

And so the day ends with the kiss. The mother blows out the candle or turns off the light, and tiptoes out.

Some children may need extra help in going to sleep, and the following are some aids that parents have found helpful.

1. Keep a nightlight burning in the room well out of reach of the child.

2. Leave the bedroom door ajar and an electric light on in the passage.

3. Leave the bedroom door and the kitchen door ajar while the mother sings as she works in the kitchen. Music from TV or radio would be the wrong approach when, in fact, what the child needs is the life of mother's own voice, and the love and assurance that this gives.

4. Sit by the child's bed and knit, read or sing, or stroke his back until he has fallen asleep.

5. Give a hot water bottle.

6. Dress him in a nightgown of a natural fabric because this is more soothing than artificial fibres.

7. Have a plain-coloured wallpaper (see chapters on clothing and on the temperaments).

8. Take down any picture in the room that shows an ugly scene or a distortion of the truth for these can contribute to listlessness and sleep problems.

9. Hang up one or two pictures of a Madonna and Child by an old master such as Raphael or Fra Angelico. One mother was unable to get any such pictures or postcards in her town and so she cut a page out of an art book.

10. Make a mobile of, say, gold-paper stars and fasten it on the ceiling above the child's bed.

11. Buy a metre of surgical gauze or some silk and stick a few gold-paper stars onto it. This can be fastened on the wall behind the child's head or next to his bed.

Normally, a few days or weeks of difficult evenings are only a phase: either the child is sickening or the restlessness and fear in the evening are a sign of a new stage of development. In both cases, the mother can answer the child's immediate need by giving him some extra help in such ways as described above. This will not spoil him, for not to help him could spoil him in a different way. Gradually the child will be able to sleep again and this will be the living manifestation of the trust that he has in his mother and in his surroundings.

Morningtime

And now we come to the morning time. When I was a child, how I loved those mornings—and consequently the whole day—when my father quietly came into my room not turning on the light or drawing back the curtains, and woke me with a kiss. I loved him for sitting on my bed, stroking my head and whispering close to my ear so that my younger sister, who was already sitting up in her bed, would not hear. He might say, "Today will be a difficult day for you. Your little sister cried yesterday and that needs to be put right." (No mention that I had hit her.) "I will help you ... Would you like me to help you?" The pause before the question was so good. It took away any pressure there might have been in the previous four words. He suggested that I should ask her if she would like to play mothers and fathers (she was four years old and I was six), and that she should be the mother and tell me (the father) what was to be done in the house. My little sister loved it, and so did I. Of course, each mother or father has a different way of dealing with similar situations, but this way suited me.

And I loved Sunday mornings when my father stood on the landing of the first floor with a hunting horn to his lips, playing different calls. Bedroom doors would open, and before his four children could jump up at him, he would have run back to his bed. We would run after him and all of us would scramble under his blankets while my mother would give us a sleepy smile. Once we were in bed, this was the time when my father told us stories from his childhood.

It felt good to know that my father was awake before we children were awake. In many homes it is the mother. the soul of the house as she has often been called, who is the first to awake and listen through the dawn and ask herself about the coming day. "What will this day bring for us? Will John throw another temper? How do I arrange the day with shopping and ironing to do when I'm so tired?" Any attempt to increase consciousness is a source of strength for facing the situations that may arise.

To wake up in a room that is still dark belongs to the tenderness of the morning, and I have heard six-year old and even five-year old children suggest that they love to wake up with curtains still drawn. After all, the senses at this time of the day are as yet delicate; they begin to operate slowly and naturally. The soul after its long sojourn during the night wants gradually to reorientate itself to the material surroundings of the day. This way of waking up allows the door of sleep-consciousness which the child is just leaving, to be closed gently.

It is important for both children and adults that the experiences of the night-consciousness be allowed to stay more or less actively for a while just below the level of the day-consciousness. For here rest the hints, understandings, re-assurances and sense of the spiritual world. Therefore the alarm-clock needs to be kept well away from the young child for it is such a cold, stern and literally shocking awakener. After such an awakening, the child could be disgruntled for hours afterwards. Instead the parent can hum a melody or sing a seasonal or morning song.

Most children cannot cope with a question during the first ten minutes of the morning. This is because the answer demands more day-consciousness than the child can easily muster at this point in time. But, like the evening time, the morning offers another opportunity to the parent to foster his child's awareness and sensitivity to the time of day and to the people and environment around her. He can draw back the curtains and perhaps stand with the child in his arms before the window and look out at the day. Only then would he turn on the electric light if it is still dark.

For some parents, the early morning with its very personal quality has proved to be the best time to recall something from the previous day that needs to be completed or to be put right during the new day. For the child who is six or over, a light conversation just before or after breakfast might be the better method and time. But whatever the case may be, a simple and lightly conducted practice within a joyful mood of affirmation of each child and of life, can strengthen, both individually and as a family group, the underlying sense of being on a path of development.

Often the child who is awake and up before six every morning cannot understand why the parent sends him back to bed, especially when he is bright and beaming like the morning sun. This can also be the child who is asleep at 7 p.m. in the evening and, as we know, is much the rosier and the more active for his long sleep before midnight. I have known a number of three-, four and five-year old children who played for well over two hours in the morning before the parent came to dress them,—and then they were so tired after breakfast that they had to sleep for one or two hours, It was a phase. Nevertheless, the parents had to find ways of getting the children and themselves as happily as possible through this phase.

It is my experience that the baby who is fed on call, who sleeps in the same room as the mother, and who sleeps even in the same bed as the mother and has his nappies changed under the mother's blanket so that neither parents nor baby are fully awake or cold, is closer to the mother's rhythm of getting up in the morning. It is more likely then that when eventually he is in his own room, the child will snuggle back under the blanket and "wait until I come". The toddler who is neither dry nor clean during the night will need changing once he is awake. In cold weather the parent can dress her child in woollen socks and a woollen jumper, and, after a few well chosen and firmly spoken words, she may go back to bed while he plays with the toys that were put at the foot of his bed the previous evening.

When the child cannot be contained in bed any longer, the parent can show him in the course of a few mornings and evenings how to put on his warm slippers and his woolly dressing gown. To make the dressing gown easier to button up, it can have the largest possible press buttons sewn onto it, a four-year old can soon learn to close such buttons. The parent can then say, "When Mummy and Daddy get up, they dress, and when you get up you may get dressed, too. Here are your slippers and here is your dressing gown. When you are dressed you may play." This can be insisted upon. But this will be easier if the child has had close contact with the parents from an early age and has led a rhythmical life.

Water is a wonderful agent to bring about a change in consciousness, whether this be toward sleep in the evening or waking up in the morning. Therefore, children usually need little encouragement to have their faces and hands washed after getting out of bed. Contrary to popular belief, warm water is far kinder and more effective than cold water for the child who finds it difficult to wake up and incarnate into the day consciousness and who therefore, easily feels cold. It is always better to brush the teeth after breakfast. The slow child will need the parent's help in getting dressed, and often such a child does not like to talk or listen to talk before breakfast. Of course, of immediate help is a bit of fun like putting the vest or undershirt on upside down, the skirt back to front, the left shoe on the right foot etc. Humour helps a child to incarnate and it also helps to establish love and respect for the adult who is creative and surprising with words and deeds.

One more thing needs to be done. The hair to be brushed or combed. Where the hair is long, this can be a painful process which sometimes has to be accompanied by singing or by the parent's childhood stories. But this activity is another such one that has also deeper meaning, for to bring the hair into order is also to bring order to the head and to the thinking.

A way of concluding the morning's bathroom ceremony is for the parent to accompany her last stroke of the brush or the comb with the words, "There—that looks like Sally", and to give her a kiss and say, "Good morning,Sally". This can help to make a child feel deep down that he or she is recognised in his or her essential being, and then the child will run happily into the kitchen for breakfast.

The Seasonal Table

Many of the homes I know have a plant in the sitting-room. Very often it is the parents' pride and joy. Next to it can stand a greeting card from, say, a grandparent or friend, or a seasonal picture, a table lamp, a candle, a few shells from the summer holidays, a few rock crystals from a walk—in short, one small place in the house is made into a special place. As birthdays and festivals come and go, so this seasonal bower changes: it may serve as a background to the birthday table, or perhaps to the Christmas tree. The family can make a practice of standing in front of it every morning, or on Sundays, and mother or father can speak a short morning verse, read a seasonal poem or a special passage from a book, followed by a spoken or sung grace.

In other homes, mother or father read perhaps from a book that might lie on the breakfast table, or speaks a verse which is followed by singing a grace before the family starts to eat breakfast. But whatever the practice, such morning rituals can help a child to build upon its sense of family and home, and to feel integrated with the best that mother and father can bring to the life of the family.

After the grace, breakfast begins. A happy breakfast means, in the first place, an unhurried breakfast. This is often difficult on weekdays when, already in the early morning, the mother can feel overwhelmed by the demands that the day will bring. After the soul has been turned away from the earth during the night, the first meal of the day is a time of reuniting with the substances and life of the earth. The more this reunion is acknowledged the better will it serve us. For the young child, this means that the food on the breakfast table will nourish him better if he can eat unhurriedly.

In countering any feeling of pressure, it is a help to create a quiet atmosphere by laying the table a little differently each morning. Fresh flowers or leaves can be put on the table, or a nice picture post-card or a small toy. The butter can be decorated, or the spoons can perhaps be placed in a star formation in the middle of the table. Even a little joke can be played by turning the cups upside down. Such little gestures invite parents and children to relax and enjoy breakfast together. On Sundays it is easier to linger at the breakfast table, especially if the parents have laid the table in a special way because it is a special day.

The end of breakfast, when the family is refreshed and ready to start the day's work, or play, is a good moment to say together, "Thank you for the meal".

And parents and children will be more in tune with each other during the day because, together, they have practised listening to the silences of twilight and dawn—times when soul is closer to soul than at any other times during the day.

3.   FAMILY MEALS

Bons Voors

To share a meal together is one of the most uniting activities for people. Sharing the same food weaves a link between people—especially at home. When we have someone at our table whom we do not like, it is hard to "stomach" and we will avoid it if possible!

When we sit at a table—physically close to one another—we need a lot of social awareness, while balancing the attention for the food and a certain amount of conversation between all family members and guests present.

Nowadays the art of eating together seems to get lost or skilfully attacked. New customs have developed whereby we just grab a snack from the fridge whenever we feel like it. Modern kitchen design has created small counters where people sit on barstools like chickens on a bar. Instant foods have taken away the joy and the art of good cooking, so why bother? The time to lay the table, the to-ing and fro-ing to a proper dining room, thereby giving this element in the day its own space, seem apparently a waste of time. So the time and the space for the meal are squeezed into odd corners. A common pattern has come about, whereby everybody takes his food on a separate tray to be swallowed, while watching television.

But really—we all know there is nothing like a table well laid or a lovely meal to be enjoyed in good company!

The Table

It is important to look at the shape and the material of the table. Nowadays most tables are square or rectangular, but the round or oval shape gives us the opportunity to see everybody at the same time. The shape of the circle expresses, as in the symbol of a ring, the quality of unity and totality. The centre leg under a round table, compared to the corner legs of the square form, provides more freedom for the legs and can avoid a good many fights in later years! It is a great advantage if the table can be lengthened in some way in view not only of one's own children, but of the many friends they bring home. Many hours are going to be spent at the table eating, but it also will be used for other activities such as drawing painting games, making huts underneath, so the material is worth taking into account. Materials such as glass, which is cold, or formica, which is efficient but so very neutral, or beautiful veneers that easily become damaged might not give the same pleasure as the sturdiness of a solid sort of wood. (The round table of King Arthur could support a horse with a man on top.) With a solid wooden table one does not have to worry about "disasters". Over the years the family history will slowly get engrained into this centre point of the household: marks from doodling forks, the stain of a pan, angry imprints of a child... a nice clean cloth can always cover the daily life-marks whenever necessary for official use or celebrations!

When we set the table there is a wealth of opportunities to be creative. Just as one nicely cut red radish can brighten up a plain salad, so can a single flower, a candle or colourful napkins create a different mood. A nice earthenware milkjug makes the taste of the milk different from what it is in a plastic, useful, unbreakable container. When a well-loved jug or egg cup—made by a child—breaks, it can be the reason for tears well spent! To eat from dishes and pots that one grows fond of and that have to be cared for, makes materials *matter*.

To have for birthdays and celebrations a special cloth that is "always" used at those occasions, gives these days a special colour and taste. The table invites us to be creative—whether it be a flower—a special message under a plate—or a straight-forward but colourful meal. (In my childhood our grandparents used to give us a packet of the best butter on our birthdays which could be used in as many fat layers on a sandwich or pure as one wished. It was a highlight of the day. (How the other siblings would sit with jealous eyes and a burning desire for when it would be their turn!)

With its daily returning routine, the table turns into a tool for making an art of daily life.

A Grace Or A Verse

Sharing a meal is so much more than eating food. Even if one does not have a religious background, one can ponder how to begin and end the meal in an appropriate way. The respect for the food, said in a grace, verse or song, raises the physical aspect to another level. It also provides the advantage of starting together at the same time! Scandinavian households it is quite common to thank the cook at the end with "Tag for matten"—"thank you for the meal". To instill in children an awareness not only of respect for the products of nature but also for the provider and the person who has been cooking, helps them to learn that things—food, work, people— *matter*.

One example of a verse is:

> Before the flour, the mill,
> Before the mill, the grain,
> Before the grain, the sun and rain,
> The beauty of God's will.

To experiment with different verses or songs of the various seasons, or with a special birthday verse, is one of the privileges of family life.[1]

Space

The physical closeness evokes endless battles at the beginning. Dangling legs, bumping knees, legs and shoes that have to be discovered by the youngest, who creeps as a mouse under the table tickling everybody until an explosion follows! The handling of forks and knives, elbows which invariably meet other elbows, are a slow process of learning to cope with space. Battles are fought over: "This is my place", "No, it is mine", or, "I want to sit next to granny" when she is visiting. It is all part of the sibling struggle to find one's right place next to the other.

Time

Learning to deal with time is another aspect the young mother has to grapple with, before "reasonable" family meals are established. Feeding the baby before or after a meal, while cooking away and answering your friend's urgent phone call at the same time. Having a meal with a tired husband and screaming infant is something which might need some thinking out and shifting of priorities!

Discovery

The first years of the small child are full of discoveries of the sense world. How different is the touching of porridge and fingering of spinach. The delight of squeezing bananas or the plashing with a full hand in the waterlake of a tumbled cup, are a necessary path of discovery before mother gets angry and wise in avoiding these upheavals to a certain extent. The joy of discovering the laws of gravity by endless tipping of milkcups and throwing down crusts out of a high chair will be followed by the surprise of meeting the social laws of mother being fed up with porridge on the floor and very clearly saying no at some point. On the other hand every parent discovers the essential tool of distraction! Aeroplanes and buses which bring spinach into the mouth or elephants and cows bringing in rejected crusts of bread.

The sense of taste is developed in the maze of flavours and smells either liked or disliked. Only gradually a variety of foods is introduced. It is not necessary in the beginning to explain to a little child why the grown ups may be having different foods. Nor is it wise to confuse the little one by giving him the choice of what to have on his sandwich. Our household had the rule that a spoonful of whatever was on the table had to be eaten, with the result that the children just about like everything. Another rule, which got bent, but worked all the same, was no dessert unless the main dish was finished.

The entire realm of discipline and table manners is a fine balancing bar for parents learning to be consistent. On one side are the steep rocky mountains of being too dogmatic and too strict, where the child in his battles incurs resentful wounds. On the other side are the treacherous marshes of being too flexible, too anti-authoritarian, where the child fails to learn the safety and security of a proper yes and no, and "this is the way to do and not to do".

Conversation

The age of "children should be seen, and not heard" is definitely over. In those days nannies ate with the children in the nursery, while the parents dined, indulging in long conversations. Parents have to learn to let go of the sort of conversation they used to have before the children joined their meals. Too much adult conversation is disastrous for a meal, since the children will start their own conversation, their language changing very quickly from verbal into the physical. We found it quite a pain to let go of that space for talking about the events of the day, which could easily lead into an interesting discussion. But in giving up that amount of adult talk, we slowly gained something new. Instead of going into abstract discussions, we were confronted with the immediate, with the present-listening to the children's remarks and funny stories of the day, while regulating and giving each a chance to speak. The concentration needed to keep the mealtime on to the right track can change the more intellectual inward orientated way of the adult into a more outward way of observing and enjoying of the "here and now".

Another aspect is the way adults speak in front of the children. When speaking about daily events one needs to realize how the first pictures and images of the world are brought to the young child. How the father speaks about his work, about successful events or about his disillusions, how the mother speaks about small events such as the milkman being late or the electrician never turning up, affect the child deeply in an unconscious way. How we look at life, whether we speak with respect or disrespect about people and society—those are the bricks and tools for imitations by the young child. Many of these bricks are laid at mealtimes.

In later years, meals can become a focus where the members of the family bring their experiences of the day or share long conversations over dessert and many cups of coffee.

Games

One of the habits that developed over the years in our family was the singing at the end of the meal. This proved also to be a good method of keeping the children at the table until the very end. Everyone taking a child on his or her lap, and singing away nursery rhymes—songs, ballads from olden days. . . How wonderful to have a guest, an au pair or grandparent to provide an extra lap for the singing! But also what joy for such a guest or stranger to be totally admitted into the circle, participating in simple songs and games they seldom get a chance for. Simple finger games, riddles, memory games at the end of a meal can make mealtimes fun and really shared activity.

The Empty Chair

The table is a place where one can experience real joy but also real pain. How awful and awkward becomes the mood when a child for some reason is sent up to his or her room or to finish his plate in the hall! The younger children wide eyed and often in tears. The food without any taste and everybody just longing for the meal to be over or the conflict to be finished and reconciled. An uneasiness between parents, the wrong words during a family visit, or a serious fight between siblings are hard to swallow at mealtimes. The empty chair when someone has died or when parents separate cries out at the table, at celebration times in particular. But theoppositeholds true, too. There is nothing like sharing a meal with one's family or with friends. . .!

Guests

It is usually a real nightmare to have guests when the children are small. The combination of cooking, preparing children for bed and receiving guests, trying to have an intelligent conversation while mopping up the knocked over sherry glass is nearly fatal for an ordinary housewife. When the children are slightly older it can still be very embarrassing at times, but it has also more positive sides. The sharing of a meal with a family can be a great joy for a single person, or for people without children. It breaks the daily routine and gives children the chance to take good care of their guests, when sitting next to them at the table. "First the guests" is a nice weapon to throw at one's siblings. In particular for one parent families it is important for children to learn, when guests are present,that grown ups have adult conversations and that not all attention is focussed on the children.

In our household, guests were very important for bringing in new games and riddles, which everybody enjoyed!

No wonder that mealtimes can be so difficult in the early years with babies and young toddlers, since they are a training ground for life in so many aspects. They are a setting in which adults still have to strive over and over again to achieve a balance in themselves and others. A balancing of all the different senses such as taste, sight and hearing (the amount of noise!). But also the more inner senses need to interweave, such as an inner sense for the right amount and the flow of the conversation, a sense for the mood and the atmosphere of the daily as well as the special occasion. Finally a sense needs to be developed for the different needs of the various members of the household with regard to time,space and attention!

All these elements form the ingredients for a good meal. In preparing the food, the laying of the table, the children washing their hands, lie an expectation: "What are we having today?" A space is created, which if well cared for, is filled time and again in a thousand different ways. . .

Blessings on the meal!

4. RELIGIOUS LIFE IN THE FAMILY

Bons Voors

The ways in which the convictions or belief of parents are expressed in family life make a strong imprint on the children. So much so that nowadays people question whether such an imprint is right or wrong. They may even feel insecure or guilty of imposing values on their children.

Erikson, an American psychiatrist, describes how children growing up in families with strong convictions are usually healthier, stronger and more resilient than those who grow up in families where there was no such thing. Even if the child will reject those values when grown up they have provided him with a certain view on life, certain values— something that can be rejected! On the other hand there is an attitude of "laissez-faire", of indifference and neutrality—"it does not matter", "anything goes", a colourlessness which is a colour all the same.

This is a helpful thought when we are struggling to find our own ways of expressing values as a family in a society where the support of certain forms, values and religions of former days has gone overboard.

Certainly, when we start on our path as a family, searching for ways to relate to the mystery of Christ within ourselves and with others, testing and experimenting with ways to celebrate and to express that relationship in the daily rhythms and in the festivals, it is often the children who help us. The young children, who are still so close to the spiritual world, pull their parents along, but the parents have to set out tracks, a ritual or a way of behaviour, to give the children a hand in order to make the reflections of this relationship visible and recognisable.

When we consciously try to shape and renew rituals and forms within a community or within a family, there remain the pitfalls of habit and of social pressure, the danger of: "This is the way to do it and not to do it." While puzzling about all this, an Old Testament story sprang to mind:

> And David danced before the Lord with all his might, and David was girded with a linen ephod. . . And as the ark of the Lord came into the city of David, Michal, Saul's daughter, looked through a window, and saw king David leaping and dancing before the Lord: and she despised him in her heart. (II Sam. 6:14-17).

When David—the shepherd boy who had become king—brought the Ark, the physical expression of the spiritual world, into his home, into Jerusalem, he danced with joy in his heart, with music and songs, being clothed in simple linen, totally uninhibited. He was in a direct living relationship with his God. But his behaviour was frowned upon and despised by his wife, Michal. King David ought to have behaved, he should have known better than to dance half naked in front of the people. But as the scripture then says: Michal bore no children, she remained unfruitful for the rest of her life. Established rules and dogmas of "should"s and "ought to"s do not bear fruit.

The unfruitfulness of Michal in being aloof, looking from a distance through the window, not daring to commit herself, and the joy and the dancing vitality of David, who enters fully into this living relationship with God, are both components one can experience within oneself and in the family. As parents we have to strive to find this living reality and to offer our children certain forms through which it can come to expression. But it is a mutual and slow path of development for all.

When our first child was born, he was not christened. When the second child was born, we had arrived at the decision to have both children baptised. The oldest, then two and a half years old, said out loud in the church after their baptism: "Now Daddy must be baptised." In a way he was right. We had also taken a plunge into our spiritual path with them.

One of the next steps on this path was when we chose to adopt a tradition of the shepherds' meal on Christmas Eve. But the children led the way! Let me briefly describe it.

We all dress up as shepherds and sheep and stumble around in the dark house. Eventually we find a fire (in the living room), where we have a very simple shepherds' meal that has been prepared beforehand. As the shepherds go to sleep on the carpet one of us (often a child) becomes an angel with a candle in his or her hand to bring the message of the newborn Child in Bethlehem. Singing appropriate songs, we climb over the dark hills of the staircase and finally find the stable under the brightly shining starlight of the Christmas tree.

Over the years this has led also to playing the entire Christmas story during Advent and over the Christmas period, quickly changing roles with just a few simple garments. It is a play in which anybody who happens to be visiting gets included! In the beginning one feels very self-conscious and awkward being an angel or Mary, but for the children, who have just come from those spiritual realms, it is completely normal. In the confrontation with their earnestness we grope our way towards this living quality in our hearts. On this slow, winding, wonderful path we can find a new connection with the festivals and with the seasons. Our awareness of the larger rhythm within the year can become visible on a shelf or in a corner of the room where the treasures of each season find a home.

In any ritual we establish a moment of conscious connection with with God and the spiritual world, as with the ringing of a bell. The sound that arises through the activity of ringing revives that connection over and over again. But both the dancing quality of David's songs and the unfruitful ways and habits of Michal are always there.

Just as you have established a certain way or ritual with a festival or a meal, you find that the oldest child has outgrown that particular form and you have to change in order not to become unfruitful. Nor can you adopt certain patterns from others, however right and wonderful they may appear in their setting. The many meaningful rituals at bedtime, important in marking the transition from day into night, such as candles and stories, prayers or songs, never got a very strong foothold in our family, simply because I feel tired and unholy at that hour of day/night, although I have often felt I "should". But fortunately or unfortunately one can not be more holy than one is! One can only ring one's own bell, as a person and as a family.

We did manage to deal with the transition from the night into the day. After many years of hectic breakfasts, which everybody took at different times, according to duties in the outside world, we decided it would probably make a great difference to start the day together, before everyone took off. So we looked for a song or a melody. After trying several melodies, which disappeared because they did not work, we found a simple Alleluia which is very short and can be sung in a round. It starts at a high pitch, so not only do you have to arrive at breakfast at the same time, you even have to reach up to that high note to greet the day! It does make a difference! It shapes one conscious moment in the on-goingness of time to say hello to the day. When writing this article I asked my son: "Why do we sing before a meal?" His delightful answer was: "Oh, we are telling God we are having breakfast, so He can join in." And he added more dutifully: I guess to say thank you."

Ultimately it is not only the highlights in the year, the festivals, the seasons table, the Sunday, the daily rituals that establish the "religious life" at home. As moments of struggle and joy, they are certainly very important keys to open up this path into the spiritual world and they create opportunities to express this, touching on the mystery of the Christ. But any moment in the day can suddenly light up in its sacred quality. A quiet story with a child, a quarrel resolved, the beauty of a coloured leaf, the awe for a dead bird. Any event in the day can transcend its grey cloak of habit and matter-of-factness. But usually it does not happen, because we do not give each moment its full time and weight, and our eyes and hearts are not always open with wonder and respect to see what lies before our feet.

To train these faculties of awareness and wonder, this sense of the divine order in the ordinary, the mystery of the Christ within our own hearts and the ability to perceive that living reality in others, we need to ring the bell regularly.

Just as we find that after a while the beautiful autumn season table turns into a dusty desert, the sword of Michael becomes bent, the once shining conkers shrivel up and grow dull, so it is with our inner life: the place needs sweeping, the plants need watering. The inner and the outer life are the same. They both need to be spring-cleaned after Christmas. They both want loving care and steadfastness.

To dance with joy before the countenance of God, as David did, to renew this living reality in one's heart and one's environment and to get stuck in the traps of rules and habits and the endless pitfalls of unfruitfulness of Michal, is a slow, winding wonderful path in family life!

5. WHY FESTIVALS?

John Davy

Every people on earth celebrates festivals. Most of these have roots going back into the distant past. They seem to be an ancient characteristic of humanity itself. They united whole communities, and were at the same time linked with the rhythms of nature. They were also "religious"—they were concerned with the meaning of human life on earth.

What are our individual, family and community festivals like today? In the so-called advanced countries, urban, industrialised, scientifically-minded, we are severely alienated from nature. And religion, too has tended to retire into churches and private belief. As this has happened, our festivals have become puzzles, problems, even ordeals. How many adults in "Christian" countries can be heard explaining to one another at the end of December how glad they are that Christmas is over. "We only do it for the children", they may add. And doing it for the children means the grind of Christmas shopping and eating too many sweets.

We still understand the idea of "celebrating". We are always throwing parties, but these are no longer tied to the rhythms of nature. We may celebrate our birthdays—but do we look forward to them as our children do? Traditional festivals were collective birthdays, moments of heightened experience and renewal. Adults' birthdays are seen by many as gloomy milestones along the road to death.

Yet we still hanker for those heightened moments. We may find them, too but they are not linked to particular times of the year or month or week. A particular evening is graced and blessed; a party comes alive or two people meet on a new level. There are moments in nature, too, when our inner mood is awake and responsive to a sunset, a view of mountains, birdsong, the sounds of the sea or a waterfall. Then, for a moment, the prose of everyday life stirs into poetry. We sing and dance inside. But do we shout and dance for joy outwardly? The place and time may not be appropriate. Other people would not understand, might take offence. Our festival has to be private, personal, inward and isolated.

Children are closer to the older experience of festivals. On their birthdays, we wish them "many happy returns of the day". A birthday is something to look forward to; each time it returns, you celebrate a step in "growing up"—towards what? Towards a grey adult world without festivals?

To be able to participate in a real adult festival is a deep joy for children. Who most enjoys a traditional "white wedding". with church, reception, confetti and all the trappings? The brides' attendants, of course. Five year old bridesmaids can sparkle more than the bride herself. But all too often, our festivals are not suitable for children: We like to see them safely in bed before the party begins.

So we become strangers to nature and to festivals, and our children are deprived of what used to be fundamental of rhythms and experiences which assure them that real life includes poetry and song as well as prose. The festivals of the past were truly *re-ligious*—they reconnected individuals and peoples with the heavens, with their origins, with the greater meanings of their lives. The rituals of the priests were also "celebrations". But many of us now are also alienated from traditional religion. Or if we are not, our religious celebrations are no longer particularly festive: There may be some dignified singing, but there is not much dancing in church.

We can lament this separation from nature, the fading of festivals, the turning inward and private of religion. We can attempt a pagan revival and sing to the full moon. But neither response faces fully the modern fact of the tension between the child's and the adult's relation to festivals, or explores its meaning.

For we really are separated from nature in a way that we used not to be. This goes even into our reproductive physiology: Although the menstrual cycle has an approximately lunar rhythm, we are unique in our capacity to procreate all the year round. Unlike the animals, our "weddings" do not have to be integrated into the cycle of the year. This is a biological "alienation" which is part of our history. It may be, as Steiner once remarked, that long ago, in prehistoric times, all children were conceived in spring and born in mid-winter. But as far as we can tell, this has not been so for several thousand years.

More recently, we have grown apart from nature in many other ways. From being Mater (mother), the earth has become Matter, raw material for mining and exploitation. Our Nature is no longer peopled by spirits, and to speak of "the face of the earth" is no longer even poetic, but a mere verbal habit, the corpse of what was once a living everyday experience.

We have paid a price—but we have also been given a gift beyond price. We have acquired the possibility of freedom, of creative choice—and with these, responsibility.

The festivals of the past were rituals to enable the Gods to guide human life on earth. They are silent now. They do not punish us for failing to perform a rain dance or greet the full moon at the autumn equinox. Nature gets on with its work and we get on with ours. But—and it is a mighty "but"—we have also become, whether we like it or not, the new gods for nature. What actually happens to the earth in the next decades, let alone centuries, to all the living things, to the life of the seas and even the weather, will depend on what we do—and particularly on what we, the citizens of the industrial and scientific cultures, do. As the adolescent leaves home, so we have separated ourselves from a life which was once integrated into nature's rhythms. For both, it is essential for growing up. But we now have decisive and actual responsibility for the future of the earth. Are we ready for it? And can we possibly carry it without new festivals?

As the old festivals lifted peoples towards the eternal verities of their cultures, so we need festivals which lift us towards the meaning of being human, towards what we can *become*. For if we cannot become more than we are now, we cannot hope to care rightly for the earth which the Gods have now evidently handed over to us. Furthermore, in celebrating our humanity, we must begin to celebrate for all humanity. The festivals of the past, although often related in many themes and practices, were nevertheless bound to particular tribes, religions and territories. As such, they gave identity to a group—but they also set it apart from the whole. Blood, possession of land and religions were the engines of much conflict in the past, and can still be so today. Yet now we have seen the whole earth from space, alive but vulnerable, and needing above all our care and understanding. The earth can no longer bear our wars. Correspondingly, our responsibilities reach beyond our race, nation, territory, blood or particular religion. So we need to find festivals at once religious and united with the life of nature, which can alsouniteus simply as human beings. Such a task calls for the creative artist in us. Our prosaic selves cannot rise to such an occasion.

Is this too grand a vision? I think it is entirely practical, in that we cannot have festivals without a vision. But we can start in a small way, in our families, with our friends, and above all with children, who are natural poets, singers, dancers and celebrants, given a little encouragement.

As we try, we shall also turn naturally for inspiration to the festivals of the past and to the religions of our own cultures if we still feel such connections. We may then rediscover the way in which religious festivals were woven into the rhythms of the year. For in the festivals we make, the collaboration of nature and human celebration must continue. So in midwinter, there is the secret, inward turning point of time which opens the way to longer days, a stirring of seeds in the soil and a strengthening sun. In a Christian culture, we may then naturally celebrate the birth of the Child who came for all mankind. Jewish families may light the Hannukah candles. But they, too, will be celebrating a kindling of new light in the midst of darkness. Every family may find its own way to kindle a light of hope for the future of all the newly born, of all children, of what can be newly born in us and in all people.

The spring equinox, the balance of day and night, is also a threshold, a crisis or crossing. Soon after, nature bursts forth from its winter imprisonment, rises from its grave. We do not have to be orthodox Christians to celebrate this time not only as a nature festival, but also as a time to consider the challenge of love: By nature, we love ourselves, our kin, our nation. But for the brotherhood of humanity to become possible, love of self must die and resurrect as love of the world. (Children are very deeply stirred by the wonder of the caterpillar which "dies" into the pupa and bursts forth as the glorious butterfly.)

Towards midsummer, we may need conscience. As we are drawn out into nature, we easily lose ourselves, and become mere consumers of the sun. The disciples of Christ retired to an upper room at Pentecost, and there found a voice and words which could speak in the hearts of all their hearers. This can be the fulfillment of the seed, the little light planted from heaven at midwinter into the darkness of the earth and the intimacy of each human heart. Amidst the blinding light of midsummer, we can seek also for an inner flowering, a power of shared understanding which can make a wedding festival, a community of life for all mankind. Individual midwinter candles are transformed into one holy and healing fire for building human communities.

Harvest time, the autumn equinox, was once an occasion not only for gratitude to the past, but also for meeting fear of the future, of the winter ahead which some might not survive. Nowadays, in a threatened world, adults need festivals to conquer fear, festivals of courage. And children have their dragons and nightmares too. There are many legends of St. Michael (who has many other names in other cultures) and of his way with dragons and devils. As parents, one of the most precious gifts we can bring to our children is encouragement, belief in what they will give to the future, in what they can become. But for this we have to find our own courage for life.

So we may find our way round the year, seeing how the drama of the sun and the earth resonates with the dramas of human life. I have not aimed here to spell out in detail ways of making new festivals with children. Other contributors to this section describe what they have tried. But our festivals cannot be recipes or prescriptions from without: We can only become festive as we awaken the artist, the poet, the singer, the dancer, the dramatist, in ourselves. Then we can also take hold with gratitude of ideas from others.

My concern has been rather to seek a *motive* for making new festivals, a motive which calls from the future, which could bring festivals in which all can participate irrespective of religion, race or nation, festivals which lift us towards a sense of what we can become as human beings so that we may learn to care rightly for the earth and for one another.

For Rudolf Steiner, and perhaps for all the contributors to this book, this awareness contains the real meaning of Christianity. As the sun of nature shines on the whole earth, so the future calls for a sun to shine from human hearts which can warm and illumine the whole world. Such a sun cannot be possessed by any particular group or religion. It will illuminate all religions which have come from the past, and celebrate the divinity in all humanity.

While the heavens ruled not only nature but all human life, there was no freedom. The festivals were cosmic necessities, the gods created through us and we danced to the stars' tunes. Now we are growing up and have had to leave home. It can seem cold and lonely. But if we find a little creative and festive sunlight in our own hearts as we go through the year, and let it help us make festivals with our children, their faces will light up and their hearts will begin to dance, You'll see.

I. A Walk through the Year with the Festivals

Caz Iveson

Travelling through the year's festivals with children is like experiencing the rainbow—no sooner has one colour faded than the next one appears. Ceremonies which have their roots deep in mankind's past flower in the day-to-day life of caring which is the home, and can be a source of healing in many troubled times. Here is a picture of how an ordinary family of a mother and children walked together through one such rainbow year.

It is a blustery, biting cold day in early spring. Mother is wearing at least four woollen cardigans, and baby Daniel can be recognised through his padding only by his scowling face! He doesn't grasp yet how important this day is—this Sunday called Palm Sunday—and the ceremony which his older brother and sisters hold dear. For two days Paul, Jane and Caroline have worked to prepare the crosses—simply made with two stout sticks, bound together with coloured ribbons. On each stick hang buns of sweet bread made into shapes of rabbits, cockerels and hens, and dried fruit strung on threads. Braving the cold wind the group sets off in procession, singing *Hosanna, Dona nobis Pacem* and well-loved spring songs learnt at school. Occasionally nibbling at the tempting bread, they tour the paths, fields and gardens around their home—their boundary—to see that all is well, and where the first daffodils are soon to appear.

"Wasn't it nice of Mrs. Jones to join in—I thought she'd think us crazy, but she asked us back for hot fruit-juice", said Paul. "Alleluja. . ." he hums to himself later in the day, as he butters for himself and baby brother another piece of Palm Sunday bread.

Later in that week the children will have helped to put the crosses on the Good Friday buns, and while the buns are baking they sow small seeds of summer flowers in their own patch of ground outside. The daffodils are beginning to open, in spite of the cold, and the first colour is appearing on the shrubs. It is joy to be outside again and

"Look—there! I told you I saw primroses—let's pick some for the Easter garden. . ."

While one big sister prepares the eggs for hanging—blowing them and painting the shells—the other, the baker of the family, uses the eggs for the chocolate Easter cake. She will put all her ingenuity into its decoration too, using flowers, leaves and chocolate! The brothers play around the table, where stands an Easter bowl, with sown winter grains of wheat, sprouting into bright blades of green.

On Easter day they will find, early in the morning red-dyed eggs in this bowl of green, the mossy indoor garden full of tiny flowers, sweet eggs and branches hung with painted eggs.

Outside. . . oh joy! The Easter hare has visited the grassy nests and clumps of daffodils, and left, cleverly hidden, golden and silver wrapped chocolate eggs to gladden the heart. Inside, mingling with the smells of the special meal, the scent of flowering currant lends its own freshness to the sunny, spring-cleaned room.

From Easter on, for this family, the accent is on gardening; preparing the soil, sowing and enjoying the flowers as they gradually emerge—tulips, the little red ones are Paul's favourites; the many-clustered grape hyacinths, primroses and celandine which the girls often pick for the table of mother's and their own bedrooms. Some friends have a white meal at Whitsun—all white clothers, flowers, even food! A common meal with many friends out of doors, for May is the best month for warmth.

Family walks now begin in earnest—who will find the first bluebells, gather the most elder-flowers for midsummer juice—heavy and potent with pollen, made with lemon and honey for cool teas, or medicine for colds. Jane loves to pick and press small flowers and leaves of every kind; once she and her best friend Ann picked posies of flowers, dressed up as gypsies and presented the neighbours with their collection!

When the local farmer delivers manure for the garden, the boys have a festival with wheelbarrows and wellington boots. The cat brings in a dead fledgling which is buried with all due ceremony and plenty of flowers, and moments of solemnity occur when, caught in a summer storm, the children can behold a rainbow, sometimes two, glowing in the heavy sky. So the summer and its festive nature passes with outdoor picnics, parties and fetes, Morris Dancers and strawberry picking, jam-making and wasp-swatting and, at the turn of the year, the great festival of Harvest and St. Michael—Michaelmas.

School begins again. All the children one year taller and broader! And mother is making the harvest loaf, in the shape of the wheat-sheaf. "Can I make the mouse?" asks Paul. Little Daniel makes one too, and his own version of the wheat-sheaf, which the birds will eat. . .

While the children celebrate Michaelmas at school, mother is picking blackberries with a friend, glad of the break and a time to chat, before the work of making jam and fruit-juice begins again. The apples have to be dealt with too—all very well for the children to be knocking them down and picking them up by the boxfull. . . There will be pounds of jam for the Christmas market; apples are in heaps on the table at harvest meal; while the marrows and pumpkins fill every corner of the store cupboard.

For people who have any garden produce of their own, now is the time to share. The boys run out after school and at weekends, to knock down conkers and gather in their store, rejoicing in the shining, polished surfaces of the fresh spilled nuts—a festival of conkers! For little Daniel, it is his first experience of grapes—harvest bread and purple grapes—that is his Michaelmas festive meal.

The evenings draw in and rain, falling it seems daily, keeps the family inside. Outside to inside, rainbow-coloured autumn leaves on the table and the first fire burning in the hearth. The two girls will spend a day this halfterm holiday making the Christmas puddings and cake—the boys will fight over the bowl—licking as usual!

But soon, preparations must begin for another walk—at the darkening side of the year, Martinmas, it is time to make lanterns. The wind is blowing, not cold but wet now, and strongly from the west. But in the house the children are intent and warm to their task—the making of new lanterns. Coloured card, glue, scissors, tissue paper, litter the table. String, and the highly prized wire and stapling machine, are fiercely guarded by the older ones—the girls and their best friends.

Little Daniel, too young yet to be trusted with these treasures now that he can walk, is settled early by a candle, lit in last year's lantern.

Mother and Jane, the artists, are creating new designs; Paul will make his simple lantern by a method tried and trusted in kindergarten ; twelve-year old Caroline frets a little because hers is not so beautiful, but laughs it off with her friend's joke...

The evening comes. After a hot soup supper, the boys and girls gather, well protected against the wind, to light the candle in each lantern. For a brief moment they can see the effect of the coloured windows lit up in the dark, before the door is opened. They set out bravely, trying not to fuss, shielding the fragile lights from the gusts. Although a few people know already, for most of the neighbours it is a complete surprise to find them at the door, singing *I go with my little lantern* and the tale of St. Martin, who gave half his cloak to a beggar. . . The battered paper lanterns swing and spin on their sticks, the procession moves off. Some criticism is voiced. "Is it really a good idea for the children to do that? . . I don't think the neighbours approved. . ." But "Thank you for that lovely experience", said some-one else. After all, Christ hid himself in a beggar's guise, and against wind, rain, cold and fire the family are celebrating the facts of life, the fact of being human, on the earth.

Caroline keeps her singed lantern for Daniel; Paul will use his every night at settling time till Advent. The artistic endeavours have gone up in smoke. . .!

And at Advent time: "It is so snug in the house, coming home from school," says Paul. Advent: four weeks for making presents, decorations for the house, almost a festival every day with little nice things to eat, a fire in the hearth and singing every Sunday.

A festival of the house—a festival of the home, of being together, rubbing shoulders, teasing, breaking and mending, hiding and finding.

The older girls now take their instruments and play music with friends, but hope they can also have a turn at opening a window of the Advent calendar. Teenagers now, they still look forward to the Christmas stocking, doing a puppet show, playing with the boys.

The older ones go away for Christmas; the youngest is left. He makes, in peace and undisturbed, a long line of wooden toy animals, his own, which bit by bit walk towards the crib under the tree. They have travelled from the mossy Advent "garden" on the little table, where four candles have burnt, to the Manger, above which the twelve tree-candles are now alight.

The tree is decorated simply; with shiny red apples, hanging from boughs on which red and white paper roses are tied. The gold star gleams at the top, just under the ceiling. Soon, in twelve days time, the others will be home, for Three Kings day. It is like a second Christmas Day for this family; each child will spread his gifts under the tree— each one will, in turn, choose a parcel for the other. The legend of the little fir-tree, or a similar story, solemnises the burning of the branches. . . and Christmas ends once more. . . all but for one thing, an image of the Christchild which will remain till Candlemas, the 4th February.

And still the small weekly and daily festivals remain, the preparation of vegetables, the woodgathering, baking, storytelling, singing at bedtime, because home is where the festivals flower.

11. Easter - Another Birth

Caz Iveson

It starts somewhere back, in the darkness, when we leave Christmas behind. Having observed the Birth with due ceremony, and sweet-meats and candles put aside, we turn to face the journey back to our own country, like the Kings; returning to our ordinary life, places, kingdoms (. . ."the old dispensation, with an alien people clutching their gods"). In winter greyness, staleness, and low in forces, we succumb to illnesses of various kinds ("I should be glad of another death". . .).[1]

But, in the darkness and contraction of the earth, there are seeds, roots. The day comes, it is there, not fixed, when the earth turns and murmurs in its sleep. . . the day when the birds sound different. . . they were there before, but we were not allowed to hear, perhaps. It is as if cobwebs were pulled away from our seeing eyes, and we are breathing bright air, becoming inwardly light, like the buds, breaking with their own light, and the sky becomes a chancel for the chanting bird's song (. . . "A green treble". . .).

You don't need to make an effort to affirm that you are alive, just look where you have arrived. Everyone has heard of spring-cleaning. Why? To clean away the dust and dirt and cobwebs of that old year, old self, old body, old house. Why fast for Lent otherwise? Give up, heave off, old ways, old clothes and habits; you peel off an old skin, old fat, old self. Make shelf-space for the new year, to hear with new ears. The earth is turning, murmuring; listen while it wakes. It is about to sacrifice itself again for our need. Work the soil, weeds away; finger the earth's garment and repair it, sow with new seeds. This is our Mother, and we are one with Her, growing each in their own way, the Son's way. We need to listen, be obedient, allow for change, do reverence. Look, the children will clean the mess away, paint, cut their hair. Your home, self, can be like a temple, light within and without; sickness and healing are cleansing.

Then you can place there your branches of sharp colour and stringent scent, in the clean bright room. They belong inside if breathing space is

made. And the outer symbol of all this new growth is the egg, of birth, of womb; like the seed, potent with life, given up to life. Decorate it, clothe it, cook, eat, enjoy it. This is the demonstration, manifesting life—life over death, another birth.

III. Easter with Older Children

Signe Schaefer

At a certain stage in family life when children grow older, Easter stories of hares, of sun and moon, and of golden treasure within an egg, may begin to pale. On the one hand, a more esoteric appreciation of Easter is not yet possible, but on the other hand, Easter Day is still a special day. The children of course continue to want chocolate eggs but the magic of the hunt is no longer there. When our own children were twelve and nine, we wondered how to approach the celebration of Easter in a new way, without a forced sense of piety which could prejudice the children against Easter, yet offering an uplifting, rejuvenating sense of spring, of life, and of resurrection.

To make the day extraordinary from the very beginning, we decided to get up early and have a sunrise breakfast picnic with another family. We chose a high spot where there are magnificent views in all directions, yet with a ring of trees to keep us from being too exposed. It was exciting to be off from home by 5.30, sleepy faces glowing in the dimness, listening to the joyous dawn chorus of the birds. It was far from warm as we walked to our meeting place, and though the sky was lightening, the clouds were thick. At first we clumped together, waiting for "something" to happen, but when it didn't, both children and parents began to scamper through the trees playing He (Tag). Then laughingly, we picked up the brightly coloured eggs that had been surreptitiously hidden during the game.

Wondering if the English clouds had won the day once again, we finally settled down in a protecting nest of bracken—seemingly grown that way for our Easter pleasure—and began our breakfast. We had hard-boiled eggs, sausages kept warm in a thermos, hot cross buns and juice. Suddenly, the sun broke through the clouds, and we were all caught by the wonder of it. Brightly the rays shot out, warming our faces and uplifting our hearts. Quite spontaneously the children began to sing songs in praise of spring and the morning, even recalling some songs from their kindergarten days. If we adults had tried to organize them into singing, they would surely have rebelled!

By half past eight we were home again to our more "traditional" house and garden Easter egg-hunt. And it was also time for Easter baskets, with hand-made surprises for everyone. This year we made clay hares and swans for the children, and the children coloured and decorated special blown eggs for us. These small items that we give to each other, have become the means through which, each year, we bring Easter back into our home. Such presents may be felt-covered flat cardboard eggs with a cut-out window to show a moving picture behind; or large golden cardboard half-eggs with a small bird on a twig and a felt sun and puff-of-wool cloud inside; or large painted clay eggs made by our daughter, and clay birds made by our son, and many painted blown eggs for the "Easter tree". These Easter tree eggs we have collected for many years, and each year we try some new technique. We generally put a branch in a vase in water on Palm Sunday and add the eggs throughout the week. By Easter Day, the buds have opened and the new green leaves shimmer between the hanging eggs.

This year I also made a "nest" of sweet bread, baked with several egg-shaped stones in the centre. I then filled the bread with hard-boiled eggs that we had coloured the day before, and this made a very festive table centre-piece until it was devoured later in the day.

We had invited several relatives and friends for an Easter meal, and we suggested that they each come in a fancy "Easter bonnet". I hoped this would encourage a mood of festivity in spite of the inevitable jeans that I knew the children would wear. And it was a great success, and fun for all. Everyone had gone out to pick flowers, decorating the silliest hat he or she could find, and there was great anticipation to see what the others would do. We could all feel the joy of spring in the gay colours, and the laughter we shared gave a spark of life to our whole afternoon.

It was truly an Easter Day which lifted all our spirits. From the early morning right through the day, without needing to talk about it, we all experienced something very real of rebirth, of joy and of love.

IV. A Whitsuntide Question

Bons Voors

"Mum! What does Whitsuntide mean?" asks our seven-year-old son, while we are painting. "We had Whitsuntide celebrations at school", said our five-year-old daughter who had just brought home a rather fat, woollen dove from the kindergarten. In her voice was an air of having already celebrated Whitsuntide, and the hint that you cannot celebrate it again. "Hmm! I'm not sure about that", I thought, and I felt I was not certain of an answer , even after many years of theological training. I have also read and learned many wise words which I could repeat. Yet, unless I can give them colour and tone, they carry no weight. They are like ten doves flying in the sky. But what matters is to get one down into one's heart or head.

Children are ruthless in their straightforward questioning—questions straight as arrows, touching the essence, are being shot at you. "Mum! What is a hostage? Why does the other man point his gun at him?" "Why do they put bombs in the mail?" "Why is Churchill a great man: he is rather small?" "What is Whitsuntide?" And there is Mum, hesitating, with rather an undefined view of the world.

To explain the daily world in a single sentence so that it is comprehensible to that particular child, to try to open up the world of the spirit without at the same time closing it off, are matters which require a great presence of mind, especially since the children come to you while you are slicing the onions, sorting out muddy boots, or sitting over a quiet cup of tea. I find these moments very challenging. For while the child is waiting one searches oneself for an answer that, in all its simplicity, is of the same honesty and straightforwardness as the child's question.

What is Whitsuntide? The children give the answer. For while pondering the question of what to do at Whitsuntide, the meaning of this festival becomes clearer. Having to give form and expression to the day with the children and family is a great help in discovering and rediscovering elements of truth about any festival.

There is the wonderful Easter image of the caterpillar who gets transformed through the deathly cocoon period into a most magnificent butterfly. Then at Whitsuntide there is the image of a multitude of butterflies, dancing and dallying over the flower cups like little sisters whispering secrets to one another. It is just as difficult to catch butterflies without damaging their wings as to catch the Holy Spirit with words. In the same way as the butterfly hovers over the calyx for just a fraction of a moment, touching the most essential inner part of the flower in order to allow this precious substance to fructify another flower, so the Holy Spirit, above the heads of the people, dances like flames of fire, and touches their hearts so that they can pass the Spirit on to others.

And how shall we celebrate Whitsuntide? After a festive breakfast with cuckoo flowers and other white flowers to decorate the table, we begin to paint. Our paintings are full of butterflies and flowers. While I try to paint with some intensity, my son looks at my picture and severely comments, "There are no sunflowers yet, Mum, and the hollyhocks are not blossoming, either!" Well! If we truly observe reality, we see that parents are taught through their children. Likewise, their questions touch our spirits and excitedly shake us into awakeness.

All sorts of things happened that Whitsuntide Sunday. Yet the entire day had the colour of lightness, and it was as if a butterfly had just for a moment touched down on each of our heads and had entered our hearts.

V. The Festival of St. John

Marieke Anschütz

It is a real summery day when we decide to spend St. John's Day out in the country. It takes some time before all six of us are ready for the trip. The tyres of the bicycles are inspected and pumped up. The pannier on mother's cycle bulges with bags full of rolls, bottles of lemonade, apples and some other sweet things. The troupe sets itself into motion.

It is still early in the morning. The leaves of trees and bushes are shining with freshness. The light green colours of spring have become darker: summer has begun.

After about half an hour we come to our destination in the forest. We ride, in silence, one behind the other, when entering the avenue of trees. Above our heads the branches of the highest trees meet and intertwine—they are forming a roof, a domed one, as of a cathedral. After a while, we get off our bikes, lean them against a verge or a tree and follow a small path full of promising surprises. How utterly quiet it is here! The sun is warm on one's face. One can hear the fall and drop of a fir-cone, the rustling of a thrush scratching for worms amongst the dry leaves, a jay-bird scooting away in front of us, and the flapping of its wings amongst the silent trees.

Suddenly, it gets lighter: we come to an open space bordered by two enormous fir-trunks along the edge of a path. From the cracks in their trunks little fungi emerge. One of the children picks at a loose piece of bark, is startled by two shiny eyes in the dark space between trunk and bark, takes another look, carefully, and then comes to tell us, almost whispering, that "a little toad is hiding there" as if the forest itself is not supposed to know anything about it. Then: the discovery of the bilberries. They are picked by the handful and the gathering of a harvest begins, a harvest which needs containers. We pick armfuls of the long grasses that are in full bloom in the clearing. With some diffi-culty, we weave a kind of basket—a container worthy of holding the forest's gift. We taste the dark blue fruit and look into each other's mouths to see whose tongue is bluest.

We also make dolls of the long grasses: little ladies and gentlemen who can be made to dance, and bow, and walk. When the sun has reached its zenith, we fetch the bags with the provisions. Sitting on or leaning against the trunks of the fallen trees, we eat our slices of bread and the grass dolls are not forgotten either.

Warm and satisfied we return home. Around the large kitchen table we cut potatoes and make holes in them with a knitting needle. Into the holes we push the long, flowering grasses—waving heads of hair. The table begins to look festive. Some potatoes are left as they are, so that they can be surrounded by grass decorations and hung up. Mean-while, the bread dough has risen. Full of zest and zeal, the children help to shape small loaves, a whole tray full of them. Whilst the bread is in the oven, I put a large pot of vegetable soup on the stove. Outside, father is tidying up the pile of dead wood which the children have gathered during the week. Branches that are too long are axed into manageable lengths and a magnificent fire is soon burning amongst the large, loosely stacked stones in the hearth-place around which we organize our stools and chairs.

We are enjoying our primitive meal whilst it is slowly getting darker. Whilst the light outside is fading, I tell a story of heroism of the spirit and of cowardice of the heart, of curses and blessings, and above all of love and loyalty which can be experienced as a balm in the trials of the soul.

High above our heads the first bright stars appear in the sky to greet the shower of sparks from the fire down below. The day of St. John has come to an end.

Since Prehistoric Times

In the spring, the sun climbs higher and higher and draws us along with her, out of our homes. It is as if we are growing upwards, out of the dark winter's night towards the light, together with the plants whose saps are rising, whose roots grip the earth, whose leaves are unfolding, whose stems are bending in the wind and, as a crowning gesture: whose blossoms attempt to meet the sun.

When the sun has reached its zenith, summer starts. Shortly after, on June 24th, we celebrate the name-day of John the Baptist. The pre-Christian summer-solstice feast, celebrated when the sun reached its zenith, was erased as it were by the feast of St. John, moved forward; it does not coincide with the planetary constellation now. The summer-solstice feast is as old as the world; only in later centuries when Christianity was establishing itself, the feast of summer solstice became interwoven with the feast of St. John. Old customs blended with certain aspects of the life of St. John the Baptist. In this old form, the feast is still celebrated in many regions of Europe. In village communities it is a feast in which the entire population participates, especially those boys and girls who are on the verge of adulthood. The young people jump over the fire in order to show that they master the heat of the fire and the fire itself. The young blood in their veins is like flowing fire and many a young heart is enflamed in love during the night of St. John.

John the Baptist

From St. John's Day onwards, the sun diminishes in power. At first, this is almost not noticeable, but then in autumn, the process quickens, until just before Christmas, the sun has reached its lowest point in the sky. This leitmotiv of "diminishing", we find again in the life of St. John the Baptist, as has been stated in the Gospels: "He must increase, but I must decrease" (John III, 30). From the dry, burning hot desert where John the Baptist was active, we can hear —through the ages— his voice, the voice of one "who is calling in the wilderness" and saying: "Repent ye; for the kingdom of heaven is at hand", repenting meaning "turn inward, search within, examine yourself" (Matthew III, 2). The last prophet of Israel announced a new era. So that the new message could be absorbed, he prepared the human being in word and by deed. He spoke to them in a—for those people in those times— refreshingly new way. He did not judge, but he drew their attention to that small point of inner renewal which everybody could recognize within his own life situation. He baptized his followers in the living, flowing waters of the Jordan. Thus he prepared the way for Him, whom he considered to be his superior, "the latchet of whose shoes I am not worthy to stoop down and unloose" (Mark I, 7). Thus, he created small oases in the inner deserts of Man: green places and clearings where all manner of things could grow and where, later, the seed of Christ's words could be sown.

The Meaning Of This Feast Today

Christ said about John the Baptist that he was greater than anyone else born int this world: "Among them that are born of women there is none greater than John: yet he that is but little in the kingdom of God is greater than he" (Luke VII, 28). On Russian icons, John the Baptist is often depicted with huge wings: "Even as it is written of Isaiah, the prophet: Behold, I send my messenger before thy face, who shall prepare thy way" (Mark I, 2). John, the divine messenger, stands between Man and angel.

He summoned the human being to "turn inward", to change his ways, at times with hard words that hurt. When, however, one is rudely awakened to reality, this can be a disagreeable experience, an experience which forces one to turn inward, to a confrontation with oneself. The question arises then: "what have I done so far? How do I go on? What shall I do after this summer?" It is a curious paradox that during a period in the year when we tend to lose ourselves in Nature and our surroundings, we are called to turn inward. It does make sense though, to direct our attention to the necessity to keep ourselves upright in the hubbub of daily life, in all manner of situations, under various

conditions and in the midst of all that comes towards us.

St. John's Time teaches us that our attempts to stand upright will only succeed if we keep trying to make space for a "quiet spot" in the day, where we can be ourselves and can meet our Selves. Not only and particularly during St. John's Time, but also through the entire course of the year.

VI. THE FESTIVAL OF MICHAELMAS

Hanneli Glasl

A year without festivals is like a week without a Sunday. Festivals are, indeed, shining lights toward which we look and live. In fact, to celebrate the festivals is a necessity. They are spiritual food, and we as parents and educators have to take care that our children do not get stones for bread. In every season and its appropriate festival, we can recognise a certain aspect that is special to each one of us, and for which we have come to the earth. Of course, we have to be alert to this special quality which we have made our own, yet this very awareness can fill us with gratitude. Such awareness can be the starting point from which the educator can work with the multitude of images that are given to us in the festivals. The more we work in this way, the more ingenious and creative we can become, and the world begins to open up to us.

So what are the images which come to us when we consider Michaelmas that falls on the 29th of September? Whereas in other festivals the soul of man has a central place, at Michaelmas the spirit of man is called by the Archangel Michael to act in freedom and with moral courage. Therefore, the image of Michael shows us different qualities. On the one hand, we see him as a courageous fighter with his sword held high, and on the other we see him as a balancer of souls. Michael gives us the weapon of courage in our struggle with the dragon of egoism, untruth, and the tendency to be pulled too much into the earth. For example, when in Autumn we look around at nature, a wealth of colour catches our eye. Once more the sun-forces light up in the trees' foliage and in the ripe fruits. But slowly the leaves drop, the animals hibernate, and the seeds fall to the earth. A process of digestion and rotting takes place. Yet, if we yield too much to nature, we ourselves can become depressed. In order not to be pulled down with the events of nature, each person can decide to call upon an inner strength to fight depression. In fact, we can practise being interested in our fellow-men, not out of curiosity, but out of warm heart forces. These forces enter into various aspects of our lives and alter our perspectives.

Thus, as well as being a fighter, Michael holding a pair of scales, is portrayed as a balancer—an image which belongs to this time of year. So do we need to be reminded to keep within bounds and to keep ourselves in balance. Yet, what of our balance? What do we do with our own harvest? Do we weigh that, too? When we have a quiet moment at the end of the day, do we look back and review what has happened, what went wrong, and what we achieved? Where our children are concerned, do we weigh the bright moments with the difficult ones? Do we see what is weighing heavily and what needs to be worked at the following day? And how do we digest all this? Indeed, when striving for balance, it is a help to stay within ourselves and our immediate surroundings.

For our children Autumn is their own great feast. What a delight to run against the wind through wildly whirling leaves! The children find out that this element needs to be wrestled with.

When it is finally September 29th and we celebrate Michaelmas, the children seat themselves around the table to make their own "bread dragon". The stomach of the dragon is filled with appetising dried plums, apricots, and other such fruit—one should not forget one's own stomach, of course. The dragon's scales are made out of almonds or crisps which are stuck deep into the dough to prevent them from falling out. Finally, the wide open mouth is filled with an apricot for the tongue. Now, the dragon is put into his red lair—the oven. Anxiously, the children watch through the glass door of the oven, and see the monster gradually swell up as it cooks.

Around the fireplace, the legend of St. George and the Dragon, or one of the many stories of his fight with the dragon, is told while each child decorates his or her own candle with coloured wax. Each sculpture takes the shape of a huge dragon with many heads circling around the candle. Later, when the candles are lit, each flame is the shining sword of Michael who devours the dragon. The table is decorated with all the treasures of the Autumn—colourful leaves, an abundant fruitbowl with red-cheeked apples, grapes, gourds, nuts, in short, all the harvest that the Autumn offers to us. When the "bread dragon" comes out of the oven, often with black burned scales, it is a real victory to eat him for he is too beautiful. But the evil needs to be tamed and transformed! After the meal, the afternoon is filled with all sorts of activities.

Every year we try to do something different and, generally, it is the children who indicate the direction. One year we did a table play of St. George and the Dragon. The figures are so simple that a child of six or older can manage to make them with just a little help. Toilet tubes formed the main body of the figures while each head was made out of paper screwed into a ball and covered with pink crepe paper. Hair was made from wool and the clothes were cut out of pieces of paper or other material, and were glued on to each toilet roll. Arms can be made from pipe-cleaners which enable St. George to hold his sword. To prevent the dolls from continuously toppling over, we stuffed the bottom of the rolls with some clay covered by tape.

It was fun making the scenery for the table play. The castle was a triplet of gold cartons with a beautiful window made of transparent tissue paper. A candle burning behind the window makes the castle even more exciting. The dragon lake was made of blue material. Behind the lake, we placed bricks covered by green material to look like mountains. On top of the mountain stood Michael with his sword in hand, and below, in the foreground, was St. George fighting the dragon. The dragon was made of a long green sock, knotted at every other inch interval, and his wide open mouth had a dangerous tongue protruding. Every child had a chance to take part in the play while the story was being told, such as making the background noises. One year, we adults played the St. George's story ourselves. The dragon was a big marionette made of newspapers with leaves from an American oak tree glued onto it.

Children love a hunt. If a child has its birthday in the Autumn, you can organise a hunt to the cave of the dragon. Each child may make his own sword and decorate it with golden stars. At various places in the house or garden, certain tasks are handed out. When the children are about to find the dragon with the help of an adult dressed up as Michael, they have to go through a narrow passage. In this passage a triangle is hanging up. This has to be touched by the sword that each child is holding. The sound of the sword and triangle is a reminder of the singing sword of Michael. The dragon in his lair is thus tamed, and the treasure near the dragon is found. The dragon hunt can, of course, be worked out in many different ways and can be adapted to any age group. What is important, however, is that by the time the children enter the cave singing Michael songs, much has happened in their souls for it takes a lot of courage to tame the dragon. But, if they succeed, then the children have really grown, and they walk more upright. After the achievements of the dragon hunt, there follows a picnic during which both lemonade and the great dragon bread are consumed.

Older children can make kites. In Indonesia, the custom was to draw the string of the kite through glue with glass splinters in it. These would then stick to the string. While flying the kites, the art was to cut through the string of one's adversary. This is, of course, only possible if the joy in making kites is so strong that one does not need to cry about the loss of a kite. When the older children are busy making their kites, the little ones can make dragon slings. A dragon sling consists of a conker with a hole through which a string is attached. A colourful strip of paper is fixed onto the sring. When the sling is swung around in the air, it makes miraculous designs, or, tossing it up, it lands with elegant curves in its tail.

What is essential to the success of Michaelmas or, indeed, of any festival? It demands a tremendous effort. But we can find that the effort is rewarding and that we can rejoice when we succeed in calling forth in the children some of the forces of courage and of heart warmth that belong to the Michaelmas time. This process of struggling, succeeding and rejoicing also has a strong effect upon ourselves. Although we are busy, apparently with the outer aspects of things, the inner process is being aroused. For that reason, festivals make a chain of bright moments throughout the year.

VII. A TIRED MOTHER'S IMPRESSION OF MARTINMAS

Bons Voors

In many countries there exist traditions connected with the theme of light and fire in the beginning of November: All Saints' and All Souls' on the 1st and the 2nd of November respectively, Halloween, Guy Fawkes in England and St. Martin's in Holland, Germany and a number of other countries. They all include an element of lighting a fire, a candle or a light.

The bright summer days are gone, the rays of the sun do not warm us any longer, the autumn leaves are swept from the trees and return to the earth. All of nature is in a process of contraction, the seeds get covered and wrapped up by soil and dying leaves, the days get shorter and so we put on more clothes and hurry home through rain and hasten to be back before dark. We turn inward. After the last beautiful autumn days with their radiant yellow and red fiery leaves, the bleakness of November begins. Many people fall ill or just do not feel well. There seems a general mood of exhaustion and weariness now, after that new vigorous start in September. Where is all our energy gone, where is our harvest, where is there light to guide us in the dark?

It seems that we have to light a candle within. All the sunshine of the long summer has turned in the autumn into those glowing red and yellow leaves. And of all that fire that slowly burns out in nature, it seems that there is just one tiny little spark left to light a candle in a pumpkin or in a lantern.

On St. Martin's Day, November 11, we walk in a procession with lanterns along the dark streets, we visit some friendly houses and sing them a song. With a biscuit or a tangerine in hand we continue our journey. But the wind is fierce! We have to relight the lanterns again and again. One lantern is caught by the flame and the swiftly burning paper has to be stamped out. But the journey goes on. Where to?

This year we again walked with our lanterns through the village. Until the very last moment it was uncertain if we would. Nobody felt like organising the walk and caring for it in the right way. Tired mothers, combining family life with too many activities, single mothers weary of festivals; mothers with jobs and outside obligations. No, this year we would not do it.

But then. . . Shall we?. . If you call. . . Let everybody bring some. . . It could be in my house.

And so everybody started to make lanterns. As a concession one or two were allowed to buy a lantern. At 5 o' clock we started out.

Do you know how fragile and futile the light of twenty lanterns looks when cars with full headlights come zooming by? Encountering the modern world with your little light makes you feel very vulnerable and rather foolish. Then we turned into a darker lane, trying to keep the snake of little lights together. At the first (pre-arranged) house we stopped and sang. Two mothers were waiting at the door, a baby on one arm, in the free hand a candle, on the ground a basket with biscuits. The little babies' eyes reflected the lanterns and the starlight. They seemed to be of the same quality, to speak the same language. Then the troop moved on. Rowdy, full of noise, the mothers warning, reassuring and relighting candles. But who relights our candles when the storms of life try to extinguish our flames, so thinly protected by the physical body?

We walked through a wooded park. No street lights, no cars, no houses. Shapes of trees looking up at the last minute in the lanternlight. How well carved the stars and moons in the lanterns, how beautifully the colours of the painted tissue and the bright patterns in the simple cardboard, softly shedding enough light in the dark night to guide us on our path! The smell of the wet leaves, the blowing wind in your face, the darkness of the night and everybody feeling very happy with his lantern.

After a few more open doors, where we sing and gratefully receive some strengthening food for the journey, we return to the streetlights and the cars to come to someone's house, where a fire is lit, and hot chocolate waits steaming in mugs. Cake is passed around. A child is prompted to play the tune of St. Martin on her fiddle. A mother tells the story of St. Martin: "A long time ago (in 332 A.D.) there was a young boy serving in the Roman army. He rode in the twilight back to the city of Amiens in France. On his way he met a half naked beggar shivering with cold. He stopped and with one blow he cut his cloak in two, giving one half to the beggar. That night he covered himself with the other part of the cloak. In a dream he saw the Christ, clothed in the half of his cloak he had given away. Christ said: Martinus, what you have done unto the least of your brothers, you have done unto me. (Later this Martinus did many other remarkable things and was looked upon as a Saint in many European countries.)

After the story someone sings a French St. Martin's song. Cake and drinks are passed around.

It is not all perfect: some children fool about and have to be hushed. It is not all that holy, but we try. The wind and the rain also try to blow out our inner candles through interruptions, by linking thoughts: "Let somebody else organise it", "There is a good programme on TV", "I don't dare play the violin". But we try, and the candle burns and sheds a light of the most beautiful quality. Finally, we all go home, tired but very content with the image in our hearts of these tiny lamps battling with November darkness in our heart.

Having overcome physical weariness by our own inner fire, we have to wait and protect the light for a while. On the first Sunday of Advent one big candle will be lit, and each following Sunday another, as a token and as a preparation for the Light that at Christmas shines into the world, and which enables us to relight our own candles whenever the wind has been too strong.

VIII. ADVENT AS A PREPARATION FOR CHRISTMAS

Elizabeth Sheen

Of all the Festivals in the year, Christmas may seem to be the one easiest to celebrate. So much preparation takes place in the commercial world that it is sometimes hard to begin one's ones own activities at the time which *you* feel is right. I will try, through relating some experiences of my own, to help mothers, fathers, grandparents, aunts and uncles to find their way towards celebrating this festival in a new way. This "new" way is something which crept slowly into my life after my marriage.

I was brought up in a fairly typical English, middle-class Protestant home and, like most children, looked forward with great excitement to Christmas. It was a magical time with fairy lights and glass balls on the tree, carols, wrapping presents, writing cards, hoping for a new doll or a puppy and getting together with friends and having a "good time". We went to Church in the morning, ate and drank too much and flopped in front of the T.V. for the rest of the day. Then in my 24th year I joined my parents at a Rudolf Steiner School where my father had become the music teacher. I arrived just before the end of the winter term from a large, dirty and depressing city. After the long journey I slept long and deep, then on waking heard what I thought must be angels singing through the sharp morning air. I jumped out of bed and looked out of the window; there coming across the fields of frost was a group of children wrapped in brightly coloured coats, hats and scarves, singing as they came. It was a very moving experience, after a difficult period of my life. I discovered later that this group was the senior class from the school and that they had been singing carols outside the teachers' houses all through the night. My mother welcomed them into the house and gave them a hearty breakfast.

There were many, many different impressions flowing around me; actual things that I could observe but also "feelings" that here things really were done in a different way and for a good reason. I began to feel a "truth" in what was being done in and around the school. I soon noticed things such as the Advent wreaths appearing on the first Sunday in Advent; the lack of tinsel and electric lights on the trees; but also I heard, in talks with the teachers, new ideas; I began to look at the dark days of Winter afresh; the trees are not dead, look at the buds beginning to swell, even in December, perhaps it is a time of Life! Nature's forces are working inside the earth to bring us the beauty of Spring. So, too, must we try to bring inner growth and light into our lives so that we can prepare to receive the gift of the birth of Christ. How we prepare for this event is so very important, especially for young children, who respond so readily and eagerly to the images we present to them, rather than to detailed explanations or traditions passed on for tradition's sake.

I was especially fortunate in that my husband had grown up in a a family surrounded by those things I was now hungry to learn about, and he was able to lead me towards preparing things for our young family.

He took charge of the making of the Advent wreath; small branches of evergreen wrapped around a wire frame, hung with red ribbons and holding four red candles, one for each Sunday before Christmas. In order to keep it fresh and discourage the needles from falling, he put strips of towel, soaked in water plus wet grass around the wire before attaching the greenery, and every three or four days we would give it a good drink in the bath. We even had fresh grass sprouting one year.

How well I remember the first time we lit the first candle with baby Tamara; the tiny pin-prick of light growing into the darkened room, a small ray of hope that sends the heart leaping. When the candle was lit we sang a few carols, if possible those with words appropriate to the time, such as, *People look East, The Birds* and *The Angel Gabriel*, all of which can be found in the *Oxford Book of Carols*. I began to realize that it was rather inappropriate to sing of the Three Kings before January the 6th, and Good King Wenceslas felt more suited to the days following the birth of Jesus.

Before lighting the wreath we had prepared the children for bed, read their story, washed and cleaned teeth and then turned out all the lights in the house. When the carols were over, (usually one for each child and each parent) we gave them a candle in a holder and they were lifted up to the wreath to light their own candle from it. Then they would walk solemnly, one behind the other, through the house to their bedrooms, singing softly as they went *"Over Stars is Mary Wandering"* [1] which came from their school Advent play. We then sat on their beds to have their prayer by candlelight and when they had blown out their candles they were beautifully ready for sleep. I once had the pleasure of doing this with a young friend who was staying with us; when I asked him if he had a prayer at home, he smiled at me with shining eyes and said "Yes, but never with a *candle*." We also liked to take the opportunity during these days to invite others to join us in singing the carols, especially elderly or single friends who perhaps have rarely had the chance to share in such an event. Other frequent visitors were, of course, grandparents, godparents and teachers of the children.

At one point I was shown by a Handwork teacher how to make Advent Calendars. When Tamara was about three years old I made my first one, from black card and tissue paper; I had twenty four coloured stars on either side of a large picture of Mother Mary standing on the moon, weaving a garment for her child. This was made from layered tissue paper, carefully glued. So began a tradition that for the next ten years or more I made a new Calendar every year.

One year I felt sorry for the youngest child, who found it so hard to wait three mornings for his turn, so I made a double calendar, a house for the girls and a shop for the boys, with the traditional stable scene in the middle. Another year I made a collage of St. Nicholas riding through the sky on his sleigh, and at the bottom was attached a pocket for each child. Each night I placed a tiny gift in each pocket, to be discovered in the morning. There were a couple of panics when from the comfort of my bed I realised that I had forgotten to put anything inside! There issued a mad dash round the house searching for three similar gifts! The home-made presents were especially appreciated, I dipped miniature candles and a pipe-cleaner king was kept by Tamara for many years.

Even when the children were still quite young they wanted to make their own presents. I avoided taking them into the nearest town, as by now I did not want to expose them to all the commercialism that simply would have bewildered them, and I think home-made gifts from children are the nicest one can receive. They began with simple things such as toilet roll cylinders covered in material or Contact, with a piece of card stuck on the bottom, to hold pens and pencils. These were very useful for Grandpa or Godfather. Collage pictures went on for many years—a background of hessian, lots of scraps of material and glue.

Calendars were popular too: I remember one which was of the same scene painted at different seasons of the year. We did a lot of candle-dipping, with careful supervision from an adult even small children can obtain good results. As soon as they could knit they made doll's blankets for each others' dolls, (yes, the boys as well), cushion covers for Grandma (which are still in daily use), hats for cousins, etc. One child confessed apologetically during a wrapping up session that she much preferred giving presents to receiving them. She loved watching her Grandparents' joy at her great efforts.

There was one preparation which did not involve my husband or me, the two eldest children, when they were still quite young, decided they would like to perform a play for us on Christmas day. Looking back on the years that followed I can say that the play was almost the highlight of the day for parents and children alike. They practised in secret, found their costumes, occasionally asked me to make a star for the Angel or fix a candle in the lantern for Father Joseph. When there were only two of them, the theme was usually Mary and Joseph in the stable. Joseph was once heard to remark; "Joseph doesn't say very much, does he?" His eldest sister was singing away, rocking the baby and holding the stage in no uncertain way.

Later, as the other children grew, we had a full length version of the old Miracle Shepherds' Play just before Christmas. Our youngest daughter had to do a quick change behind a screen from the Angel into Mother Mary. We also had a Kings' Play, a play about some children who had nothing to give to Jesus, and many more. Each seemed more lovely than the last, and sadly we have now watched our last one as the children have grown too old to enter into such an activity.

My husband preferred the Continental tradition of decorating the tree on Christmas Eve and, not before, as it really replaces the wreath. We were also quite sure that we wanted it to be a surprise and as I was lucky enough to have my parents living near I would take the chilren there for the afternoon while my husband decorated the tree. A discreet phone call determined that all was ready and so we went home and prepared the children for bed. No one was allowed into the sitting room until they were quite ready. My parents would creep in first as they loved to see the expressions of wonder on the children's faces. At last the door opened and in they went to a truly magical transformation. All the everyday clutter was tidied away to make room for special belongings; tissue pictures shining in front of candles, wooden candlesticks made by the children's cousins, a revolving lantern, lit from within that sends a star and an angel moving round behind cut-out scenes from the Nativity and coloured with tissue paper. The tree itself, decorated simply with thirty red paper roses and three white ones to represent the thirty three years of Christ's life on earth, and some golden signs. Delicate straw stars go beautifully with the green and red and candles complete the picture.

Beneath the tree on the floor is the very special stable with the Holy Family, the Ox and Ass, three Kings and three Shepherds with their sheep, made out of wood. These were made for us by one of the children's cousins when he was about eight or nine years old. When he showed them to us for the first time, Tamara was still a baby. He explained that she could put the figures into her mouth quite safely and take them to bed with her if she wanted to. Oh, how sensible to make something durable that small exploring hands could hold and move about without fear of being told not to touch! We still use these figures and have grown to love their simplicity more and more; it matters not that the crib is at least three times bigger than Mother Mary; children do not notice such discrepancies.

Just as most small children believe implicitly in Father Christmas, the Easter Bunny or the Tooth Fairies, so our children believed that it was the angels who brought us our tree, I think they felt it was too beautiful to have been created by man alone and who knows, they may be right! So on the 6th of January the angels remove the tree in the night and leave behind a very special little gift for each child beside a large coloured plant on a bright red cloth in place of the tree. The angels sometimes wrote, in special writing, a message to each child about the year to come. One year Tamara was in floods of tears at the thought that the tree was going away, so the angels left her the tip of a branch with a red rose on it and she kept it beside her bed until all the pine needles dropped off!

I tried when possible to find appropriate stories to read at this time; *The Christ Legends* by Selma Lagerlöf, certain chapters from the Laura Ingalls Wilder books (it is so interesting for our lucky children to hear how happy those girls were with so little!), *Little Grey Rabbit's Christmas* by Alison Uttley, which has a beautiful passage in it of a candle-lit tree in the middle of a wood, surrounded by gifts of food for all the woodland animals.[2] Alison Uttley's own childhood memories of a farmhouse Christmas as told in *A Country Child* has become a classic. As they grow older I would love them to hear Laurie Lee's description of a Christmas in Spain, Milton's Hymn on the *Morning of Christ's Nativity* and the Christmas story as told in the Gospels. [3]

6. BIRTHDAY PARTIES

Bons Voors

Festive occasions have an eyeopening effect on me. Every event on a festive day, regardless whether it turns out to be a disaster, a shining diamond or an O.K., but rather dull event, stands under a brighter light of awareness. Days and weeks can go by unnoticed, but a festival stands out. It stops you in your routine tracks. You have to think and plan, buy presents, extra and special food. But how, for heaven's sake, do we fill the day and what did we do last year?

These are the thoughts that rise up. They link you with the same events in former years: you review them again with a critical eye or with loving memories. Festivals make a thread with different coloured beads over the years. One can trace a development in oneself and in the family in dealing with these celebrations.

Let me tell you about two birthday parties of one of our daughters. We have had quite a few birthday parties by now, but the one last year—when she became five years old—was a fair disaster. There was a large chest full of dressing up clothes and long evening gowns and swords. We had called in to help us a friend who was very gifted in decorating faces into butterflies, clowns, princesses. . . Well. . . experience taught us that five-year-old girls who have just put on their best party dresses and feel already like princesses, are very reluctant to change into old garments. For quite a few the face painting was too scary to join in. The dressed-up princesses and kings got caught in their long robes while playing games on the wet grass. The birthday girl burst into tears in the middle of it all and did not want to share in any of the games. So. . . although well meant, it was all too much. Too many children, too much upheaval, too much excitement, and for this birthday girl too many surprises.

This year, when our daughter's sixth birthday was coming along, she took part in all the preparations. She decorated the white paper cups and plates. She helped with the making of velvet hairbands for the guests as little presents to take home. She insisted in coming to the woods to collect horse chestnuts and acorns. She loved making models of conker animals and little acornmen with beechcaps, and spiderwebs of conkers and matchsticks with thread. Thus the habit was broken that "everything has to be a surprise for the birthday girl". What is exciting for one child, can be quite overwhelming for another. In this case she was not left out of excitement beforehand and prepared for what was to come.

Another element taken into consideration was the time factor. For once I had listened to the often-made remark of my daughter: "Mum, don't be so hasty!" So we lengthened the usual time for birthday parties and did not squeeze all its activities of conkermaking, games and birthday cakes into one fat sausage. We made plenty of time for her and her friends to breathe in and out between activities by not nervously interrupting when they played with the dolls or when taking turns with the new skippy ball. Our daughter was the radiant centre of all her friends, enjoying the day at her own speed and her own way of dealing with the world.

Two days later our youngest of three went to a birthday party. She was the only guest for her four-year old friend. The older children said: "But that is not a birthday party!" Whereupon the youngest answered, absolutely content with her afternoon of playing with the dolls, "It was a birthday party and we had jelly!"

So I realise again and again that a party or a festive event is not a following of strict codes, is not the cramming of activities into one afternoon, is not being scared that things will go out of control.

It means watching your child, observing and listening where it is in its development, what its rhythms are, how much it can take. It is not glueing one's own expectations and patterns on to the child, but watching the being that comes towards you.

Sometimes your eyes are open, but often you see only in retrospect. And next year. . .? Oh, next year is completely different.

III. CHILDREN'S WAYS

1.   THE TEMPERAMENTS

Ann Druitt

Her name was Susan and she sat two rows in front of me in the class, I sat in the back row, the "bright" row, and the not-so-brights sat in the very front, under the teacher's eye. Susan sat somewhere in the middle. I thought she was odd. Actually, I thought she was *very* odd. She was pretty: soft, blonde hair bobbed around her face, tied on one side with a large white bow, her pink and white complexion was sprinkled with tiny freckles, and out of the soft round plump face with its almost baby nose, for a nine-year-old, gazed two very pale blue eyes with long curled lashes. She wasn't fat, nor yet actually plump, but everything about her was soft. . . and she was *slow*. That was the odd thing about her. She was so very, very slow. She walked. . . so. . . slowly. She talked so. . . slowly. . . When she answered questions in class I grew so impatient that I would blurt out the end of her sentence for her. As for gym, it was no surprise that she could not vault the horse, the real achievement obviously lay in fulfilling the run-up! Of course we would tease her, but she never seemed to get the joke, nor did she seem to mind that she was the butt of our teasing. She smiled good-naturedly and went on her sleepy way.

By the time Junior School days were over, the very experience of Susan had transformed itself into a question "why are some people *different* from me?"

Then came the self-scrutiny of the teenage years, and with it a new personality to preoccupy me. Mary was tall, always taller than the rest of the class certainly, but in the early years of senior school, before other growth patterns adjusted the discrepancy, she positively towered over us. We noticed her rounded shoulders and slight stoop and attributed these to her conspicuous height, but she carried her head well and her willowy frame had a gentle grace about it which was sympathetic. Her fine fair hair and soft grey eyes accentuated the gentleness, and the serious gaze which greeted one as the eyelids slowly lifted, spoke again of sympathy—sympathy needed and sympathy ready to be given. How I envied her long tapering fingers and elegant neck! I felt so "stubby" in comparison. But more than that, I envied her serious demeanour, her rock-like integrity and her ability to apply herself to her books with a natural and uncompetitive interest. I suppose if I had been honest with myself I would have acknowledged that she was a rather dreary wet-blanket when it came to planning some of the more daring pranks for the class, and one rarely enjoyed with her the camaraderie of a good giggle. Her height carried with it a cool aloofness which could be irritating, she did often appear "huffy" and yet I wanted *so* much to be like her. Why was I so frivolous when she was so sober? Why was I so uncontrolled when she was so self-possessed? Why couldn't I study like her instead of looking out of the window all the time?

Mary became a model for me, and although I worked hard and long at it, I have to admit that, in all probability, none of my friends even noticed.

Knowing Mary posed a new question, "why am I different from other people?" This was a frustrating experience, but the very frustration was enough to fuel a quest that would last for many years to come.

Life posed the questions, and learning provided the clues—but not the answers to my satisfaction. Psychology, astrology, phrenology, all had enlightening things to offer, and in particular brought the "type" more into focus, but tantalizing clues they remained. Somehow, somewhere I had to find the picture which would gather up all these oddly shaped fragments of wisdom and speak finally of the whole, of myself and humanity, of the normal and the abnormal, the individual and the "type", the "given" and the potential.

In true Sherlock Holmes style I hunted my quarry through the dusty shelves of second-hand bookshops and through the gleaming thought forms of first-class intellects, until one day I was introduced to Rudolf

Steiner's work on the Four Temperaments. The "Four Humours" I had already been acquainted with, by virtue of Shakespearian studies, but it was a fragile relationship—I couldn't quite cope with those nauseous biles, for instance—but in Steiner's work new life was poured into these medieval concepts and disposition became something more than a matter of indigestion, it became a matter of. . . ah! the mystery is solved, the quest is realised, the answer is. . . Elementary, my dear Watson."

Very soon after taking up the challenge of attempting to understand the elements of another's personality, we realise that what meets us initially in that person and often determines the nature of our relationship, is much more that *through which* the individuality shines, rather than the pure personality itself. This is especially so with children and young adults. We feel differently on gazing at the same sun as it shines through different coloured glass, and in exactly the same way an individuality strikes the world differently according to the "colour" of its soul. And here we come to the elementary nature of the problem. The Four Temperaments colour the human soul each in its own unique way, and each according, as the medieval scholars knew, to the laws of one of the Four Elements of Earth, Water, Air and Fire. These Elements were considered by the Greeks to be mixed states of physical condition interacting throughout nature—therefore within the human being also— always seeking equilibrium. In the process of characterizing these Four Elements we come closer to understanding the nature and interaction of the Four Temperaments: Melancholic, Phlegmatic, Sanguine, Choleric.

From the earthy element, or mineralizing quality at work in the world, we can build up an impression of how the Melancholic Temperament works within the human being. Picture to yourself a rock lying on the sandy beach, alone, self-contained, hard and cold to the touch, very still and seemingly unmoved by what goes on around, weighed down by its own mass, sinking slightly into the ground below. Ask yourself how long has it been there?. . . what is it thinking? One's fancy enjoys the thought that it might have been there for centuries and is dreaming still about events of long, long ago. . . it certainly isn't busy planning what to do next.

A rock speaks to us of ancient times, and the melancholic child often appears before us as "a little old man" or "a quaint oldfashioned lass". The face is pale and the gaze of the child is veiled as if the eyes, although open to the world are, in fact, gazing inward. A dreaminess is there, expressed occasionally in a sigh. The weight of Earth in the body causes the eyelids to drop a little, the shoulders to slope as if bearing a heavy burden, the feet appear to sink slightly into the earth at each step. No child is still for long, but the very melancholic child will not enjoy energetic games as much as those pastimes which require inward activity—drawing, listening to stories, writing poetry. The inwardness of the melancholic accounts for his isolation, the inability, often, to relate harmoniously to others. At times such a child may become the butt for childish humour, the unfortunate victim of practical jokes which cause him deep unhappiness. The skeleton is the most concentrated mineral element in the body, and one might expect the bones of a melancholic physique to be prominent; around the forehead and nose, shoulders, wrists and hands, ankles and feet, the bones do often seem to lie unusually near the surface, indicating something of the "thin skin" that the melancholic experiences both in a physical and an emotional sense.

Once the rock has warmed through by the midday sun, however, then its isolation can be alleviated, for its company is sought by birds and animals looking for a quiet place to "be". Long after the sun has gone down, such a rock will continue to give out a gentle heat to the comfort of its immediate environment, and is considered by all a blessing. So we look for ways in which we can warm a melancholic child both physically with extra warm clothes, cooked food, maybe a hot water bottle in bed, and also warm his soul with encouragement, understanding and sympathy, confirmation of his being, persuasive enthusiasm and *very* gentle humour. The lack of vitality of a melancholic child is often a source of concern to the parents especially if they are anxious to avoid molly-coddling, but these "warming" measures can be achieved with the minimum of fuss if the parent recognizes that this child really needs them, even if his sisters don't. This little rock cannot "give" to the knocks of life and he therefore will feel all the bumps and bruises, and tweakings of the hair as you comb, really *more* than his siblings, and allowances should be made accordingly.

How grateful we feel for the mineral world—for the *terra firma* beneath our feet that is so reliable once we have the measure of it. How obvious that the Church needed to be built on a rock! The clarity, precision and structure that a melancholic personality is capable of bringing to the problems of life out of his own inner connection to the methodical laws of crystal growth, is a gift indeed. He, above all the other temperaments is most likely to apply himself to unravelling fundamental questions, to measuring the foundation stone of life to the benefit of the whole community.

We all suspect stones of hiding something, when we go looking we leave "no stone unturned", and the magic of opening up a rock to find a cluster of crystals at its core is something that everyone should have the chance of experiencing. But perhaps the greatest joy would be were we all to have Michelangelo's gift and be able gently to peel away the rough, hard, cold exterior of the stone and reveal to the world the beautiful being that lies within, waiting to overcome his isolation, and reach out and speak directly to another's heart.

To study the Element of Water, or fluid quality, as we are aware of it in nature can be of help in trying to understand the Phlegmatic Temperament. The raging sea whipped to a froth by the wind, the dew hanging from a spider's web, the unseen movements of sap in the plants all reveal aspects of the phlegmatic personality which is perhaps the most complex of all the Temperaments.

Consider first a droplet of water—smooth, round, completely self-contained, a little world all of its own: there sits the phlegmatic child engrossed in a toy, or maybe his fingers only, impervious to pleas to get dressed for a walk, or to come and meet the visitor. His chubby form gives the impression of an extra layer of softness all over him concealing the boniness of his skeleton, and in complete contrast to the melancholic physique. His often very pale eyes are like tranquil pools of water, peaceful and happy, so calm sometimes that one can wonder if anything ever ruffles the surface of his soul—is he perhaps even "lacking" in some way? But this tranquillity is misleading. The mountain stream that rushes and tumbles over the rocks has the tranquillity of the lake as its goal—one can almost hear the sigh of relief as the last rock is passed! But the smoothness of the lake conceals the complex rythms at work in the hidden depths below. Outer tranquillity enables an inner dance to develop undisturbed, while the glass-like surface of the water, unruffled by outer influences, allows the possibility of ordered reflection. The ability to reflect on life's questions is one of the talents of a mature Phlegmatic Temperament, *if* he has become interested in so doing. There lies the rub. It is often difficult to capture the interest of the phlegmatic. Gerald Moore, the accompanist, describes in a most amusing way in his biography, his parents' desperate attempts to interest him in this game, or that activity, all to no avail. The melancholic person feels his isolation acutely, but a phlegmatic feels most comfortable when left to himself, his maxim is "anything for a quiet life" which may often become the excuse for profound laziness. Parents anxious to help their deeply phlegmatic child might find that the company of other children is of most benefit to him; he must be brought into inter-action with the other Elements to overcome his natural inertia.

However, there is an important characteristic of the element of water which works strongly to overcome the potential dullness of the phlegmatic, and that is—it adapts itself to other forms, whether a jug or a hole in the road. It can be a source of great surprise to us when our self-effacing phlegmatic child shows talent as an actor (something which is extremely difficult for most melancholics). The reflective nature is naturally gifted in this direction, and from its selfless vantage point can evolve a rare type of humour which is never unkind or destructive, but always refreshing. Yes, water refreshes us, and the phlegmatic who is active in society has the ability to freshen others, to free them from their hang-ups, to calm them from their frustrations, to soothe away their anxieties, and bring stability and confidence in the future. All this is possible because of the inner harmony granted to the phlegmatic temperament through his relationship with the movements of his body "sap", or lymph system, especially the gastric juices.

The lymph system is the chemist in us, gathering in, distributing, eliminating, regulating, and naturally *needs* substances upon which to work. These substances come in the form of food and drink. One of the first observations a parent is likely to make of his phlegmatic child is his friendship with food. Other children may often be hungry, or greedy, but for *this* child his bowl of porridge is an *experience* which is to be enjoyed to the exclusion of everything else. In fact, the all-absorbing nature of a phlegmatic's digestion process prompted Rudolf Steiner once to recommend that it might be necessary for a phlegmatic child to go without breakfast if he was to be awake sufficiently to the world to take in his morning lessons. This reverent attitude to food is well illustrated by the following conversation between a small boy and his phlegmatic sister: "Did you know, Helen, God could strike you dead this very minute if He wanted!" "No He couldn't, 'cos I'm having my tea." It seems in character that the Buddha, depicted always as an archetypal phlegmatic in form and facial expression, is said to have died on the banks of a river after eating an indigestible meal.

The strong instinct for order, born out of the regulating nature of the lymph system, can be a boon to the mother of a phlegmatic, for this makes him, already at an early age, a wonderful "tidy-upper". Even through the teenage years a certain neatness and order about his person, is likely to remain.

Vera Lynn describes her father as being an "extremely easy-going man who could get into a towering rage if someone forgot to sugar his tea", and this illustrates another aspect of the Element of Water, its hidden potential for violence and destruction. To obstruct the deeply phlegmatic person's rythms of life by insisting that he hurry, or impede the ebb and flow of his gastric juices may call up a storm in his soul, which takes everyone by surprise. But this is a rare occurrence. Usually, potential obstructions are carefully fielded by evasive action or by a very characteristic "soul deafness". through which any ripples on the surface of the phlegmatic's life are simply rendered ineffectual by the deep pool of his being.

When something does happen to sink to the bottom of this pool, however, there it is preserved in its entirety. Like "a fly in amber overta'en" those impressions which have been admitted to the fluid world of the phlegmatic's imagination are encapsulated there, and may become the solid foundation for future impulses or, less happily, an impediment to flexibility which proves very difficult to shift. This devotion to the "known" can be of help to parents in handling certain situations. Naturally shy of innovation, a phlegmatic child can be encouraged to accept change by the parent pointing out that so-and-so (perhaps an elder sister or beloved relation) does it this way. My own fairly phlegmatic son loves to copy in his drawing activities—starting with the "known" and embellishing the theme with his own rivulets of activity.

This apparent lack of originality is the mainstay of the phlegmatic's social talent for stability. He is always able to build on the situation which has been given him, and will never disrupt communities or organisations or families by iconoclastic demands. He is therefore constantly sought after as reliable friend, comforter and adviser. Of all the four temperaments, one is truly able to say of the mature Phlegmatic: "he leads me beside still waters, he restores my soul".

Now let's look at the Element of Air at work in the world and marvel at its sociable nature, its complete lack of isolation. It belongs to no one person or place, but is shared by all. See what a sacrificial quality is there, how it allows itself to be used by the world, to be transformed by people and plants; how necessary is such generosity to life! Air is the archetypal messenger, the bearer of all sound—speech, music, birdsong or harsh noise, all are treated equally. Air is in constant movement itself and the cause of movement in other things. It is busy locally and travels far distances with ease. Held too long in one place it becomes stale and bad; forcibly compressed it is likely to explode.

The lightness of air characterizes the Sanguine Temperament in both form and personality: the bright twinkle in the eye, the spriteliness of step, the "airy" manner, the expressiveness of the hands moving constantly in the free spaces about the head, the cheerfulness and optimism of the heart. Gravity, so deeply experienced by the melancholic, gives way to levity—in both senses of the word. The sanguine child not only prefers to skip, or jump, or run on his toes than to walk, he also needs humour and gaiety sprinkled liberally over his cultural diet and spicing his relationships with others. A delicate "taster" of food, with a bird's appetite and a butterfly's preference for sweetness, the sanguine child seems to be nourished more by his five senses than his three regular meals.

The body opens itself to the air through its many orifices, and the sanguine child experiences the inner and outer worlds through all of them with equal devotion. His mouth will be more often open than shut (in complete contrast to the phlegmatic) and if not savouring words and sounds will be well occupied with licking fingers, nibbling pencils, chewing shirt collars or other obscure isometrics designed perhaps to develop mobility of expression or firmness of jawline, who knows? Not the sanguine child, for sure, who will be totally unaware that he was doing anything at all. The ears also are open and ready to catch a name whispered at 100 yards, or hear the rustle of sweet papers three rooms away. Likewise the nose becomes a centre of intense activity, from the usual rebarbative childish habits to use as a resting place for biros or the ends of pigtails, and then on to a sort of clearing house for smells of which the rest of us are happily unaware. All this, coupled with the birdlike movements of the eye shows us that the sense world is never dull for the sanguine personality, which can present problems in the schoolroom. Quick to grasp anything new, difficulties arise for this child when staying power is needed to follow something right through, but it is possible for him to find motivation through love. So strong are his heart forces that where a loving bond is established with a parent, teacher or even another child, this can cultivate perseverance where constant admonishments fail.

Air as a bearer of the sun's light and warmth calls forth the flowers and the fruits of the earth. In the same way, the sanguine child will respond to the light and loving touch of encouragement and humour, with a willingness to please and to achieve. The wrong way to handle a sanguine child is to "sit" on him. He will only find a way of wriggling free and, most probably, like the air in a joke cushion, make a rude noise as he goes.

When we watch the air's movements made visible by steam or smoke, we are entranced at their complexity and beauty. Here is an artist at work in mobile, ever-changing form. A parent may find this mobility exasperating sometimes, but should consider it as a challenge to avoid the command "Sit still!". This is an impossible command for a healthy youngster to obey anyway, but for a sanguine child, to be still means to die a little. Just as the phlegmatic needs to experience the harmonious inner dance of his digestion, so a sanguine needs this outer expression of the mobility of his being to feel alive and well. He is, in his childish fidgeting and prancing, laying the groundwork for what in future years may become artistic brilliance, perhaps in dance, music or drama. On the stage, the phlegmatic is reliable and accurate, but the sanguine is an actor with flair and ability to "breathe in" the character of another, and "breathe him out" a little larger than life, and even more convincing.

The sanguine's creative spirit sees potential in every situation. Just as one's eager breath stretches the fact of the ordinary little rubber balloon until it becomes something captivating, marvellous, impressive and free, so will the sanguine child blow up life's little happenings until they reach the size at which things become unforgettable. If a corrective story is ever needed for an over-sanguine child, he will listen enraptured to the disasters that befall the hero as he carries his activities first to excess and then into the realm of the ridiculous.

The air that is used by all weaves between individuals and whole nations an invisible web of relationships, and it is in making relationships that the sanguine personality excels. Not only does the child need to feel surrounded by many friends, (the thirst for company is a strong characteristic of this temperament), but the mature adult is able to develop a real gift for bringing other people, and also facts and ideas, into relationship. Communication is one of his talents, words fascinate him, and many a sanguine has built a happy nest in one branch or other of the media. Unlimited practice at this sort of work has been acquired in childhood, of course, at mother's knee, or elbow, or shoulder, or neck, or whatever piece of her will respond to this gay little bird as he follows her around the house twittering at every step—or hop. She will have to learn techniques of coping with this breeze of words which ruffles her hair. If she is sanguine herself, then let "Like cures like" be her motto and talk back as hard as possible. If she is not, then this will prove far too exhausting; I found that taking a very deep breath before responding to a question often did away with the necessity of answering altogether, because something else would by that time be claiming my little friend's attention. That's the lazy way. All one can say to encourage the parents of a sanguine child is: you will have a *very* amusing time of it!

The Choleric Temperament is the last to be considered here although most cholerics would admit to a preference for being placed first in

most things. This temperament comes about when the Element of Fire has the upper hand in the constitution of the—"unfortunate human being" were the words which sprang to my mind, but this is a great mistake, and only exposes my *own* prejudices! It cannot be said often enough that *all* the temperaments are worthy of praise and respect, and only become a handicap if the balance between them is very seriously upset. All four temperaments work within us, one usually very much in the background, one or two in the middleground, and one or two much more to the foreground.

The Choleric Temperament has the advantage, or the disadvantage, whichever way one may choose to look at it, of drawing its "owner" very much into the foreground socially. No one ignores a fire, its majesty captures everyone's attention and people naturally gravitate towards it, grateful for its warmth and light perhaps, sometimes in awe of it, or simply mesmerized by its activity and its energy. This energy is the hallmark of the choleric child and cannot in any way be compared to the constant activity of the sanguine. The latter has a lightness about it, a slight carelessness; the choleric, on the other hand *cares*, he is undeviating in his purpose, and can be quite fanatical about achieving his aim. Even at rest, the energy latent in the smoking coals is apparent in the clear, direct, penetrating gaze of the, often dark, eye. A firmness around the mouth and jaw, with lips not just closed but sealed tight, often gives the misleading impression of clenched teeth and suppressed anger. The muscles of the compact, even short frame reminds us of an athlete or gymnast ready to spring into action; and it would be no surprise to us to see sparks fly from his heels as they ring out on the pavement.

Other children are aware of this subtle force and usually defer to it. This is advantageous for the choleric child in that he can rise to his instinctive role as leader and allow full play for what he feels are his superior skills. With an audience to admire him and plenty of children around to be organised (at which he excels) the choleric child is supremely happy—as indeed is everyone else. On the good days, that is. On the bad days, he is rejected as being simply "bossy" which makes him utterly miserable and confused. He *knows* the best way of doing things—why won't the others listen to him? He *wants* to help them, he *loves* his friends, they could have such a good time if they weren't all so stupid. This unfortunate state of affairs can occasionally lead to the child destroying a game or project from which he has been excluded "just to show them" that he still is the boss. But this uncontrolled raging of fire is rarer than it might be because the choleric child has a very keen sense of fair play and is a prompt critic of injustice wherever he sees it.

Fire is quick to come to life and can also be speedily "put out". In the heat of his enthusiasm the choleric child is often careless of the finer feelings of others, but when his own soul is wounded he feels this deeply, and his inner flame is doused. He needs always to feel the approbation and appreciation of others, which acts as the fuel that he must have, not just to complete his self-imposed task—that will be done anyway—but to give him the warm afterglow of achievement which will perhaps spark off another project later. It is difficult for other temperaments to appreciate that the choleric *needs* to feel superior, and is most at ease and works best when he is secure in this position.

A fire is methodical in its work, and given the right circumstances it is willing to work without rest until its aim has been achieved. No task is too big for it. So one can see that to cope with the energy of a choleric child one has constantly to provide challenges which are *almost* outside his grasp, and he will pit every ounce of his being against failure. Don't offer this child the clothes horse and a blanket to make a house, he will need scaffold planks dragged up one by one from the cellar. An exercise of this kind will tire him out comfortably, and then he might be willing to listen to a story or be amenable when there's company for tea.

The tenseness of the choleric, and his overwhelming frustration when things don't work out his way leads to obvious social difficulties, but these are balanced out by his ability to generate warmth in a group. Not a naturally demonstrative child towards those he loves, this warmth is communicated through his enthusiasm for things and spreads easily to others. Life experience usually mellows this temperament and it is possible for the choleric to emulate the candle flame, around whose strong and steady glow a group may gather for warmth, work and mutual enlightenment. One has also to keep in mind the most virtuous activities of fire-purification and transmutation. The choleric has a potential for clarity of thought and far-sightedness that is able to bring cleansing and healing to many of life's "sticky" situations; his capacity to inspire others and imbue them with his own activity of will can transform not only the outer things of this world, but the inner lives and destinies of those who are near him.

With this in mind it is easy to see why a choleric child needs to have access to adults for whom he can develop a deep respect—for they embody something of the ideals towards which he is always striving, those ideals which he openly acknowledges as superior to himself. And when, as a result of the struggles of a lifetime, he is able to achieve such ideals in some measure, then this achievement will be for him as precious as the alchemist's gold—the gift of the noblest quality of fire working within him.

The temperaments colour the glass through which our personality shines, and the effect is most pleasing when the colours glow clear and bright without one of them being too "loud". A painter learns quite quickly that by strengthening another colour in a painting a "loud" colour will be quietened, and so it is with the colours of the soul. Trying to rub one colour out will only make a mess and muddy the picture, so, for the parent, it is helpful to acknowledge that one must always work *with* the temperament a child is expressing and not against it. This builds the child's confidence in his own being and will give him the strength and assurance to deal with self-knowledge as an adult. The three gentle tools a parent may use to balance out a temperament are: special stories, certain foods and colours; but the supreme corrective measure is normal social intercourse. The interaction of the temperaments is something I have not dealt with here, but it adds a new dimension to the child's awareness of himself and others. When one sees how the fire can warm the rock and water soften its hard edges, how air can make the water bubble and fire may even lift it out of itself, how air feeds fire yet earth controls it, how water sinks down into the earth, one can appreciate that the morality inherent in all this social interplay impresses itself on the child and leads him to a deep respect for those elements that he inwardly most lacks: then he is able to admire the phlegmatic's ordered room, the choleric's prowess, enjoy the sanguine's company and appreciate the melancholic's thoughtfulness.

The study of the Four Elements within and without the human being fashioned for me the key to the solution of one of life's mysteries "Why is everybody so different?", and also led me to appreciate its twin "What is it that joins different people into groups that we recognise by the word 'type'?".

I began to understand Susan's comfortable lethargy at last, not just as an oddity, ripe for ridicule, but as a characteristic that has a legitimate role to play in the order of things. Mary was quietly removed from her pedestal and placed among the ranks of ordinary folk with their weaknesses and virtues, their strivings and their achievements. I was able to appreciate the many colours that mingled, blended, and sometimes clashed in our family, and to see myself in a clearer light and to say "I want to be like me", and have some of the perceptions which might one day enable me to be just that.

2.   CREATIVE DISCIPLINE

Margret Meyerkort

Discipline and authority are two words which make many contemporary parents uneasy. Our instincts tell us not to interfere, to leave children free. We want them to express their individuality, we like to ask them what they want instead of telling them what they should do as our grandparents did. Before asking ourselves which line to adopt in the guidance of our children, let us look at the reasons behind this rapid change in upbringing. It seems there are mainly two. First, the astonishing mobility in our society which made us question and reject the old constraints. All human relationships have been evaluated anew: marriage, parenthood, sexuality, the place of the aged, homesexuality, the relation between producer and customer, so, of course, the whole question of the relation between the child and adults is also being reviewed.

But there is another reason. Most parents to-day know how not to bring up children, certainly not the way in which they themselves were brought up. So we often question our right to impose our values and forms of behaviour on our children. Are we not brainwashing them at the most impressionable age? Are we not programming them in our image? The sensitive parent is full of doubts, the overworked parent is simply frightened by the immensity of the task and as often as possible withdraws from the uncongenial charge of correcting his or her child.

This is an unhealthy situation. The young child instinctively expects guidance. Without the certainty of his parents and teachers he loses his security. Growing up is difficult enough. Growing up without help means being left alone to flounder. Constantly being asked what he wants creates bewilderment in his mind. He feels let down by the adults. The solid ground under his feet shakes. He lives in uncertainty and this feeling of insecurity weakens him in body and mind.

Through Margaret Mead's work in New Guinea during the Thirties we gained an insight into the wonderful life of the Arapesh. It confirmed our instinctive awareness that, basically, man is good, that once, at the beginning of time, paradise really existed. The whole of Arapesh society is permeated by love. You do nothing for yourself, everything in community with others. You do not demand, you learn to give. This really *is* paradise, but the modern American and European can get back to it. Most of us do not want to do everything in community with others, we also want to be independent individual personalities, a state which the Arapesh can never reach. But if we chose to live like the Arapesh and bring up our children as they do we could not hold our place in a technological society. And if we were to opt out of this society and take our refuge in a rural community which we built up according to our ideals, we would soon notice how our complicated modern selves bring tension into a community which was expected to manifest only harmonious relationships.

The door to paradise is barred and bolted. We cannot even go back to the certainties of the Victorian age, much as some of our politicians would love to force us back again. Lost traditions cannot be artificially resuscitated, lost instincts cannot be recycled. Instead of instincts and traditions we must develop consciousness and consciously meet the child's paramount needs. They are easily stated: security and an awareness of growth. Security presupposes stability, love and a certain amount of protection. You would prevent your child from electrocuting himself, but to be overprotective means to destroy his potential for growth, thus debilitating him.

Love alone makes the child dependent on his mother and on other people, because first as a child and later as an adult he could not do without someone who loves him all the time. Therefore he cannot become self reliant. If the child is in difficulties and his instinctive reaction is to call "Mummy" or "Daddy" he will not learn. There must be times when the parent says: "Don't call me for the next five minutes"; or, "I think you can climb down the tree yourself", or, "You can try getting this nail out yourself". A child who is over-protected can become scatty and nervous, he can show a lack of concentration and become essentially insecure. As adults these people can show difficulties in dealing with the complexities of modern life because they have too little experience of how to stand on their own feet.

This means that the conscientious and conscious parent will have to play an active and positive role in the education, the leading forth of his child. He will realise that if he is frightened to influence his child—his morals, his habits, his tastes—somebody else will take on this role, the ten-year old boy next door, television programmes, advertisements. For many years I have worked with the following suggestion of Steiner's and have had encouraging results: in education it is not a question of avoiding what is wrong but of doing what is right.

The parent will realise that without love, stability, regularity his child will be weakened, possibly made insecure for the rest of his life. But equally, the parent will realise that he has to take conscious risks to provide space for growth. This means that the parent will erect boundaries against which the child will push and thereby develop his strength. These boundaries are not irremovable, they are constantly being widened. Thereby we give him a first feeling for the process of time and an awareness of his own future growth. "No, this is not right for you. Not yet. But when you go to school next year you will be able to do it".

Not only boundaries change, but also the *way* of guidance changes from year to year. The baby's boundaries were narrow and guidance consisted largely of nurturing the physical body. I tried to lead the toddler by ordering the rhythm of his day. The playgroup child was led by taking his hand. I directed the kindergarten child by being an example to him myself, while the child aged seven and more responded to a guidance which came in·the form of a story.

My intention was to lead the child, not by stamping the prejudices of one generation on the other nor by giving the child an adult freedom which can result in immaturity, but by conveying a firmness permeated with love.

Within this general framework a few practical hints might be useful: each child must be treated differently, according to his own personality and out of the unique child—parent relationships. Children appreciate a mother who says: "Yes, I do not treat you both the same, but I treat both of you fairly".

This was Sally's experience:

"The family sitting at the table for lunch included ten months old Peter in his high chair. While his mouth was full he played with his food. He dropped slices of carrot on the floor, he dropped the teaspoon on the floor and then threw the cup on the floor.

The cup broke. Peter leaned over the bar of his high chair, looked at the various items on the floor, looked at me, and continued to finger his food.

Similar activities happened repeatedly. Already on the first occasion I was irritated because in the morning I had swept the floor. Sometimes I quietly cleaned everything up straight away while at other times I left matters lying on the floor and cleaned up later.

Help came when a friend told me that life proceeds in phases. Peter was in the 'throwing-down' phase and would soon proceed to the 'breaking' phase. Also I began to see life as one large phase during which we acquire understanding of ourselves and of existence. At the beginning of life we gather experiences principally through our will. It is the child's will to take hold of life—and I began to understand what Peter's grasp of my soft hair had been for the baby some months ago. The child wills to discover life: he has to find out what water does, from the tap, in the sink, on the floor! He has to know how strong things are—by standing on the wastepaper basket, tearing paper by poking, searching, reaching, pulling, pushing all sorts of things. The child wills to explore and invent. All the time Peter expressed his will through the activities of his limbs. For some years to come he was a *doer* without showing as yet any purpose in his actions.

When the third cheap cup was broken and Peter received no milk but heard my repeated 'all gone' he tried to imitate the sounds of my words. The boundaries which I set him at this young age were largely boundaries which I set myself: firstly that whatever was within the child's reach was not dangerous and was inexpensive; secondly, I tried to sense an oncoming difficulty and to divert his attention. Thirdly, I was aware that his development was the more even and corresponded to his own forces—the fewer artifical stimuli, car rides, visits and so on he had."

Carole found John a demanding toddler:

John was fourteen months old when he learnt to walk. I offered him as little assistance as possible but was there when he was in danger. It happened that after one or two or more wobbly steps he stood still and began to whine. When he realised that no help was coming he let himself down on the floor and after a short cry in the sitting or lying position he crawled to me into the kitchen. He pulled himself up at my skirt and with tears on his face began to grin and laugh as if to say: 'I know what to do and I can do it.'

We both laughed. I took him on my lap and we had a Humpty-Dumpty game.

I wanted to strengthen his sense of discovery and his determination and therefore decided not to rush forward for every little whine. Once John walked well he wanted to investigate cupboards, drawers and bookshelves. His activity consisted of emptying out baskets and boxes and climbing and creeping inside them. Later, he dragged cloths across the floor from one place to another. He would throw them into one pile and himself on top. He also enjoyed sitting among the saucepans and jars and taking lids off and putting lids on. I locked my precious articles away and put older ones into the containers instead. When I did not want him to take the books out for the third time one morning and neither distraction nor song nor a cuddle worked any longer, I introduced a short, definite 'No, John!' and raised my finger. For a while he accepted the seriousness in my voice and my raised finger as the end of his activity. He turned to something else.

I used forms of negation rarely. Rather would I help him find out what the house consisted of or pretend not to have seen what for me was chaos.'

Children's moods can often be anticipated. If there are difficulties about going to bed give a quiet warning a few minutes in advance that soon we are going to bed. It is unreasonable to expect children suddenly to drop a beloved activity. Some mothers have to issue two or three warnings at regular intervals and the third time set an additional boundary: "When I call you next time I want to be heard", or: "When I call you next time I want you to come". If you have to say something which the child will probably not like, do not moralise or expound. Say it in a few words in a calm and even tone. Better still, act. An honest "no" in a quiet voice is much more effective than evasion, a long explanation or a reluctant "we shall see". The more we fail to carry our underlying, never-to-be-doubted love into a difficult situation—we can achieve this through the tone of our voice or an appropriate gesture—the more we increase the emotional tension of the moment and undermine our future relationship as well. Wherever possible try to defuse a threatening conflict by humour.

I should like to quote at length a mother's account of how she managed to steer a child who had entered a negative phase. She already had experience and realised that her proper attention could shorten this stage of her child's development. She used to carry her child screaming and struggling into his own room. She put him on the floor and said:

"This is your room where you can scream. When you have finished come again to my room."

Recounting this she remembered:

"I listened to the sounds which came from his room. Often I found him asleep on the floor after ten minutes. A few weeks later, I would go into his room when the sobbing had subsided. I busied myself with his clothes or cleaned the window. Robin was playing. Without looking at him I said quietly and with my normal tone of voice: 'Now it is time for us to go for a walk', or 'It is tea time. We have to lay the table for Daddy', whatever was appropriate for the time of day. Robin sometimes nodded, sometimes he grunted, once he said: 'Can bear come for a walk?' All through our little conflict he did not experience an angry or resentful mother, but knew that I loved him."

The mother concerned had erected a boundary: no screaming outside the child's bedroom, and this meant an increase of inner strength for the child without any breakdown in the loving relationship between the two.

The mother continued:

"The hardest test for me were the occasions when Robin refused to eat the food on the table and threw a temper. I insisted quietly on his eating, at least a certain amount of what was on his plate or going without, and I did not usually give him snacks between meals. Only a couple of times did he go without a meal. I tried to cook what suited his age and constitution, and often we prepared the meal together. By the time he was five years old I had greatly increased the range of food which he liked, but continued not to ask him what he wanted to eat. Now I can hear him ask for the spinach which a few years ago would have thrown him into a temper. In retrospect, I am sure that few things strengthened his confidence in me more than my quiet insistance over the meals."

The mothers I met wanted the children to grow responsive to the surroundings. The question was how to do that. By asking the child continually what he wants to eat and wants to have, one educates him into an egoist. The world will neither supply the child's and the adult's needs nor will it give them what they want. An egoistic education prepares the child for a world which does not exist.

Another aspect of the child's age of resistance is this:

The child looks at the mother to get her attention and does precisely what the mother does not like. He tests the growing awareness of "I am myself, I am not you, not you...but I—*am!*" against the other personality, against the other "I". This is fun for the child and asks for a lot of humour on the part of the parent. It also brings the beginnings of loneliness is therefore painful and asks for songs and being held on Mummy's lap. It also creates a feeling of strength and power in the child. Hence that coy look on Susanna's face in Claire's story that follows here:

" Susanna aged three and a half, went into the kitchen and when I came in later she had chopped up a piece of soap. I commented:

'Such small pieces of soap. I wonder whether we will be able to wash our hands with them?' Before supper time Susanna heard every member of the family complain about the size of the piece of soap and she herself did not get a strong lather either. Next day we poured hot water over the bits of hand soap and made a lather for washing some clothes. I put a new piece of soap into the soap-dish with the words: 'This is for our hands. The soap powder over there is for our clothes. We will use that tomorrow when we will do more washing.'

In this way she had experienced the difference between the kinds of soap.

When I was unable to interrupt my housework and do some baking which she wanted I said: "Later, not now." When she had taken hold of a knife, I took it out of her hand and said: "You may have the knife to cut up the vegetables for lunch. I will call you later."

With an older brother and sister in the house Susanna needed to be clearer as to what belonged to her and what belonged to the others. "This is Mark's book and it lives on Mark's shelf. If you want one of Mark's books let us ask him." Saying this, it had then to be followed up when Mark returned from school. I tried to accept and respect her problems as if they were my own. This meant that she had all my tenderness and that this tenderness was not deprived of strength."

I was once invited to a family with three young children. The second child of four years of age had started in my kindergarten a few weeks previously. He was a quiet boy who observed people, insects and animals. With a shy happiness Mathew sat between his father and teacher at lunchtime. He had helped his mother make the apple pie we had for lunch. After a few spoonfuls Mathew tipped his plate carelessly into his lap. Apple and pastry fell on the floor. I saw out of the corner of my eye that he turned his head to me and had blushed tomato red. His father cleared up everything without a word while his mother and

I continued the conversation. As a matter of course his father put another piece of apple pie on Mathew's plate. When he had eaten half of it I turned to Mathew and we spoke about our breadbaking in the kindergarten.

The surprise of what had happened in spilling the plate and the subsequent shock had brought the child to his senses. The only value of a reproof or punishment is a clearer consciousness. This clearer consciousness had come about and a corrective word from the parents was therefore unnecessary. When the children had gone into the garden after lunch the parents told me: "We want our children to grow and be able to give and take. We believe we can prepare them best by taking opportunities of helping each other in front of the children and of helping the children themselves."

My attitude and point of departure in matters of handling young children was the same during my years of teaching; namely to serve the children in introducing them to life. In the classroom and with children other than one's own this was easy compared with a family situation. Nevertheless, I want to relate some of my actions and the reactions which I received from the children.

Barbara knocked over the vase of flowers. I got up saying: "Oh, an accident!—I'll help you—I'll get a cloth." I mopped up the water and put the flowers into fresh water.

Richard upset the tin with the sewing pins. I got on the floor saying: "Oh, an accident!—Let me help you pick them up." This I did together with another child who out of her instinctive imitation got on the floor with me.

It did not take many months before one and more children said in response to my movements: "I'll help you." Teacher and child were putting matters right together. What was interesting was that Richard watched while Barbara helped me pick up the pins he had dropped and Barbara watched while Richard helped me mop up the water she had spilt. There was never any laughing about each other's mishaps. We tried to be open towards one another and very slowly to learn to respect each other's unique differences.

It did not take many years before five and six year old children came to me and told me what had happened to them or called out for help "I've had an accident."

Young children respond to being shown how to act and live rather than being told. I tried to teach through the example of my actions and left the teaching through words and logic for a later age.

Also in the kindergarten we need not necessarily continue with traditional reactions. While a Steiner kindergarten is not a formless entity where the children should do nothing but express themselves freely it would also be wrong to foster fear, guilt and lack of openness in the children. So it is good to rethink some conventional responses in order to help the children to develop more easily into free and responsible adults.

Children all too easily learn to simply keep the rules of the teacher and hide their true feelings. This leads to dishonesty. To moralise to the child can make him behave as an adult in a deceitful and hypocritical manner. Similarly, if the child is offered a reward of a piece of chocolate or of an outing, or of a late evening for doing the "good" deed of making her sister's bed or of cleaning out the rabbit hutch. Be it moral blackmail or emotional blackmail the child may be threatened.

The need for exclamation and "verbal explosions" in many situations is obvious. Usually we break out into stereotyped forms which sometimes can be extremely vulgar. I felt that creativity—which stimulates an individual response to each incident and to each person—can be of help. Therefore when I made a mistake in front of the children I was able to make up a humorous word such as "Crumbumblelees!" or "Jimmie-jammie-jangle!" when I had dropped jam on my skirt!

I dealt with those children who swore at other children in a similar way. When six-year-old Nigel had made things difficult for me I quietly said, tipping out his water-logged rubber boot next to him: "You waterskating elephant!" Or, when he had upset the first rising of the bread dough, "You purple apple pie!"

I still don't know how to deal with the child who brings vulgar language into the kindergarten. Whenever possible I tried to ignore it and to divert the child's attention. But there were those situations when a six-year-old provoked and defied me. I quietly took him into the cloakroom or bathroom and said: "You can speak 'toilet' language in here and when you have finished come and join us again." Usually the child returned after a few seconds. No mention was made of the incident by anyone in the room. Very, very rarely did I have the same child go twice into the cloakroom. Altogether I have had little problem with this sort of thing. A couple of times I had to go two minutes later into the cloakroom and, again in a quiet matter of fact way, help the child to return to the group. At no time did I have a parent who spoke of new or greater difficulties with her child at home on account of my attempt to deal with this problem in a mixed group of young children.

I did not mean to condemn vulgar language. It was my intention to put it into its place. But then I was creating a dark area there where I would rather have had a neutral area. I certainly did not want to strengthen the feeling in the child that such obvious and natural things as are pronounced in what is called toilet language are contemptuous. In some homes the parents say from time to time to their children: "For five minutes it is "toilet language". This seems obvious, from the point of view of many schools of psychology. However, it is a question of whether this need is really so great in the child concerned. I know many adults who did not have such a need in childhood. Is it really good to bring this language into the consciousness of a few children—or more children in a kindergarten—for the sake of possibly helping one child? Perhaps for once the old-fashioned method happens to be the best. I state that this is not the way his family speaks. But I say lightly, if possible in the form of a rhyme.

Are there other helpful words for the parent and the teacher who looks for help in education? I have chosen another four words:

1. *Gradualism.* I want to put my five-year-old child to bed earlier. It is of no use to start this new form of life as from next Sunday. The child will certainly rebel. But week by week the child goes into his room five minutes earlier until he is in bed at 7.30 p.m.

2. I do well to consider what is *reasonable.* Has my six year old child developed enough stamina to tidy up his room on Saturday mornings? Does this educative measure fit into the family life and does my health or my shopping routine enable me to stick to it? I need to be conscious of possibilities and priorities when I choose a new task or experience for my child.

3. The child will benefit from my being *consistent.* I do not threaten, neither do I use blackmail.

4. When I want to establish a boundary for the child I try to be as *conscious* of myself as possible. I try to put any form of emotion behind me. It helps when I can speak with a quiet voice. I do not allow myself to be moved from the stance I have taken, and if necessary I repeat what I have said. Thereby I assure the child of the enduring relationship I have to him.

The old form of discipline produced many moral and upright people. It also produced cowards and bullies. We hope to help young people of to-day to grow into free human beings, capable of taking initiative and responsibility. For this they need a basis of physical and moral strength, of confidence in themselves and in the world. If we do what we can to provide this basis we have reason to expect that, with proper guidance, the road to freedom will open up once puberty has been passed.

3. SPECIAL STORIES FOR SPECIAL TIMES

Joan Marcus

Introduction

Storytelling is an art, which parents often feel they lack. But it is not that people are unable to make up a story, they are simply not used to it any more with the wealth of good and bad children's books available in bookshops and libraries. But children do love it when you make up a story and often adults only need a bit of encouragement to plunge into the deep end. Many parents discover to their astonishment that they can tell a story. They discover too that it is not so much the dramatic action which makes a story alive, but the details (how granny always wears a purple shawl with a silky fringe and how she always nibbles little peppermints out of a very special silver box. . .).

Stories told at bedtime, stories told at teatime create a very different atmosphere between the storyteller and the child to that when the adult reads out of a book. An intimacy is created by being able to look at one another, the adult being inspired to create something by the wonder and usually the full attention of the child.

There are occasions in particular where no book or written story will provide an answer to a certain question or a difficult situation.

Children will often ask questions which cannot be answered by logical reasonable answers since their faculty of reasoning is not yet developed in that way and should not yet be appealed to either. A story can be a wonderful help in such a case. Also, dramatic events can happen, which ask for a different kind of explanation to: "Yes, Granny is dead and she will never come back", or "Daddy has left us, that's it, you'll just have to get used to it".

A story is not meant to make a truth "woolly" or be a way of avoiding the truth. It should lift up the facts, enliven them in a picture in such a way that the child can understand what is happening.

Many a situation can arise—be it jealousy over a newborn baby brother or sister, aggression in order to get more attention, the death of a pet, loss of a parent of friend or whatever, where one of the solutions might be to tell a story to the child to help to come to terms with such a difficult situation. A story will not deal with the reasoning powers, but it will speak to the soul, which will understand the message and at the same time be nourished and comforted.

Joan Marcus has written some stories that she made up when difficult situations arose. These are examples of what father or mother can do. You might well ask: Yes, but how does one find the right image or picture to give to the child?

It might be that the question of a child needs the inspiration of that moment to tell a story, but very often one can think one out over the next few days. When a difficult characteristic trait of a child is involved or a longterm event such as a separation or a hospital operation, there is also the possibility of sharing your problem with someone else.

Building up a picture together in order to understand what is at the bottom of the problem or behaviour. Looking at the beginning and the end of the child's day: when is it happy, when unhappy or anxious. Who looks after him: what are his favourite games or pets, etc. It can be a tremendous relief to share such thoughts with a friend, often finding out you are not the only parent with such problems. Practical solutions can arise out of such a sharing, new rhythms established, but also inspirations for a story to tell to the child. A story that might be told for quite some time with slight extensions or small variations. The very stubborn five-year-old will love to hear over and over again the story of the little donkey that did not want to move an inch forward or backward and finally brought the waterjugs home for his master. The utter delight to get spelled out how stubborn that donkey was and the sigh of relief if he finally started moving again! This way of building up, either alone or with someone, an understanding of what lives within the child, consciously looking at his or her day and night and who takes part in that, will not only give clues for a right image to tell to the child but this focussed love towards the child will help the child also in unseen ways, strengthened by the help of invisible forces.

Bons Voors

There are various ways of communicating a story to a child. It depends on the nature of the gifts of the narrator. For instance the following story was told for a little boy of five, whose best friend was killed by a lorry. I wrote and illustrated it very simply and made it into a little book which I gave to the mother for the boy. Apparently he carried it around with him everywhere and showed it to all his friends who had to read it to him time and time again, until it was well thumbed and grubby.

I: The Death Of A Friend

"Once upon a time there lived two little boys who were great friends, the elder one was called Michael and the younger one was called Bobby. They played together after breakfast until they went to bed at night. They loved each other dearly.

One day after tea they went out to play and as they were chasing each other and laughing together, they came to a wood. They soon stopped running because there were so many trees and the path was narrow.

After a while they came to a big wrought-iron gate which they opened and found themselves in a beautiful garden with sweet scented flowers, all colours of the rainbow. Butterflies were fluttering from flower to flower and the bees were humming contentedly.

Hand in hand they wandered along the banks of a stream and watched the fish swimming in the rippling water. They lay in the grass and gazed up at the blue, blue sky. They watched the sun disappear behind a cloud and then reappear in a golden glow and red and purple clouds. Soon it vanished and one little star appeared and then another. It was twilight. The younger child said, 'I wish I could stay in this garden for ever', but the older boy said, 'Quickly, we must go home, it is already late and our mothers will be worried.' So they speedily made their way to the gate. Michael passed through but before Bobby could pass through, a great wind arose and blew the gate shut. It closed with a clang.

'Oh, what shall I do?' said Michael, 'I can't go without you.' He tugged at the gate in vain. Bobby peeped through and said, 'I can't come with you now but we will see each other again soon, I know.' Michael pulled at the gate again and again. Heavy-hearted and as it was getting dark Michael hurried home through the wood. He was crying and would have stumbled and fallen if it had not been for a light which showed him the rough places and the tangled roots of the trees. As he came out of the wood a voice said, 'Don't cry, Michael. You will see Bobby again in your dreams.'

Michael was miserable without his friend and grew sadder and sadder. He didn't want to live any longer and wanted only to be with Bobby.

One night Michael had a dream that he was in the same beautiful garden and Bobby came running up to him and said, 'Oh Michael, I've been waiting for you for a long time. Let us play star-catching with the angels—it is my favourite game.' They ran and played, throwing the stars lightly from one to the other. Suddenly an angel handed Bobby a star to give to his friend. Joyfully Bobby touched first his forehead then placed it in his hands and finally touched his heart where it glowed. 'Now you will always have a light where I have touched you. There is so much for you to do, Michael, and I will always be near you to help if you need me. I must go my way and you must go yours, have courage!'

When Michael woke up he felt much happier and had the will to live. He came down and ate a good breakfast and smilingly went off to school. He felt warm inside and knew now that his friend was near him.''

II: Jealous Of A New Born Sister

A very common occurrence is the arrival of a new baby, which is welcomed, but often resented at the same time by the other siblings.

I had a little girl of four and a half in my Kindergarten group who had a little sister and then a baby brother. When the brother came, the parents were delighted that apparently Tara had accepted the new baby without any difficulty. But at school matters were quite different. I watched her playing with the dolls. They were undressed, smacked and dumped unceremoniously into the corner. I picked them up and talked to the dolls one by one, remarking how cold they must be. I dressed them again and tucked them up in their cradles. Tara looked on rather sullenly and without comment and then I took her on my lap and we talked quietly about her home, her Mummy and Daddy, her little sister and the new baby. She said she didn't like the new baby because he cried so much and woke her up in the night, so I suggested that she should sing to him. I cradled her and sang to her and the next day I told the following story. This is a shortened version.

"Once upon a time there was a little child in the Heavens who was waiting to be born. She looked down onto the earth because she wanted to have brothers and sisters; she didn't want to be alone. In the Heavens she always heard lovely music; the stars used to sing to her and she was in no hurry to leave, but the day came when the family was ready for her, so she said goodbye to all her friends and with the sound of music in her ears she made her way down the starry pathways to earth.

When she arrived, everyone was very kind to her but she cried and cried because she didn't hear the music anymore. One day, when she lay in her cradle crying, her big sister came and sang to her and soon she fell asleep. When she was asleep she again heard the music of the stars and she was happy, but when she woke up there were other sounds—loud banging, people shouting, machines going—and she began to cry again very loudly. Her big sister heard her and rocking the cradle started to sing quietly to her, and soon she was listening, for it reminded her of her other home.

The baby's mother would often say to Big Sister, 'Do go and sing to your little sister, you are the only one who can quieten her and make her happy.' One day Big Sister was allowed to take her out of the cradle and hold her in her arms, and then both Big and Little sisters were as happy as could be."

Such stories tell in imaginative form the story of birth. It is in this way that a child can understand in the depth of his being a little of this mystery.

III: The Death Of A Grandmother

Ian was a sad little boy of four years and nine months in my group. He rarely smiled and obviously something was on his mind.

His mother told me that his Granny had died a few weeks previously and she had tried to answer his questions as best as she could, saying that his Granny was happy in Heaven now. But recently Ian had said, "Mummy, when I grow up, will you be old?" "Yes." "If I'm a Daddy then will you be a Granny?" "Yes." Then he had burst into tears and would not be comforted.

I told a story, something like this:

"Once upon a time there was a dear little old lady who had many grandchildren. She used to wear an old blue cloak and the children hardly ever saw her without it. She grew old and wrinkled and sometimes she said to the children, 'One day I shall go on a long journey and you won't see me again, but don't be sad, because I shall be going to the land of the Angels and one day we will meet again, I promise you.'

Some months later, when the children went to visit Grandma's house, she wasn't there. Her old blue cloak was spread out on a chair and all around were lots of presents with the children's names on them. There was a pendant and chain, a crystal, a knife with a mother of pearl handle, a little wooden box and many little gifts that Grandma knew the children would treasure. On the table was a candle which lit up a picture of Grandma smiling, with her family and friends around her."

I shall never forget Ian's face when the story was finished. He said quietly, "So my Grandma is happy with the angels, too." It was as if a weight had been lifted off his shoulders. He stayed quietly smiling long after the others went out to play.

IV: Sleeping Difficulties

It seems nowadays children have far greater sleep problems than in days gone by. This is due no doubt to many factors, the speed of life, noise of traffic, radio and T.V., eating habits—i.e., watching T.V. while eating. We all know that emotions affect the digestion. Then there is so much adulterated food, and because of the pressures and difficulties of sleeping, parents resort to sleeping tablets.

Many doctors are aware of the affect of T.V. on children and if they are going to watch, advise leaving two hours before going to bed free from T.V.

Here is a story which I know has helped:

"Once upon a time there was a little boy who just could not get to sleep when he was put to bed. His Mummy or Daddy would tell him a story and then light a candle and say his prayers with him. He would blow out the candle and his parents would kiss him goodnight and then leave him to sleep. But no, as soon as his parents left him, he would get out of bed, play with his toys and jump around. This happened so often that his parents refused to tell him a story, but he still would not settle down.

Now one night, as soon as his parents left the room he sat up in bed and thought, 'Now what mischief shall I do tonight.' Just then he heard a tapping on the window-pane. At first he was a little frightened and then he became curious as the tapping continued, so he went to the window and opened it.

In hopped a big white bird who said, 'Little boy, if you would like to sit on my back I will take you for a journey.' 'Oh, yes', said the boy and without more ado he was soon sitting on the big white bird's back and flying over his garden and over the streets and houses. He could see some of his friends already lying in bed. He wanted to knock on their window panes, but the white bird would not stop. 'Look at the rooks all settling down in their nests at the top of the trees', said the bird. He looked, and there were the noisy birds tucking the nestlings under their wings and then making quiet sounds to tell them it was time to go to sleep. Soon they were silent.

The boy saw a mother rabbit hustling her young ones into the burrow. A squirrel disappeared into his drey. All the birds and animals were soon silent and settling down for a night's sleep. Only the night-owls, bats and a few little creatures who come out in the dark were awake. The moon and stars shone and wondered why our little boy was still awake when everyone else was asleep.

The little boy wanted to go back; he was tired, but the bird flew on over the trees, fields, streams and moorlands. 'Oh, please take me home', begged the boy, 'I'm afraid of slipping off your back.' The bird heard and swiftly turned round. The boy had to hold on tightly because the big bird flew so fast. Soon they reached his window and the boy clambered off the bird's back. Sleepily he thanked him, said goodnight, and fell into bed and was asleep in the twinkling of an eye."

This story told gently, and perhaps with the repetition of; And the crow said, Good night little one, sleep well. And the rabbit said, etc. This story has worked for many children.

4. A KEY TO THE IMAGES IN FAIRY TALES

Almut Bockemühl

Speaking As The Basis Of Social Life

Children want to play. Through play they enter into the world. Through play they learn. At no other time do they learn as much as in the first three to four years of life. Everything becomes a toy, it will be taken hold of, handled, licked, and in this way thoroughly experienced. Just as the child through playing experiences the visible, touchable, tasteable world of objects, so in a similar way he enters into the life of language. He hears sounds, he hears words and imitates them. He plays with the words. Only later will he find the meaning in the imitated word, a very mysterious process. On the waves of the spoken word enters the thought. So the word is much more than just a sign with some informative value.

And yet a word is always a communication, a contact from soul to soul. When one is talking to a little baby—often spontaneously—while changing or feeding it, it does not yet understand the thought content, but it understands our devotion, our love or impatience, and reacts accordingly. Speech is the foundation of all social life.

In our time, when such great disturbances occur in our social lives, speech defects of children are very much on the increase. Certainly one cannot say that they have not enough opportunity to hear speaking. On the contrary; through the media we really suffer an inflation of words. In stores, in railway stations or air terminals, but mainly at home through radio and TV one is continually bombarded by words. One is fascinated, yet we can easily ignore the fact that not one word is personally meant for us. Besides when one is in a darkened space, where the TV is on, one is isolated from the real world and the real human contact. So it happens, that children, in spite of all the masses of words, are lacking in human contact through the word. Humans are the only living beings who have the gift of the word, therefore the exchange of words is a necessity of life for man, without them we would wither away.

Rhythm As The Element Of Life—Nursery Rhymes

Through the ages, little children have learned to speak through play. Mothers and nannies helped them. That is how we have such an abunddance of children's rhymes and children's songs. In our day less and less of this is passed on by parents to their children. Instead we have in the bookshops different collections, from which we can get inspirations. But one should be selective in what is offered. Neither the trivial kind nor the instructive kind are suitable for little children. Rhymes with strong sounds and rhythms are best.

> Diddle, diddle, dumpling my son John,
> Went to bed with his trousers on,
> One shoe off, the other shoe on,
> Diddle, diddle, dumpling, my son John.

Rhythmic repetition is the life blood of the small child: not only rhythm in the daily life, but also by rocking, swinging, riding on your knee, singing and speaking.

If we watch how the plant pushes forward leaf by leaf, regularly and yet never exactly in the same way, then we can see how rhythm is an attribute of the living. And it is the same way in the plant, as it is with speech, speaking comes to life through rhythmical repetition. There are funny little stories built entirely on this which the bigger children, who have grown out of nursery rhymes, can find tremendously amusing, such as: *The Big Fat Pancake,* or *The Little Gingerbread Boy.*

With time, about three to four years old, the child starts to distinguish his own inner life from the outer world. It starts to think. Then the content of the stories will be of ever greater importance; the real fairy tale age begins. The content of these stories has grown out of the living nature of speech, as the flower grows out of the plant, and can speak directly to the soul.

Whether it be a rose or a sunflower or a violet, each blossom speaks to our soul in its unique way. The green leaves have not this kind of expression, they refresh and enliven us. But as no blossom can arise without earlier strong leaf formation, so just in this way it is necessary to nourish the small child with the rhythmic element for out of this its imagination or phantasy will develop, and with it a capacity for lively and strong pictureforming. And only a lively imagination will enable a child to listen to a story with rapt attention and concentration.

Naturally the rhythmical does not suddenly lose its importance. The leaves of a plant do not suddenly disappear at blossom time. The child wishes to listen to the same story again and again. Until the sixth year, we don't need much variety. The tension in a story often increases by the third repetition, the highest point often is emphasized and becomes a kind of ritual through a little verse.

Concerning The Truthfulness Of Stories
The picture consciousness of the child at the fairy tale age.

If one understands that the child has in fact a deep-seated need to be told stories, then the question emerges: Why should one really go back to the old folk tales which belong to times long past? Would it not be sufficient if the purpose is only to stimulate the child's power of imagination, simply to tell fantastic tales indicating that these stories are not reality? Or, on the other hand, should one lead the child better into life through more realistic stories?

The Swedish poet, Selma Lagerlöf, reports that in her childhood, her grandmother sat all day long in her room in the corner of the settee, and when the children came to her, she told them fairy tales. When the story ended, she put her hand on the child's head and said, "All that is as true as I can see you and you are seeing me."

We all know that animals do not talk, dragons, unicorns or glass mountains don't exist, the dead do not come to life again. What reason had the old woman to emphasize the reality of her stories with such urgency? She was deeply convinced that there are forms of truth other than the so-called "realistic" ones. Just as it is true that the Arctic regions are bitterly cold while summer heat prevails in Africa, so both the outer physical world and the inner soul world are realities. Fairy tales belong to the soul world, a world which is not simply fantastic but has its own laws just as the physical world has. Its laws are such as can apply to a world of pictures. The soul world, or as Rudolf Steiner calls it, the imaginative world, is a world of moving, living pictures. Out of this source flows the wisdom of fairy tales. Out of this spring also flows our language. It is full of picture wisdom and was even more so in earlier times. We say: "Now I have lost the thread", "This dress hurts my eyes", or "In that situation she lost her head completely". Of course these sentences are not to be taken literally. We understand their meaning. In the same way, the people in olden times understood that in the pictures of fairy-tales one does not look for images of the physical world, but one looks for "images" in which soul and spiritual happenings are expressed in pictures.

Children have a very marked feeling for this difference. Thinking in pictures harmonises with their state of soul. At a certain age, approximately between the third and ninth year, they can think only in the manner of fairy-tales. This living in pictures, which we adults know only in our dreams and only then in a chaotic form, the child at that age has in its waking life. One could say that the fairy-tale stage lasts as long as the child can really play. It is no problem at play to turn into a hunter or a dog. The dog can also talk if required. He can also turn suddenly into a bird and fly off. Some children have invisible playmates. Our youngest child, with whom we travelled a great deal, had an invisible land; it even had a name. He could spread it out anywhere, wherever he might be.

When the children during listening to stories begin to ask: "Is that really true?" then we realise that the time for fairy-tales has ended. We can bridge it by saying: "Here in our world it is not like that, but in the land of fairy tales it is true". From that time on, the child will more and more lose its thinking in pictures and develop a thinking through the intellect.

How Can An Adult Find The Way To The Picture World Of Fairy Tales?

The question about the truth of a fairy-tale can be asked when a child is still small. The reason for this may be that we ourselves were not sufficiently convinced about the truth of our story. If one wishes as an adult to tell a story convincingly, then one has first to find a way to differentiate between the picture wisdom and the fantastic. We will give here a method how one can practise to find this way. One has to acquire a state of soul which lies between thinking and feeling to develop a thinking which is more strongly imbued with feelings than is our ordinary dry thinking. Then one's thinking loses its linear character more and more and becomes colourful, rich and picture-like. This of course is a gain also for those who are not called upon to tell stories to children.

It is important to cultivate an exact observation. One should have seen for oneself the things found in stories and one should not miss any opportunity to look at things together with the child. During walks I always took time to stop when a fire was burning in a garden, if we passed a little stream, if somewhere pigeons flew around, or frogs hopped through the grass. It is also very good if at night the child sometimes can look at the moon and stars from a place where there are not too many street lights, or to watch how someone spins with a spinning wheel and weaves on a loom. In this way the pictures gain colour and richness, and become alive. Nowadays we have to look for such occasions consciously. In times past they were found in everyday life.

For the child it is sufficient if we make such observations and also tell him stories. For ourselves we have to take a further step. We have to turn the outer world in the stories into our inner soul life. This means a process of introversion, a turning inside out.

"Earth, is it not your will to arise invisibly within us? Is it not your dream to be for once invisible? Earth: invisible! What, if not transformation, is your urgent task?" says the poet Rainer Maria Rilke. How can this transformation come about?

The longer we let the blueness of the sky (or any other colour) work on us, the more the impression of the colour will deepen in us. If then we close our eyes, something remains. This is no longer a sense-perception but a semblance perceived by the soul. We should become more and more conscious of this phenomenon, not only with colours, but also with other things in our surroundings. Then they will come before us not as they are in the outer world, but as in the fairy tales, they will speak to us in a quite new way and become transparent. They will become pictures and symbols. Goethe also saw this as an aim of development: "All things transient are but a parable", he says in the closing scene of Faust.

If one has a sense for poetry, for symbols, for metaphors, this can be a great help.

A thing of beauty is a joy for ever,
Its loveliness increases; it will never
Pass into nothingness, but still will keep
A bower quiet for us and a sleep
Full of sweet dreams and health and quiet breathing.

Endymion

The theme of these verses by John Keats is "a thing of beauty". He describes it in pictures as "a bower", "a sleep". Pictures and concepts are standing here side by side. But one is not an explanation of the other. Only when both merge into each other, have we understood the meaning; the refreshing and blissfulness of beauty.

In fairy tales only the picture is given. If we can merge into these pictures and identify with them, then they can become transparent and show their deeper meaning. They become a symbol. Let us imagine our soul is a stage on which the whole happening of the fairty tale takes place. Each character belongs to us, and is part of our own soul. If we add an explanation to the picture in the fairy tale, we do not gain anything. We remain on the same level of consciousness, having merely replaced the pictures with a concept, and impoverished the story. It is more important to acquire a method of experiencing the pictures. Then fairy tales can become a means of educating the soul.

The child during his "picture consciousness age", up to about ten years of age, can understand the fairy tale pictures immediately if not intellectually. They rest within the soul and let him sense the secrets of life. Later on these pictures transform themselves into powers of understanding.

It is different with the adult. He has to regain an understanding of the images through consciousness, through thinking. Thinking is the clearest of our soul faculties; understanding must begin there.

The description that follows here can never be compelling as all the images are open. After concerning oneself with images for any length of time one can develop a kind of "thinking feeling" with which to grasp the meaning.

The Fairy Tale Of Little Red Riding Hood

I will give you a simple example of how one can look at a fairy story so as to understand it as a soul process, while reminding you that this should not be taken as a finished explanation. The more one can bring the pictures alive in the soul, the more can our understanding be deepened.

"Once upon a time there was a little girl who was loved by every-body, but her grandmother loved her more than anyone else. One day the grandmother gave her a little red velvet hood which fitted her so well that she did not want to wear anything else like it, and so she was called Little Red Riding Hood.

One day her mother said to her, 'Come, Little Red Riding Hood.

Here is a piece of cake and a bottle of wine. Take them to your grandmother. She is sick and ailing; they will refresh her. Go straight there and don't run or leave your path, for you might fall and break the bottle and grandmother would have nothing.' Little Red Riding Hood promised and started on her way. But grandmother lived in the forest, half an hour from the village."

The little girl and the grandmother belong together. One part of our soul is very old, full of wisdom, but also full of tradition. When these forces of old age get too strong, then the soul is sick. It needs strengthening by what is fresh and young in us, by the eternally childlike forces, for a new beginning. The little girl wears a red hood. Red is an active, fiery, gay colour. On the head wearing the little hood are most of the sense organs, above all the eyes. The little girl lives joyfully and actively in the sense organs, as all children do.

But there is a danger if this force becomes too strong, if the pleasure of the senses turns into sensuality. There exists a power hostile to humanity which can enter just at that point. It says: "Little Red Riding Hood, look at the lovely flowers all around. Why don't you have a peep at them? I think you don't even hear how the little birds sing. You walk just as if you are going to school, and it is so delightful out here in the forest"

And Little Red Riding Hood listens to the seductive voice.

"Little Red Riding Hood opened her eyes and looked around, and as she saw the sunbeams dancing up and down between the trees, and the beautiful flowers everywhere, she thought: 'If I bring grandmother a freshly picked bunch of flowers, it will give her pleasure. It is so early in the day that I shall be in time.' She left the path and ran into the forest and looked for flowers. And when she picked one it seemed that further out was an even more beautiful one, and in going to pick it, she wandered deeper and deeper into the forest."

This part is rendered exceptionally well by the Grimm brothers, and altogether this version of the Grimm brothers comes nearest to the original pictures of the soul processes.

"Little Red Riding Hood opened her eyes", with the result that "she left the right path". Are we not involuntarily reminded of the Garden of Eden myth? "And their eyes were opened". A child will not get the right image of the "wicked wolf" if we show him a wolf in the zoo, padding around in his cage like a dog. We must try to picture the terror which gripped our ancestors when on a winter's night they travelled through a lonely region and heard the howling of the wolves

come nearer and nearer. In our story the wolf is a no less threatening power, even though he may seem harmless through the simplicity of the story. He wishes to settle in the soul and overpower it, even to destroy it altogether. Firstly, he takes the place of Little Red Riding Hood and outwits the grandmother, then he lies down in grandmother's place in her bed to outwit Little Red Riding Hood. And he succeeds only because Little Red Riding Hood is diverted by picking flowers. During a time when a person's attention is too strongly directed outwards, the adversary power settles in his inner life.

The dramatic climax is enhanced by a rhythmical element. Little Red Riding Hood looks into Grandmother's bed, but cannot yet quite realise the danger. But it is of interest that she does notice that her supposed grandmother's sense-organs (seeing, hearing, touching and tasting) are too large.

"'Grandmother, what big ears you have.'
'So I can hear you better.'
'Grandmother, what big eyes you have.'
'So I can see you better.'
'Grandmother, what big hands you have.'
'So I can grasp you better.'
'But Grandmother, what a terrible big mouth you have.'
'So I can eat you up better.'
Scarcely had the wolf said this, when he leapt out of bed and gobbled up poor Little Red Riding Hood."

The story would end as a tragedy if a new character were not to appear. It is the hunter who hears the wolf snoring. So he comes in and cuts his belly open. As he made a few cuts, he saw the little red hood gleaming, and after a few more cuts, the little girl jumped out, exclaiming: "Oh, I was so frightened. It was so dark in the wolf's body!" And then the old grandmother came out and could hardly breathe. Little Red Riding Hood quickly brought big stones and filled the wolf's tummy with them. As he woke up, he wanted to jump away, but the stones were so heavy that he collapsed and died. That made all the three happy. The hunter took home the skin of the wolf. Grandmother ate the cake and drank the wine which Little Red Riding Hood brought and soon recovered again. Little Red Riding Hood was thinking: "You will never in your life again leave the path and go into the woods when mother has told you not to."

Fortunately in every soul there is such a hunter, an inner guard, who keeps watch in the twilight of the forest. He directs the adversary to the realm where he belongs. His lawful place is in the material world represented by the hard and heavy stones with which the belly of the wolf is filled. The hunter does not kill him, which would be easy, but the heaviness of matter pulls him down. There happens what always happens in fairy tales, because it corresponds with soul and spiritual laws: evil judges itself. The human soul is restored in its threefold nature: Little Red Riding Hood, the Grandmother and the Hunter are in the house together refreshing themselves.

Characteristics Of Styles In Fairy Tales

It is advisable at first to use only old folk tales and leave the artistic stories for later years. (Even Tolkien's *The Lord of the Rings* is in this sense an artistic tale.) The form of a real fairy tale is short, precise, objective, never emotional or sentimental. Feelings are only hinted at if they are relevant to the course of the action, but they are clear and definite.

"A king and queen had no children, but wished very much for one". Although love, marriage and birth are often-used motives, the fairy tale does not use erotic language. Feelings are immediately transposed into action. "As he glimpsed the picture of the virgin, so exquisite and radiant with gold and precious stones, he fainted and fell to the ground."

It is obvious that beauty engenders love, but it is just as evident that true beauty lies only in goodness. For a while it can appear as if the evil queen were the most beautiful in the country, but the truth is that Snow White is more beautiful. The beauty which the story describes as physical is in reality a beauty of the soul.

In the same way ugliness is a picture of evil, while terrible and gruesome happenings are either pictures of the overcoming of evil, or they can be reversed in some way which in the physical world is utterly impossible. The little boy who had been cut to pieces, cooked and eaten, is transformed into a bird, and stands there again hale and healthy, after the death of the wicked stepmother. Eyes that have been put out are threaded and hung round the neck. Later they can be put back again with no difficulty. If one tells these things in the right way, children will mostly understand them rightly.

Little Red Riding Hood and the grandmother are swallowed, and afterwards brought out quite unharmed. The most impressive experience for them was the darkness in the body of the wolf. This is described correctly because it is about the soul experience of darkening, contracting and eventual liberation.

The characters in the fairy tale have no inner soul life. Everything is told in terms of pictures, happenings, gestures and action. Hence there is no contrast in fairy tales between inner and outer world. All is inner world, spread out as though on a surface with no dimension of depth. Whereas in the legends and sagas (sometimes powerful or amazing) we encounter the incursion of the other worlds into the terrestrial, in the fairy tales only one world exists. It is the other world. Therefore it is not miraculous when animals speak or transform themselves. This is taken by young children as a matter of fact, because it corresponds with their state of consciousness. The adult, on the other hand, has to take all such characters and happenings back into his soul processes.

In this other world there is no final death, only transits leading to transformation and a higher life. Everything good is a force and is rewarded in the end, even if the person concerned is often looked upon as a dunce, laughed and mocked by his fellow beings. Moral values are valid after all. Lovers who belong to each other will find each other, even if the search lasts until the end of the world. Distance cannot part them, time cannot destroy them. Sleeping Beauty is as beautiful after one hundred years as she was before. It is possible to find a relationship to all beings; and even where the world fails, a character can ascend into the cosmos—"She thought, humans cannot help me anymore, and ascended to the sun."

All this penetrates deeply into the soul of the child as a picture, and it gives him strength and confidence which will help him later on to master life.

The descriptions which are given in the stories follow strict rules. Unbridled fantasy does not exist in the stories. Where motifs of myths are used with no such conformity to rules (as in fantasy-fiction), they portray neither a physical nor a soul reality. They are then lies and illusions.

The fairy tales are told in a style that belongs to no literary classification but is characteristic of the soul world, a world that can be comprehended only through imagination and not through intellectual knowledge.

"In physical space, for example, there are certain laws for seeing. One sees an object far away in perspective, diminished. In soul space everything seems to the onlooker near or far according to the distance of its own nature."[1] It is the same in the world of fairy tales, hence their two dimensional character.

One could quote widely from Rudolf Steiner in this context. But I will give only one more example: "The more spiritual the worlds one enters are, the more do moral laws and natural laws become one. In the sense world one is well aware if one says of an evil deed: 'it burns in the soul', one is speaking figuratively. One knows that real burning is something quite different. A similar differentiation does not exist in the spiritual worlds. There is a marked difference between the spiritual worlds and the sense-world also in what concerns the picturing of the beautiful and the ugly. Lying and ugliness are the same reality in the spiritual world, so that an ugly being is a liar."[2]

The Significance Of Storytelling And Reading Aloud In Family Life

An old Celtic story tells how the son of Cobhaun Saor "cuts short" a journey. The son wished to take his father to the seashore where there was an important task to do.

" 'Son, cut short the way there', said the father. 'How could I do that', said the son, 'if your two legs cannot cut it short?' 'Now do you think that you can make your fortune and mine also if you cannot even fulfill such a small task as that?' said the father, and he returned to his house. The son went home sadly. There he told his wife. She gave him good advice, and when on the next day he again started on the way with his father, he told him a story. This lasted all the way to the seashore."

Many long hours can be made shorter for children by this means— a waiting time, a tedious task or even a meal, if it is not liked. It is good if one can, beside this, to establish a regular story hour (or a half hour) during the day. Sometimes, in a large family, this is difficult to achieve, but if it can be done, the times of quiet togetherness are of great benefit to children and parents. Only later, slowly, will the child learn to listen and concentrate on longer stories.

We have to get a feeling for how much the child can absorb. We should try to tell a fairy tale freely and not read it aloud, for a story really lives if we have made it our own. While we tell the story, we can look at the child and observe the effect it has on him.

After what has been said here about the structure of the fairy tale, its unadorned conciseness, its two-dimensional character, it must have become clear that it is best to tell the story without additions, illustrations or omissions. It does not necessarily have to be learnt by heart, but we should have deeply grasped the succession of images and we should visualise them as far as possible, exactly and in colour. If we don't like a story, or if it does not seem suitable for our purpose, we should not tell it, but we should never alter it.

In our home, the stories were usually told in the evening by the fireside. Later on this was changed to readings which were kept up beyond the fourteenth year.

The King of Ireland's Son by Padraic Colum was very popular with all the children and became the transition from the world of fairy tales to the world of fables, legends and myths.[3] We read a lot of Celtic mythology, as the Germanic and Greek myths were taken at school. Later, we started on a few good children's books, stories of adventure and discoveries, biographical stories, and then more and more really good literature. Later on the children were surprised to find how many writers they were acquainted with through these readings aloud. Light fiction we let them read by themselves. In this way one can foster a certain ability of discernment.

Sometimes it was difficult to find material suitable for both big and small children. So it happened that the older ones heard fairy tales for a longer period than the younger ones.

Anyone with several children has to find their own individual way. With the bigger children it is no longer so important to distinguish between reading to them and letting them read to themselves, but we can enrich childhood enormously by the telling of fairy tales.

5. THE HIDDEN TREASURE IN FAIRY TALES

Margret Meyerkort

A true story: About ten years ago a friend of mine was teaching a group of young Africans in Copenhagen. One Saturday morning he noticed a student he particularly valued in a white hot rage. His inquiries resulted in accusations of the white man's barbarity. The reason? The Danish hosts to the course had taken the students on their free afternoon to their very latest achievement in the social field, an old people's home. The young African felt the isolation of the old people as an insult to their humanity. For him this modern house was a squalid prison. "Old people have their uses", he cried, "they can tell stories".

In these stories the wisdom of the ages was handed to the coming generations. Before they asked questions they had received answers, answers which told them of the destiny of man, the origins and history of the tribe, the functions of father and mother, of the shepherd and the smith, of the warrior and the priest. But these answers did not only provide information, they raised expectations, stilled fears and gave directions for inner development. How disadvantaged are, in comparison, our children who often receive a superabundance of information and little nourishment for their innermost needs.

In the European tradition the fairy tales stand in a sequence of imaginative linguistic creations which, according to the child's age, extend from lullabies to nursery rhymes, to simple undramatic realistic stories in prose and then to the fairy tale proper and finally into the world of mythology. Each of these has its specific style and atmosphere. We know of no fairy story which does not end with its complications resolved. We know of no mythology which is not aware of the tragedy of man, of the twilight of the gods.

The fairy tale, then, is particularly appropriate for children of between four and nine years. But experience will teach us to grade the stories according to the age of the child. As a first story we might take *The Sweet Porridge* out of the Grimm collection. It is short, it portrays the world of the child and it is accumulative, that is based on the principle of *This Is The House That Jack Built.* Longer and more complicated stories follow: *The Star Child, The Wolf and the Seven Kids, Little Donkey;* the first kind of Jacob's *English Fairy Tales* and some twenty stories of the Grimm collection are suitable for seven year olds.[1,2] Other English fairy stories and French and Russian tales are best left to children age seven to nine.

Fairy tales in their imaginative way speak to the consciousness of the small child. For him the boundary between inner and outer reality is still blurred. Only recently has he emerged from a state of consciousness which overflowed into and embraced all the manifestations of the world. First there was only a dim awareness of his identity and nothing else, then he learned to say "I" and separated himself from other people. Only later did he become aware of the fact that a table does not experience the world in the same way as himself. He still may play with invisible playmates and experience his naughty side as something not himself like the girl who when chided by her mother said "Jenny told me to". The fairy story speaks to this sort of consciousness and so the content is much more readily assimilated and assimilated at a much deeper level than would be the case if we approached the child with the consciousness of the adult American or European. Our consciousness is objective and alienating, his participatory and imaginative.

It is just this change of consciousness which is one of the major areas of concern of the fairy tale. One of the familiar characters is the youngest son, the dumbling, the prince. The father, the king is a patriarchial figure, full of power and wisdom, like one of the old initiates. The young man has none of it. He is naive, modest, kind. He has no rank, he can only act out of his own resources. And yet, it is he who breaks the spell, who wins the princess and returns to the realm of his father. This is the story of mankind. First, living in paradise, compassion to the animals, companion to the angels. Then the step into darkness, into separation and loneliness. Finally the man who relies on his own individuality and attempts the re-conquest of what has been lost. And he succeeds.

This is but one of many insights which through the medium of the fairy tale can be inscribed into the child's subconscious and his emerging consciousness. Gradually more areas of inner experience are faced, and among them is the question of evil. Modern men sometimes feel a revulsion against the drastic punishments dealt out to evil-doers in the stories. Not so the child. He has not yet reached the stage of consciousness where foregoing the "proper" punishment seems magnanimous and joyful. Nor does he experience fear when listening to the story. The story for him is what art is to the adult: a pretence world, a world of make-believe in which, nevertheless, the greatest and most profound human issues are sounded. The child knows the character of the fairy tale: all will be alright in the end, the evildoer will be put into his rightful place and the good people duly rewarded.

The fairy story appeals to a child's imagination, and it is this imagination which we want to foster, the ability to experience the world in images and to create such inner pictures ourselves. The adult needs imagination for a number of reasons. No *initiative* is possible without imagination, without seeing the potential for growth and development in a situation which others experience as static—and therefore hopeless. No *compassion* is possible without our imaginative realisation of our friend's or neighbour's predicament. Nor can *love* flourish without it. If we look at a person in a biological, scientific manner we cannot love him or her. We need to experience a person's potential, the possibilities of his or her growth, the potential for transformation. To fall in love is easy. We are driven to it. To continue to love needs imagination. This imagination is no phantasising. It helps us to uncover his or her full stature, profundity and deepest intentions.

So imagination helps us to successful living as adults. It also lives most strongly in young children.

The moment young children get together we can hear: "Let's play mothers and fathers." They build a house with chairs and tables. They cook and go out to work:

Five-year-old Dylon is already sitting at the lunchtable in the Kindergarten. Julian comes in from the other room: "Can I hand the bowls around and be the waiter?" Teacher; "Yes." Kathrine enters; "I want to be the waiter." And fastening an apron around Julian the teacher continues; "Grown up people call this a headwaiter. You are the headwaiter." Kathrine; "And what am I?" Dylon; "The tail waiter."

Mother calls six-year old Ruth in for lunch. Ruth; "Can't you see I'm Jane." Mother; "Sorry, come in Jane." Stupid Mummy. I am Ruth."

Four-year-old Myra comes in from the garden and looks up at her mother. "Mummy, when we kill a beetle, do we kill God?"

What do these stories tell us? The children move into the world of pretence, and in doing it, they move forward into adult life; they have a preview of adult life. The stories also tell us that the children live in a world of values, which is the world of imagination. This world of imagination is full of human values out of which our existence is woven. Also, the stories show that for the young child the boundaries of the inner world and of the outer world are blurred. For the young child, the world of the person and the world of the object merge. As we can experience, when the child who has hurt himself on the table says "naughty table", and hits it. The young child has a different consciousness. We call this consciousness the participatory consciousness, or, the consciousness of imagination. It is a kind of consciousness which has no or little boundaries, which is active, creative, changing, all-embracing.

This participatory consciousnes, this consciousness of imagination, has an enormous hold over the young child. It is his life. So for us the question arises. How do we acknowledge and work with what the child naturally has and naturally is? We do not want to prolong imagination in child development, or we would educate people who in adulthood cannot stand firmly enough in modern life. Neither do we want to force the child out of his natural environment, the consciousness of imagination, with the result of immaturity, of a stunted soul life in adulthood. Here the fairy tales offer help.

The narrator, teacher or parent, grandmother or uncle, will do his bit to emphasise the unique mood of the fairy tale: intimate, inward, calm, personal. The mother might hug her child while she recounts the age-old story, always in the same words as yesterday, always with the same vital phrases. Her voice will be even, the anger of the king will be a fairy tale anger, the danger a fairy tale danger and so the slight anxiety of the child in moments of imminent danger will be but a pleasurable thrill. I know from my own memories of childhood what a great source of courage I derived from listening to such stories.

Some parents may want to increase the special mood of the fairy story, its intimacy and inwardness, by drawing the curtains and lighting a candle or other, similar devices. Most important, however, is the narrator's total identification with the story in the way of the story teller of old. If he brings his modern attitudes into play, doubt, cynicism, rational discussion, he will be unable to build up the atmosphere around the story which is so sustaining to the child.

It is the atmosphere, the imponderables, the intimations for which the child longs. The content is, comparatively, a matter of indifference. "Again!" the child says. And so the story has to be repeated, even after the child knows every word by heart and will correct the narrator if he changes a word or leaves out an incident. The story, the child feels, has a life of its own which the narrator is not free to alter. It is "true", it can support and it can guide. Occasionally, the child will ask "why?" But he does not expect a logical answer, he is only after an assurance that the narrator has completely identified with the story and is able to defend its "truth", that is, its validity for the inner dimensions of man.

So I might end with what a woman in her mid-twenties told her one-time kindergarten teacher:

"I can remember that we children were sometimes cross with you."

"Why?"

"Well, you told us fairy tales and we asked you whether they were true."

"And what did I say?"

"You said: we'll see."

"And what did you want me to say?"

"That they were true, of course, because we knew that they were true."

6. CHILDREN'S QUESTIONS

Cecil Harwood

From about the age of three children begin to be full of questions, and it is sometimes a matter of great difficulty for their parents to find the right answers to them. Every question demands its own individual answer, but it can be of great value in deciding what answers to give to have a clear idea of the kind of answer which is required. For it is altogether wrong to imagine that a little child should be given the same kind of answer as would be suitable for a child of eleven or twelve, but, in a simpler form.

The range of questions which even young children will ask is truly astonishing. Indeed, in many respects the youngest children will often ask the most fundamental and far reaching questions—on life and death, and life after death, and many subjects on which parents have often resigned all hope of definite knowledge. A child of four (to quote an actual example) has asked these questions in the space of a few minutes:—

Do men die? Will you die? Shall I die? What do the angels say to you? Are angels shy? Who made God? Do you like God? When you die do you come alive again?

It must come as something of a shock to little children if parents declare themselves unable to answer questions fundamental to a knowledge of human life, and the questions of children must be a challenge to many parents to carry their thinking to the point of becoming clear and certain on many things which they are often content to leave unsettled.

There are two things, however, to be noticed about the questions of little children; they will often ask question after question in rapid succession, as though it were not so much information they were seeking, as the satisfaction of hearing the answering voice; and they will listen with more pleasure to an imperfect answer which is spoken with love and warmth in the voice, than to a complete and final reply given in a matter-of-fact tone. It is, indeed, to a large extent true that when little children pour out their endless questions they are seeking something much deeper than the mere satisfaction of curiosity; they are seeking to bring around them the living tones of the human voice. For the voices which they hear do not remain arrested in their consciousness, as is the case with adults, but penetrate even to those deep unconscious processes which take place in the building up of the physical body. Indeed Rudolf Steiner has shown the exact connections of the sound of the *alphabet* with the formation of the different organs of the body; and hence it is that Eurhythmy, which expresses the various sounds of language and music in movements of the limbs, is not only an art, but can be used as a means of healing.

It is, therefore, just as much a matter of *how* you answer little children's questions as of *what* you answer. Pure full tones of speech (and modern voices, especially those of intellectual people, are often terribly clipped and dry) not only give a child a feeling of blessing, but help him to form his bodily strength for later life. A child is first nourished by his mother-milk, and then by his mother-tongue.

But as a guide to what kind of answers little children need, it is often to be noticed that a child will supply the answer to his own questions, and not infrequently reject the one given by the adult for another of his own invention. Such answers which children give to themselves as a rule are much more full of fantasy than those which an adult would supply. A child asks: Why does the sun take the water up into the sky? and then adds: Is it for the angels to drink? Or seeing a piece of wire-netting over the funnel of a steam-roller, he asks: Why do they put the netting on it? but immediately adds: It must be to keep the birds from building their nests there.

It is not easy for an adult to copy this wonderful power of fantasy, and a certain sense of intellectual truth may often stand in the way. But it is always good to remember that what little children need is a certain living fantasy in the answers they receive. To offer them logical explanations (however true to a scientific mind) is to give them a stone when they ask for bread.

Sometimes little children's questions arise plainly from their desire to unite themselves with words to the objects around them. A child sees a caterpillar for the first time, and asks: "What is that?" "A caterpillar." "What is a caterpillar?" But what he wants from the second questions is not a definition of a caterpillar in ideas, but the joyous affirmation of the reality before him, "*That* is a caterpillar." "A Spae-woman lives by telling people their fortunes and interpreting their dreams," says the *King of Ireland's Son*, "that is why she is called a Spae-woman."

When children have passed the age of six or seven they naturally need much more connected answers to their questions than when they were younger. They wait more consciously for the reply, instead of living in the speech which is the answer. It is at this age, for instance, that children will ask many questions about the heavenly bodies, the nature of the sun and stars, the creation of the world, etc. And ready to supply the answer are numerous Children's Encyclopaedias, Newspapers, Science books, and what not, with beautiful diagrams of the Sun, a flaming ball on a black page, many times the size of the earth, or a man cut in half showing the heart like a pump, the lungs like a pair of bellows, the nervous system like a set of telegraph wires, etc. Whether or not the these things are in any sense representations of the truth is not for the moment the question: though it is worth noticing that by the time scientific theories reach popular children's books they are often quite out of date even judged by their own standards.

There will be plenty of time for children to investigate scientific theories at a later age, when they can really understand some of the conceptions on which they are based. For these scientific conceptions arose only at a very definite point in human history, and the mind of a child is not to be compared to the wave of intellectual thinking which historically brought them to birth. A child between seven and twelve or so has in him much more of the piety and luxuriant imagination of the Middle Ages. To him the stars are not vast spheres incredible millions of miles distant in space; he feels their clear shining beauty as something very close to him. The sun is not a huge stationary mass of burning gases; its rising each day fills him with a wonderful feeling of joy and thankfulness. The pictures of the heavenly bodies in mythologies are far truer to children than the distances and dimensions of modern astronomy.

The Norse people said that wolves swallowed up the sun at the time of an eclipse, and to a child, who has a fine sense of the *devouring* quality of darkness, the nature of an eclipse is much better expressed by such an image than by a diagram of revolving shadows. For in an eclipse it is truly *as though* the wolves devoured the sun, and that 'as though' is, after all, the furthest claim made by the true scientist: Newton did not say that the planets are attracted to the earth by gravity; but that they move *as though* they were so attracted, and it is not his fault that men have made a dogma of a hypothesis.

It is, in fact, of real importance not to give a child scientific conceptions on these subjects too soon. They tend to destroy the vivid feeling and imagination proper to this age; and, because they are received before the child has developed the power of following the thoughts on which they are based, they become matters of faith instead of matters of knowledge. Very few people in their adult years have even the will to investigate the mathematics on which is based the Newtonian planetary system or modern atomic theories. In a sense a scientific age is the most credulous of all ages. A thousand years ago a man could at least say: "I see the sun move with my own eyes"; but to-day many a man has to say: "Somebody proved a long time ago that the sun stands still. I forget exactly who it was, and I don't know how he proved it, but it's a fact all the same."

When children begin at this age to ask, How a thing is made? it is worth while considering how much of the true explanation has real meaning for them. There are children's books to describe how everything is made, but from such books children often get a very superficial, it may almost be said glib, impression of the work men have to do in the world. Such works are generally illustrated with photographs which give children a very easy picture of various processes, but very little feeling for the real conditions under which the work is done. A few flashlight pictures of miners hacking at a seam, together with a section of a mine with the cage descending, and a child will soon think he knows all about a coalmine, and turn to the next page to discover how a gramophone works, or what the Great Wall of China looks like. But there is something extra-ordinarily superficial, muddled, and uncreative about such a way of acquiring information; it is really far better for children to make their own pictures in their mind's eye from living in descriptions they hear of the intense silence under the ground, of men walking to their work for miles in galleries where they cannot go upright, of the dripping of water, etc., etc. In short, they should have some such picture of the inwards of the earth as George MacDonald gives of the interior of a mountain at the beginning of *The Princess and Curdie*. And, above all, the mine should not be an isolated fact, but a knowledge of mining should come as part of the children's general thoughts at the time, in some connection with chemistry, perhaps, or history or geology.

One of the worst results of children's books of the 'How it Works' type is that a child will often collect an extraordinary amount of theoretical information and forget to observe things which come within its own ken. Many children can describe the solar system, but do not know where the full moon rises, or what planets are in the sky. They know a lot about the assembling of a motor-car, but are very vague as to how butter or cheese or soap is made. It is always best to try to keep younger children's questions as to how things are made to those objects which they can really understand and observe, perhaps by themselves making them. Generally speaking, it is much easier to impart information to children too early than tactfully to withhold it until a better season.

But a certain reticence in answering children's questions is of great help in keeping the questioning faculty alive. For it is a sad fact that the power of asking questions only too often fades away as children grow older. It is perhaps a test of whether children's questions have been answered rightly in their younger years to see how profound are the questions they ask when they are older, and if they are readily satisfied with the answers. For by the time they reach a more intellectual understanding towards the age of fourteen they should have a strong desire to probe every question in life to the bottom, and not be lightly satisfied by theory without knowledge. For children of this age there is a deep meaning in that part of the story of Parsifal where, as a young man, he first sees the wounded Knight, but does not ask of him the question he should. Many of the questions which children should have in their hearts at this age will indeed only be answered by life itself. They stand in the threshold of life, and life will answer them, but only if they put to life the right questions.

7. FEEDING THE FAMILY

Wendy Cook

To be the guardian of our family's health is a very responsible and hopefully a joyful task. This task is realised in part through the proper selection and preparation of the foods that will provide the daily nourishment for our family. Sadly for some women, cooking has acquired a somewhat tarnished image. For, in an age of "haste and bustle" busy mothers can be tempted to take short cuts in food preparation by using convenience foods so readily available. These commercially manufactured foods, which usually contain additives, preservatives and colourants can never fully engage the digestive and metabolic systems. Moreover they are often addictive and can set up within us one-sided cravings which help to make us restless and unsatisfied. The long-term effects of this can be seen reflected in unbalanced agricultural practices and in areas of our economic life. Food that is processed mechanically in factories is largely de-humanized and de-natured, and is bereft of the forces needed to sustain and develop mankind in the right way. Food that has been grown, preferably bio-dynamically or organically (without artificial fertilizers and pesticides) and which is freshly prepared in a sensitive way is by far a better support for growing individuals. In fact we have the important task of re-establishing the creative alchemical role of the cook, who selects from the gifts of the earth, combines them and brings warmth to them, so that when they are consumed they help to create the quality of our blood which is the seat of our Ego and our will.

Evolution Of Key Substances In Nutrition

Some background information about the evolution of nutrition may give the reader some useful insight into where we stand today in relation to the past in terms of certain key food substances. Milk, for example, was the earliest of human foods, it is connected with the Moon principle and is related to the reproductive process. It contains everything needed by a growing organism, for it is a liquid synthesis of proteins, fats, carbohydrates and mineral salts.

The Lily and the Rose family (monocotyledons and dicotyledons) are the great archetypal forerunners of our fruits and grains. They have been symbols of special qualities from time immemorial and were sought after by the wise men of the Orient. Zarathustra, the great leader of the Persian civilization taught his followers to breed the food crops that we still consider the most important today.

At the time of Christ, salt and salted foods started to become a craving of civilized peoples. There were even feuds which developed over the ownership of salt-springs and deposits. Thus, when minerals began to be included in man's diet this marked a new development, whereby a real earthly character arose in man's nutrition. Salts are connected with the thinking and stimulate the warmth processes and have their correlate in the Ego. Our blood, of course, is saline. Spices, in the Egyptian times, were only used by the Priest-Kings. Later through Arab trading in the Middle Ages spices became widely used. This happened at a time when man's senses were awakening and his mental powers began to focus in a new way upon the material world. Now, used delicately and with insight, spices can be used to stimulate and awaken digestive processes.

Tomatoes and potatoes are both members of the Nightshade family and natives of Peru. They were brought to Europe as curiosities and the first European potato was planted by the botanist Clusios in 1588, who undoubtedly had little idea as to how widespread potato cultivation would become. The digestion of potatoes involves the brain, this, in one way can be seen as having helped the development of the consciousness soul. However, if the diet contains a great deal of these nightshade plants there can be a tendency towards materialistic thinking and egocentricity.

Tea, coffee and chocolate also began to be used widely at this same time and also played their part in awakening a certain "self"-consciousness. They are mildly poisonous and have the effect of loosening the relationship of the soul-spirit to the body. Coffee can have the effect of giving one's thoughts a sharper definition. Tea can be seen to stimulate "light" conversation, whereas chocolate gives a feeling of warm expansiveness. Today, these stimulants are often used as "crutches" and in excess can help to impair our health.

Refined sugar has played an ever-increasing role in the human diet in our search for sweetness. Certainly beet-sugar has a more mineralized quality than cane sugar, as it comes from the root and is therefore more difficult to balance within the body in any quantity. Too much sugar can affect the stomach and nervous system adversely, causing a deficiency of vitamin B1. Much more strengthening to the metabolism are the sugars which are converted within the body; the sugars of fruits, vegetables and cereals.

Thus by tracing the evolutionary pattern of humanity's earthly nutrition we may have some indication of how to introduce foods to the growing child. First comes milk; the mother's milk being the most perfectly balanced food for the baby, then a little fruit juice is introduced, then cereals, flower teas, vegetables and nuts. Later you may introduce salt, eggs (sparingly, and if it is deemed necessary meat and occasionally fish). The teenager, in developing his personality, will probably enjoy spicy foods and want to drink coffee. In later years we will probably once again enjoy much blander foods and the elderly can gain much from the combination of milk and a little organic honey in their diet.

Biographical Notes

My own adventure into a more conscious and wholesome way of cooking for my family was precipitated by my quest in helping my young daughter Daisy to overcome a severe asthmatic condition. I felt quite strongly that there must be a more natural way of dealing with this disability than administering to the child quantities of strong allopathic drugs which had the most alarming side-effects. Upon the advice of a friend I started to look into the field of nutrition. Daisy, at the age of seven had already quite independently decided that she was going to be a vegetarian. Through my studies and cooking classes in vegetarian and macro-biotic cookery a whole new aspect opened up to me, the world of the seven grains, nuts, seeds, vegetables, dried fruits, squashes, herbs and even seaweeds! All these foods can be available to be orchestrated into so many subtle symphonies.

I had always loved cooking and was also interested in healing. This new approach seemed to bring the realms together. I have to admit that for some time I became a "bit of a fanatic", nevertheless, as I look back on this time, I wonder whether it is sometimes necessary to go through a period of what appears to be "fanaticism" where one is truly immersed in an exploration of something new, this is also a time when one has a greater motivation to break old habits. Indeed one's eating habits are very often some of the most deeply embedded and most difficult to change. Through becoming much more conscious of our eating habits we were able to distingusish more clearly the effects of certain foodstuffs upon our individual organisms. For instance Daisy seemed to benefit from the absence of a great deal of dairy produce in her diet, in fact she seemed to have a definite allergy to most milk products, so I had to learn to make balanced and appetising meals without them.

In fact over the years many things have helped to bring about a more healthful life for all of us, but in the case of Daisy the picture is more dramatic. We moved from the city to the country and both my daughters joined a Waldorf School where amongst other activities Daisy's health was helped with curative eurythmy classes. Today she is a robust, lively and sturdy seventeen-year-old, almost free of those crippling asthma attacks, and able to enjoy most activities including sports, and also she can deal with most foods.

During the four years that I helped to run the kitchen at Emerson College, I had a good opportunity to deepen my knowledge of cooking and nutrition. To provide food at Emerson College is quite a responsibility. The students come from a wide age range and as many as twenty different national backgrounds, each with a differing range of food customs. The task was to try to ensure that everyone was taken into consideration, and of course the wider knowledge that one had of different cuisines, the better. The anchoring and unifying substances were the wonderful bio-dynamically grown vegetables from the farm and garden which were usually the starting point for any menu-planning. Whatever one's concern with sound nutrition might be, the food should be appetising and beautiful so that people actually want to eat it!

In trying to understand certain aspects of balance in human nutrition a picture which has stayed with me for some years, is the picture of the human teeth. Considered in a Goetheanistic light, one can think of their shape, apparent function and number, in relation to diet. Of a total of

32 teeth, eight (1/4) are incisors best suited for cutting and slicing vegetables and fruits, four (1/8) are canines designed for dealing with flesh foods, twenty (5/8) are molars best used in grinding cereal grains. This thought is not intended in any way to be taken rigidly or schematically, but possibly to provide insight for a greater balance in choosing foods in general. For example would there be a more just and healthy balance to our nutrition if man's diet were centred around cereals, vegetables and fruits, with a smaller proportion of animal food if required? Would this also lead to improved planning for agriculture?

Perhaps at this point we could look into the question of what eating meat means in a more esoteric sense, as contrasted with eating from the plant world: "When we eat food from the plant world we have to work on this food with inner forces in order to raise it to a stage where it can be used by the human being. When we eat animal food, the animal has already worked on the plant substance to re-organize it within itself. Thus when a man eats animal flesh he leaves forces that are in him unused. He allows the animal to take over a part of the work which he would have to do had he eaten plant foods."[1]

"The well-being of an organ does not consist in working as little as possible but in activating all its forces. When a man eats only plant food he stimulates the forces which develop organic activities, when he eats animal food he fails to make use of these forces."

So, in effect, in looking at nutrition we must try to understand which forces are being developed in the course of digestion, at the same time realising that food is a support that can only be made use of to the degree that the individual spirit actively transforms it. This does not of course mean that everybody should be a vegetarian; it is often very difficult even if a person would like to be a vegetarian for a whole ancestry of meat-eating to be thrown off in a lifetime. Many people are not able to do without meat, but more and more young people are tending towards vegetarianism and indeed the economic factor is one which plays more and more into what shapes our diet.

So it is as well to be quite prepared with knowledge on how to nourish our family in a balanced way from the plant kingdom, even if meat and fish also appear in the diet.

The Importance Of Cereals And Their Quality And Preparation

Let us then look at the qualities of our staples, the cereals. These are the sun-ripened, wind-pollinated fruits derived from the Lily family and identified with the wisdom of the Isis-Madonna. One only has to look at a field of ripening grain to feel the ancient wisdom and grace that has made this food a staple for centuries. These seeds contain proteins, oils and salts and complex carbohydrates or starches. In the process of digestion they are broken down into sugars which are released rhythmically into the bloodstream, giving us a steady on-going energy, rather like a slow-burning bed of coals (as a contrast to the rather superficial bursts of energy experienced when taking in the carbohydrates in the form of refined sugar, which is partially absorbed in the mouth and hardly brings the true digestive process into play).

The seven grains, Rice, Oats, Millet, Rye, Barley, Maize and Wheat, can be seen to be connected with the seven planets, and different civilizations have developed their cultures around certain cereals, or combinations of them. We are usually lucky enough to be able to have a choice of many varieties, and if they are to play a central part in our diet it is important to try to seek out bio-dynamically or organically grown cereals which have not been dressed with chemicals. As Steiner emphasized, "It is not so much the material substance of the food that is important, but the forces that have gone into the growing (and preparation) of it which count."

As more demand for bio-dynamically and organically grown food comes about, so there appears to be a response from farmers and gardeners. It is well if we can be prepared to make an effort to obtain good quality food for our families; for some this may be more difficult than others.

Much care is needed in preparing whole grains. Too often well-meaning cooks turn out masses of greyish, soggy, overcooked grains or under-cooked bullet-like particles which will discourage even the most zealous wholefood palate. It is difficult when we no longer have a tradition out of which to work; we have to re-establish our links with nature and our insights into the properties of foods. Cereals are very contracted and dense foods. They contain within them the potential for a whole new plant and in consequence they are particularly nourishing and strengthening to the metabolic and nerve system. When we cook food we are carrying on the fructifying process a stage further. In cooking whole cereals, because they are so contracted, we generally need a long slow cooking process to allow them to expand gently and to take up the water slowly. Different grains need different cooking times and amounts of liquid and as there are many excellent wholefood cookery books available it would be as well to consult one for specific recipes. I can only touch here on some basic guidelines and qualities of the seven grains. Of all the grains, wheat, rice and oats are probably the most familiar, but do try also to get to know the characters of the less familiar ones.

Some Guidelines Towards Preparation Of The Seven Grains

Whole rice has a similar sodium/potassium relationship in its composition to that in our blood, thus making it one of the most easily assimilated grains. You may cook a pot of plain boiled rice at the beginning of the week. Use twice as much water as washed rice, and if you have a source of spring water, all the better. Add one teaspoon of seasalt and when boiling point has been reached, turn the flame down really low and use a flame spreader to prevent the bottom of the pot being scorched. A heavy pot of earthenware or cast iron with a heavy lid which doesn't allow the liquid to evaporate is best. Allow three quarters of an hour cooking time until all the water has been taken up, but do not stir during cooking. Such a basic pot of rice can then be used in many dishes throughout the week if kept cool. For example you could make a rice pilaf, where the cooked rice can be mixed with lightly-cooked, stir-fried vegetables and cooked chestnuts. As a dessert, make a special rice pudding where the rice can be cooked further with the addition of milk, some grated sweet apples, chopped hazels, sultanas, a dab of butter, a dash of nutmeg and a little beaten egg if a firm rice pudding is required. Bake until golden. Rice croquettes can be made from the cold, cooked rice mixed with finely-chopped spring onions, parsley and seasonings, formed into firm balls or triangle-shaped patties, with dampened hands, rolled in sesame seeds and deep-fried in hot oil until golden brown and crispy on the outside. They should be drained and served with a piquant sauce, such as one made from freshly grated ginger root and tamril soya sauce, thickened with arrowroot and presented on a bed of steamed vegetables. There are countless ways of serving rice, too numerous to deal with here, but if by the end of the week you should be left with some rice which is beginning to sour, this can be used as a good basis for sour-dough bread, perhaps using the combination of two other grains, i.e., wheat and barley flour.

Oats have the highest fat content of all the grains and thus have a "fiery" quality. Oat porridge made simply with water and a pinch of salt has been the staple of many a stalwart Scot, helping him to brave the rigorous Scottish climate. We may prefer our porridge with the addition of some creamy milk and honey, or cooked with dried fruits, not forgetting the pinch of seasalt which brings out hidden depths of flavour in the cereal. The best way to cook oat porridge is to steep the oat flakes in boiling water, being careful that they do not "lump" and leave overnight in a heavy pot in the oven with just the pilot light on, or even better in the warming compartment of an Aga or wood-burning stove. In the morning you may add your cream, fruit, sweetening, etc.

Oat flakes are the main ingredient in muesli and "Granola". "Granola" is rather like roasted muesli. It usually consists of oat flakes, dried coconut, sunflower seeds, chopped hazels and peanuts, all of which are lightly coated with a mixture of warmed oil (corn oil is good for this) and honey, two parts of oil to honey and a dash of salt. This mixture is then gently roasted in the oven, stirred frequently until evenly golden and crunchy.

Finally some raisins and/or chopped dates can be added when the mixture has cooled a little. This makes a delicious and sustaining break-fast and is also handy for travelling. Oat flakes are good in "flapjacks", and oat flour can be used in bread and cakes for added variety. Whole oats may need some tasty addition in order to encourage them to be eaten.

Millet has a Mercurial ability to blend itself with other flavours, sweet or savoury, in a similar fashion to rice. Wash excess starch from the grains which should be relatively plump and a rich golden yellow, not greyish. Allow to dry in a wicker basket, or something that the air can penetrate. Then sauté lightly in a heavy pot with a knob of butter or some good corn germ oil and a teaspoon of salt. Add hot water, equivalent to double the volume of grain and allow to bubble a little until some of the water is absorbed.

Place a flame spreader, or asbestos mat between the pot and a very low flame. Allow to cook gently without stirring until the millet is fluffy and all the liquid is absorbed (about 35 minutes). Millet makes a good basis for grain patties or grain savoury loaves, with the addition of grated carrots, some roasted sunflower seeds, chopped fresh herbs and some sharp grated cheese, and egg to bind if required. Millet also combines nicely with some soaked dried apricots and top of the milk to make a milky pudding which most children will enjoy.

Rye is one of the more hard-skinned grains and can be quite difficult to digest if cooked simply in its whole form. It is marvellous in pumper-nickel bread which involves a lengthy cooking process. Another way to prepare rye is to wash it and slowly let it dry and roast overnight on a baking sheet in the oven with only the pilot light on. The next day it is cracked or "kibbled" in a grain mill and then cooked into a thick porridge with just a little salt. When cooled you may add cream cheese, a little caraway seed, chopped herbs and spring onions and bake in heaped spoonfuls on a greased baking tray for about ½ an hour in a medium oven. This is delicious and nutritious if it is accompanied by a sauce made with onions and bechamel or perhaps a hazelnut-bechamel sauce and salad.

Barley is a warming sweet grain. My family particularly enjoys barley in a favourite wintry stew. The barley is cooked slowly overnight and the following day it is tied in a muslin bag and immersed in a rich vegetable stew where the barley continues cooking and absorbing some of the vegetable broth and acquiring a delicious flavour. The barley is then served in the centre of the bowl surrounded by the vegetables and garnished with emerald green sprigs of watercress. Barley bread has a very sweet and nutty taste but because barley is low in gluten, barley flour has to be mixed with a percentage of hard wheat flour to prevent too crumbly a texture.

Maize was used by the ancient Aztec and Mayan civilizations, by the American Indians and now by Mexicans and Italians. It is also a very versatile grain mostly used in the form of flour, which is cooked into a thick porridge (polenta), this can be used in many ways. I like to make a dough consisting of ½ maize flour, a little corn oil, ½ wheat flour, some beaten egg and cold water to mix. This is then kneaded thoroughly until it resembles the texture of one's earlobe. It is then rolled out thinly, cut into small plate-sized rounds, and allowed to dry out a little. These are then deep-fried until golden and crisp and then allowed to drain. These are 'tostados' which are then covered artistically with a layer of re-fried beans, a spicy tomato sauce, sour cream, finely shredded salad, grated sharp cheese, and topped off with tomato wedges and halved olives. This Mexican dish is a real family treat. The same dough can be used for 'tortillas' or Mexican pancakes which can be cooked in different ways with different fillings. Wheat is the most widely used grain, particularly in Europe. It is also the most suitable grain for making bread, pastries, cakes and pasta, having a higher gluten content than the other grains. Homemade pasta is delicious and much easier to make than one would think, even without a pasta machine. Flour which is 85% of the whole wheat makes a lighter pasta and is often used for pastry making. I can really recommend an unusual light and crunchy pastry crust, suitable for both sweet and savoury dishes. Take 3 parts 85% wheat pastry flour, 2 parts small oatflakes and one part of sesame seeds. Then take half the total weight of these dry ingredients in butter and rub this lightly into the flour mixture until you have the consistency of fine breadcrumbs. Then add a little water, mixing until a good rolling consistency is achieved. Baked in a hot oven this is excellent for flan cases, pies, tarts, sesame crackers and such like.

Bran which is left over from sifting flour can be used to make bran pickles. The bran is mixed into a paste with coarse salt and water. This paste is then layered between sliced root vegetables in an earthenware crock. The whole is then weighted on top and left to pickle for a month. Bran and raisin muffins are good for breakfast and are a good laxative, too.And thus I have devoted some space to the cereals as they really are a good starting point for planning a menu.

Planning A Balanced Menu

It is quite a sensible guideline to hold the thought of having something of the root, stem, leaf, flower and fruit included within the menu, not necessarily always in one meal, but within the space of a day or two days.

In menu planning I consider it to be very important to reflect the Seasons in our cooking. It is so easy to overlook this aspect nowadays because freezers keep food from one season to the next and cold-storage planes transport foods which are in season in one part of the world to another where they are out of season. Many people lose touch with what is happening in nature and eat the same foods all the year around. Of course it can be nice to have a little variety in times when vegetables of the home-grown variety are low, but Nature in her wisdom provides the best fruits and vegetables adapted to our climatic and environmental needs. Hence in the winter we have the root vegetables more predominant. These, with their mineral salts bring warmth, and they nourish the head and nervous system. "This is all very well" you may say when you are left for two months of the winter with nothing but carrots. Of course we are not to be so rigid, but as cooks we have to be imaginative, and as many painters have discovered, by limiting their palette they can be more effective. When we are faced with limited resources true creativity can take place. Let us look at a few of the guises in which the humble but versatile carrot can appear.

1. Roasted with oil and tamari and rosemary sprigs and bay leaves until sweet and tender.
2. Crispy deep-fried slices, dipped in an egg and flour batter (tempura)
3. Carrot and onion tart with ginger glaze.
4. Steamed with rosemary, served with butter and lemon sauce.
5. Grated raw in salad with celery, raisins, cashews and freshly squeezed orange juice..

6. Grated in a carrot cake.
7. Stir-fried with spring greens.

8. Boiled with some sweet parsnips and mashed with butter and chopped parsley.
 These are just some of the ways to bring the 'carrotness' out of the carrot!

In the Spring we have an abundance of 'leafiness'. and if you live in the country you can make use of this abundance of Nature's wild foods, for example nettles, young dandelion leaves, wild garlic, young birch leaves (for elixir) to mention but a few are all wonderful additions to our diet and are very blood-cleansing. The leaf of the plant corresponds to our rhythmic, breathing system. It is true that when the Spring comes we just want to go out and take in as much fresh air as possible in order to awaken our senses and our limbs. Therefore we will be helped if Nature's new green and vital leafiness is reflected in our diet.

In the late summer if we have gardens we gather our harvest, and if there is a surplus we can preserve foods to help us through the winter. We can make jams, chutneys and pickles, and we can bottle and freeze food of which there may be a glut. Wild berries such as blackberries, elderberries, rosehips and the wild crab apple have a marvellous and strong flavour for making syrups and preserves. All this gathering and preserving can become a wonderful social activity to do with children and friends, the more the merrier!

In menu-planning it is important to use our imaginations to see how the meal will look when it is prepared. We should keep in mind all the aspects of colour, shape and texture and should consider whether the food will be hot, cold, soft, crunchy, cooked, raw, sweet, salty, spicy or bland and so on. All these various qualities need to be subtly orchestrated, not arbitrarily nor with gimmickry directed at maximum sensory gratification, but in a meaningful way. To do this we need to contemplate with real love, our environment, our ingredients and the people for whom we are cooking, their temperaments and their activities: for example are they sitting down all day or are they working manually? All these aspects should be considered in order to make our cooking truly conscious. In cooking, eating and digesting, we are unifying ourselves with and interiorizing that which is outside of us in the world. If we have a broad, open appetite for that which is healthy and natural we have a good chance of being healthy questing human beings. But one often finds that a child who is in his formative years has been allowed to become fastidious and choosy about what he eats may well grow up with an exclusive attitude to life in general. In all of this, our attitude is so important and our example, as parents, is paramount. If we are constantly rushing and approach mealtimes as something of another chore to be overcome as quickly as possible, this will surely become a vicious circle. I am always aware, in my home, that if I prepare something in haste, it seems to be eaten in haste, for haste becomes bound up in and transmuted through the food. This is sometimes unavoidable in the lives that we lead in the present time, but it is a very sad thing if it becomes the norm. Mealtimes are an important oasis within the daily round, a sacramental coming-together in gratitude and reverence where we can really meet each other, enveloped by a feeling of well-being and a thoughfulness towards our food. The thought that it has taken a year to grow and several hours to prepare may restrain us from bolting it down and rushing off to our next activity

By the same token, the kitchen can be a place that reflects the quality of artistic endeavour, harmonious and orderly, with gleaming pots, sharp knives and wooden stirring implements. It is usually the heart and soul of the home where people tend to want to gravitate because it is a welcoming place to be. (In India the meditation room is usually next to the kitchen.)

Vegetable Preparation

Let us now assemble our ingredients. If you have B.D. or organically grown vegetables you do not need to peel them. Indeed a great proportion of the mineral salts lie within the skin, so keep a special small brush with which to scrub the vegetables carefully. Try to look at your vegetables to find ways of cutting them attractively in order to enhance their shapes. If one vegetable has been cut finely, "Julienne" style. then let the other vegetables be in larger, 'calmer' pieces, otherwise there tends to be a 'busy' feeling on the plate. If they are going to cook for a long time in a casserole, then they will need to be cut into 'chunky' pieces so as not to disintegrate during the cooking.

The climate can also play into our choice of cooking methods. In the winter we need more enduring warmth and so we will probably find the longer cooking methods of roasting, baking and casseroling to be appropriate. In the summer lighter cooking methods such as stir-frying, steaming, sautéing and lightly boiling, give a greater lightness to the food. Different cooking techniques can be used to bring contrast within a meal. For instance it would not be considered very advisable to have a meal which consisted of Tempura (deep-fried vegetables or fish in batter, followed by Apple Fritters or doughnuts as a dessert, for obvious reasons.

The Question Of Raw Foods

There are questions about the place of raw foods in our diet and there are many different views on this. Dr. Steiner spoke of raw foods as playing more of a medicinal role in our diet. On the whole the digestion of raw food takes more forces than with cooked foods, since we need to produce more warmth in order to 'cook' it within ourselves. It is again a question of climate and a question of degree. In the summer salads are plentiful and even in the winter there are salad vegetables like chicory, watercress and cornsalad which in their bitterness and pungency are stimulating to our digestive juices. I sometimes like to begin the meal with a colourful 'spectrum' salad of variegated vegetables some cooked, some raw. This is beautiful to ponder upon in the centre of the table while we say a Grace and it begins the meal by enlivening the palate. *Soup* is also an important beginning to a meal, it is light, nutritious and stimulating to the digestion. Beans, pulses and lentils can be particularly valuable in winter-time when fresh produce is scarce. In addition they are quite often popular with people who are giving up meat-eating because they have a certain kinship with animal protein. We can witness this in the extraordinary lengths that people go to, to 'spin' soya protein and transform it so that it looks and tastes like meat!

Pythagoras is said to have forbidden his followers to use beans. Aristotle says beans signify lasciviousness, thus the prohibition of using beans might mean 'chastity'! It has also been suggested that unruly conduct in general is signified by peas and beans, because of the wild and unruly growth of their shoots. Indeed many people have great difficulty in digesting beans and therefore it is a very individual matter. Dried beans must be cooked really well, having previously been soaked overnight and the soaking water discarded. They should be cooked for a long, slow time, depending on the variety, without salt as this tends to harden the skins. I find that the addition of a small piece of kelp seaweed helps greatly to soften beans, and you can use a little fennel to combat any flatulence that the beans may produce. Salt or tamari soya sauce can be added at the end of the cooking time. It is also an added precaution to cook the beans again, as in re-fried beans.

Thus I have tried to cover some of the main foodstuffs within the vegetable kingdom. I have not touched on herbs which I value in cooking greatly, since that is a whole study in itself. Nutrition is a vast subject and I am well aware of the difficulties involved in trying to deal meaningfully with such an important and emotive theme . I merely hope to share some of the insights I have gained in my searches to illuminate the subjects of cooking and nutrition, as a basis for further study. In fact these two subjects have become streams developing unilaterally and in opposite directions. The one stream in its relentless search to appease the restless appetites of the 'epicures and gastronomes' of this world, becoming quite degenerate in its lack of attention to the other stream, whereas 'Nutrition' seems to be something that is dictated by the findings of scientists, isolated in laboratories with their calorimeters, having lost all touch with Nature and the spiritual processes that are involved in human digestion. Our task is to re-unite these two wayward streams into one powerful 'life-stream'.

Let me close with an anecdote that really helped me to change my thinking about the role of the cook. I was talking to a friend, a student of Zen Buddhism, about cooking. I said that because I have always had a certain gift for cooking I seemed not to value it as much as a talent for which I would have to strive, and also that I had been somewhat daunted by the image that many people have of cooks, usually of the feminine variety, being considered rather menial creatures. Then he told me that in a Zen monastery the wisest person of all was often considered to be the cook. This helped me to begin to think differently about my task, indeed a lifetime's task and one for which I am truly grateful.

8.   ILLNESS

Gudrun Davy

Responsibility And Trust

In December 1982, Prince Charles gave an unexpected and courageous address to the British Medical Association. "By concentrating on smaller and smaller fragments of the body". he said, "modern medicine perhaps loses sight of the patient as a whole human being, and by reducing health to mechanical functioning it is no longer able to deal with the phenomenon of healing."

To counter this trend, which sees the human being as a machine and the doctor as a mechanic, he suggested that if the notion of healing were to be reincorporated into the practice of medicine, the profession could well draw new inspiration. Paracelsus, the renowned sixteenth century healer said Prince Charles, was a radical critic of some of the wonder drugs of his day-viper's blood, 'mummy powder, unicorn horn. He saw illness as a disorder of the whole person, involving not only the body, but his mind, his self-image, his physical and social environment, and his relation to the whole cosmos. "Nature heals, the doctor nurses," said Paracelsus. "Like each plant and metallic remedy, the doctor, too, must have a special virtue. He must be intimate with Nature. He must have the intuition which is necessary to understand the patient, his body, his disease. He must have the "feel" and "touch" which make it possible for him to be in sympathetic communication with the patient's spirit's."

And Paracelsus believed, "that the good doctor's therapeutic success largely depends on his ability to inspire the patient with confidence and to mobilise his will to health." Prince Charles ended by bringing to his audience Paracelsus' desperate plea: "Would we human beings know our hearts in truth, nothing on earth would be impossible for us."

When our children are ill, we know in our hearts that we are not simply witnessing something going wrong with a machine. Many doctors know this too But scientific medicine has no clear place for what the heart says. A drug is prescribed to eliminate the symptoms of disorder. This seems "rational". But this kind of rationality removes from illness all real questions of meaning—not only its meaning in the life of the patient, but also in lives of doctors, parents and others involved. The drug becomes a device for repairing the machine, the doctor becomes a device for prescribing the drug, the parent a device for administering it, and the patient has simply to be 'patient', passive and obedient to authority.

A mantle of spiritual and pastoral, as well as technical authority falls all too easily on the shoulders of doctors. This is reinforced by our own attitudes, especially if fear makes us want to hand over all responsibility and judgement to someone else. At such times we become conscious of our lay status, and uncertain of what contribution we can make, other than to sit back and let the doctor take over.

Yet our hearts tell us otherwise. Here too, many women and men nowadays sense an issue of freedom (Prince Charles is evidently one of them). In no sphere of life are we any longer content to accept authority without question. So we are reluctant to hand over total responsibility for health to others, however sympathetic as well as expert. It is complicated, of course, when it is our children who are ill. It is a central theme of this book that our children are not our possessions, but that we are entrusted with their care, while they grow up. But neither do they belong to the doctor, or to the "authority" of medical science. Our hearts can tell us, though, that such questions can only be humanised by developing a deeper power of trust: trust in the child, in nature and in the doctors with whom life brings us together.

What is trust? The question becomes a burning issue for many mothers as they approach childbirth: There is now a widespread determination among young parents to have a say in what happens during pregnancy, delivery and after birth. This certainly leads to difficult confrontations: Between the technologically minded doctor, for example, who insists on a hospital birth, and starry-eyed parents who want a candlelit delivery at home. Neither party can see the other's point of view: One gives priority to "safety". the other to a happy and harmonious birth experience. Mistrust feeds on mutual incomprehension. The parents see the doctors as heartless authoritarian technicians. The doctors see the parents as irresponsible self-indulgent dreamers who refuse to face the facts. The parents ignore the life-saving possibilities of technology in crisis. The doctor ignores the parents' heartfelt conviction that psychological, emotional and social "safety" may be as significant for the child's birth as the safety provided by machines. Yet it is obvious that a polarisation of this kind is never in the interests of the child let alone the doctors or the parents. It is the opposite of what is needed, which is that fostering of the relationships between doctor, parent and child so that all begin to "know their hearts in truth."

If trust is to be more than mere sentiment, it can only grow out a fuller and more intuitive insight. We cannot expect this of doctors if we do not attempt it ourselves. This means trying to understand the doctors' needs as well as our own and our children's. We may find that our views are very different. But I have found it a real help to ask a different question: "Why have I met this doctor at this moment?". If we can make our relationships more whole, we can better hope for a healing to take place.

I want to explore in this article some ways in which we as parents can support and reinforce the healing processes by seeking, with Paracelsus, "the intuition which is necessary to understand the patient, his body, his disease". Can we also learn to be "in sympathetic communication with the patient's spirits"? And can we also become more "intimate with nature", and learn simple means of home nursing, which together with home remedies can help children through their illnesses? I shall look first at the common feverish illnesses of childhood; then at some of the stresses of our culture; and finally at the handicapped child.

The Blessings Of Fever

One of our friends, Susanna de Souza Aranha, sent from Brazil this account of accompanying her two children through the measles:

"I can well remember the days when my eldest daughter had measles, not so long ago. What comes to my mind is that watery red face and body, completely swollen. Water ran from mouth, nose and eyes; her temperature was constantly over 40C. She did not seem like a being of this world. As she was my first to go through this illness, I had no experience and easily panicked. I felt I ought to interfere in some way to save her. But the measles went on. She came through it, and from being a horrible sight, she emerged a new girl, with quite different features. There was a new special look in her eyes, much more determined.

Two weeks later our younger daughter caught the disease. This time I had no fear, I knew what was to come. I could understand the process she would go through. I knew what I had to do to help her help herself to overcome the disease herself. Most of all my attitude was one of expectation. We all wanted to see how she would grow out of the illness and how different she would look after it. Which part of herself, hidden until now, would appear?

Most parents must go through such difficult times with their first children and even with the following ones, when they can't grasp what is going on behind their ill faces. But to know that this is ultimately a healthy process, and to share one's fears and responsibilities with others can be a great help."

The idea of "healthy" illnesses is strange to medicine which regards things like measles simply troublesome and possibly hazardous infection. Yet if we are observant, we can often recognise feverish illness in ourselves as small crisis, crossing points, "rites of passage" bestowed by nature which help us to take a step out of something old into something new. Colds and influenza tend to strike when we are low. If we don't suppress them with powerful drugs, they force us to rest. We may look back later and see that during the pause, we gathered new forces for life, both outwardly and inwardly. A feverish heat cooks us gently—Na ture takes us into her warm oven cleansing the body but also ripening new flavours and possibilities in the soul.

The childhood illnesses, especially measles, chickenpox, mumps and whooping cough (which is not always accompanied by fever) are most often contracted in the first seven years. This is the time of "coming down to earth"—learning to cope with the transition from prenatal floating to walking; from taking in food through the blood, then the breast, to eating solids with a spoon; from the all-round support of the womb to physical independence (including maintaining one's own temperature). Rudolf Steiner saw in the feverish childhood illnesses not unfortunate infections, but profoundly positive opportunities for development. The fever is like an enhanced infancy, even a pulling back into the almost tropical world of the womb, a protection from the over-rapid descent into the colder, harder body in which ageing processes are already at work. To the "eye of the heart", these illnesses can be understood as allowing the soul and the spirit to dissolve and then reform the body a little, so that it is a better "fit". Here too is a basis for later freedom, an early way in which nature can help the individual transcend inherited "hang ups".

If we see this, as Susanna did, we no longer want to suppress the fever, but seek to help it to run its course artistically, musically, not too loud and not too soft. There are many simple aids for nursing children, a few of which I shall mention later in this article, together with some helpful reference books. At this point, though, I am concerned with the task of seeing the meaning in these childhood crises. Neither we nor doctors can expect to trust these illnesses, not find the confidence in ourselves and our children's capacities to cope with them, if we see no wisdom, but only malfunctioning machinery, in what happens.

In many countries, children are being immunised against many of these illnesses. In some cases the authority of scientific medicine is being reinforced by the authority of the law. This creates further possibilities of conflict between parents and doctors. In all such situations, we have to try and transform confrontation into process of developing insight and trust—just as we can learn to transcend the first fearful confrontation with our children's illnesses, and learn to discover the possibilities of healing in it with which we can work. There can be no wonder drugs for these situations. And if the law or the medical circumstances mean that a child is prevented from experiencing these illnesses, we can work all the more to foster warmth processes in other ways—warmth of interest, enthusiasm, joy in life. (A resentful, melancholic or defeated parent is of no use to the child, whether it is allowed to have measles or not.)

One final thought on feverish illnesses· There is a stage of development which is often accompanied by fever for which no-one has yet proposed immunisation, namely teething. There the immense fiery capacity of the body to forge hard crystalline shapes and set them into position to deal with the outer world, is obvious. It can keep children and parents sporadically busy with mild crises for two years or more. It is repeated five or six years later, although usually with less drama, when the teeth change. The magic of hiding one's old tooth under the pillow in the evening and finding it changed into a silver coin the next morning acknowledges the hidden achievement, the new birth hidden in each small dental crisis.

Illnesses Of Civilisation

The feverish illnesses are part of childhood (and as adults, fevers can also offer us a brief but blessed return to infancy). But we have to meet, in addition, conditions of illness arising not from nature, but out of the unnatural conditions of our lives. These are less easy to pin point, as they are often of our own making. They are part of our modern situation. Yet this book is much concerned with some changes in the ways we live which can also moderate such ills.

The number, intensity and speed of the events in our surroundings today create an environment which bombards the senses in ways unlike anything experienced in earlier times. Even in the country; TV, radio and all kinds of machinery are constant companions. Even small rural shops and restaurants add loud piped backdrops to the noises which belong there anyway.

Adults learn to some extent to shut off—yet every general practitioner knows that a high percentage of his patients are suffering from stress disorders of various kinds. The volume of prescriptions for tranquillisers and sleeping pills is frightening, and often lamented. But it does not seem to occur to us to turn down the volume of the Muzak .

It should be obvious that if we are vulnerable, so are our children. Most parents know the look of pale and nervy exhaustion of small children emerging from a rowdy party, or gripped too long by a tense film. And teachers know the drowsiness and irritability they bring to school next morning. All too often nowadays parents seek tranquillisers and sleeping pills for their children as well as for themselves.

The hyperactivity in our environment is often coupled with another obsession, that children should "progress" if possible faster than other children. The adult rat-race creeps into the nursery. Parents are easily convinced—on no evidence at all—that children who can read or operate computers at five, or four, or three, are somehow "ahead" and thereby guaranteed success in the competition of life.

In this connection, Virginia Axline has written a most moving story, both tragic and wonderful: *Dibbs in Search of Self*. Dibbs mother was a doctor whose ambitions, for complicated reasons of her own, was to prepare her two year old son for a prodigious adulthood. She taught him to read, identify composers on records and tapes, and learn to work with scientific toys. At first the child seemed to respond to this "stimulating environment". But gradually he shrank into himself. His childhood was being invaded. He withdrew more and more from his ambitious parents. His withdrawals alternated with tantrums and outburst of frustration. The brilliant boy gradually became a mentally handicapped child. After great struggles with her own pride, guilt and despair, the mother eventually sought professional help, without revealing details of the child's past or her own medical background. Dibbs was very fortunate indeed to meet Virginia Axline at this point in his life. This wonderful Psychotherapist seemingly did very little but allow the child to play. But with the mother's reluctant permission, she recorded each play session and through the book we can follow the slow path of healing. She provided a sanctuary for the child, a play room equipped with simple toys, sand and water, and she just stayed with the child. During this one precious hour during the week, no demands were made, no judgements were passed on any of Dibbs' outbursts or reactions. He could just be himself, a small child wanting to play and be loved without any expectations. Gradually, he found an inner and outer security.

Virginia Axline combined her scientific training with the intuitions to understand her patient which Paracelsus asked for. It is the alienated intellect which is prone to the delusion that children are simply miniature adults. The eye of the heart shows us very well that we are meeting in two-year olds another consciousness and way of being, which has its own needs. Virginia Axline knows this. She had simply to create an environment, of which as a loving presence she formed a part, and Dibbs gradually healed himself. His unfortunate mother was perhaps not merely crudely ambitious. Our urge for liberation, if the head is divorced from the heart, can take queer forms, like trying to rush an infant into mastery of the adult world. The result was almost to imprison Dibbs in himself. His guardian angel brought him to Viginia Axline. His story and her book, are a profoundly therapeutic offering towards the "illnesses of civilisation" which afflict us.

The Handicapped Child And The Healthy Spirit

We have seen how "the eye of the heart" can show us meaning in the crises of childhood illnesses, and also awaken us to the illnesses of civilisation. The most demanding question of all is perhaps faced by the parents of handicapped children. Here again a wonderful story has been recorded by Mary Craig. In *Blessings*, she tells how there arrived into her normal happy family which already included one bright little boy, a second child, Paul, suffering from Hoehler's Syndrome, or "Gargoylism". This is an extreme form of physical and mental handicap. These children don't necessarily look seriously abnormal at birth, but as they grow, they rapidly develop a grotesque appearance. The condition was not diagnosed until Paul was in his second year. His mother describes vividly the shock, the horror, the search for help, the cruelty of passers-by. "Children like that should not be on public transport", said one woman at a bus-stop.

When Paul was six, Mary Craig was offered a short holiday from the exhausting burden of caring for him. Her decision, intuitive and rationally inexplicable, was to go and help at a Sue Ryder home for survivors from the Nazi death camps. What she met there—shattered and crippled individuals living lives of extraordinary courage, love and humanity— changed her life. She came home a different person. Through this new connection she later found a doctor who became especially interested in Paul and took him to his sanatorium in Poland. Paul spent three happy years there and was then brought back by his mother to die at home.

This might still seem to be on the surface a tragic story—but Paul and Sue Ryder together had enabled Mary Craig to unlock in herself reserves of strength, courage and devotion of which she had been quite unaware. She learned to look back on Paul as someone to whom she owed a deep debt—although the meaning of Paul's life for himself remained mysterious.

Mary Craig had two more children, both boys. The second suffered from Down's Syndrome: he was a "mongol". There is no connection between gargoylism and mongolism. Two such births to one mother was against all odds. But the mongol child engendered love wherever he went. The family which had suffered so much accepted him, loved him, made a space for him, and he brought them much.

This story seems to me to contain very powerfully the unexpected secrets of development in human relationships with the handicapped. For the purely scientific eye, Paul and the mongol boy were two almost intolerable human disasters. In the real life of Mary Craig, the one brought something like a re-birth, the second brought unexpected grace and joy. And what awoke in the adults flowed back to the two boys. We can almost hear Paracelsus commenting that when we "know our hearts in truth", nothing is impossible for us.

At the age of nineteen I began to work and train in a home for mentally handicapped children in Switzerland. My grand-parents were horrified. They did not feel a young girl should bury herself in such misery. In fact they sent a young man to rescue me from "that place". He was a young businessman, with no idea what it was all about. He was very surprised at what he found. The home was a beautiful place, well cared for and colourful. He was made welcome and shown around. He saw cheerful and light-filled faces, both among the handicapped children and the co-workers. He was puzzled, and certainly did not see any reason to persuade me to leave. My own experience was that as one got to know the children, one began to forget that they were strange-looking or behaving oddly. But through the oddities, one learned to know shining individualities, as valuable and lovable as anyone else. This is what many parents experience once they have accepted their handicapped children. The spirit which lives in every human being cannot itself fall sick. The meaning of illness and handicap have to be sought not only at the level of physical disorder, but in the growth of soul and the awakening of spirit which can be found both in the sufferers and in those who care for them.

Towards Intimacy With Nature

At the practical level, the modern faith in technology has tended to make us less intimate with nature. Family practitioners used their hands to explore temperatures, swellings, condition of lungs, the strength of pulse. Modern trainings in acupuncture and osteopathy require some comparable sensitivities, and underline our potential for intimate observation without scientific instruments. Many mothers in caring for their children develop quite accurate perceptions of warning signs, improvements or deteriorations in the conditions of their children. But we need encouragement to undertake simple nursing measures which were commonplace for earlier generations: Cool compresses around the calves to moderate high fevers and calm a restless child; fresh onion slices bound to the ears for earache; a piece of amber to chew on for teething; herbal teas for many conditions. A modern medical training gives little support for developing the intimacy with nature which Paracelsus urged, but as parents we can to some extent make good the lack ourselves. There is a wealth of knowledge quite easily discovered, and simple skills to develop. It is a special joy to grow some herbs oneself, in the garden or in pots. Sage, lemon balm, lovage and many others are home remedies as well as culinary plants. The herbal tradition indicates that roots work more on the head, leaves on our respiratory and circulatory systems, and flowers on our digestion and metabolism. A teething child may be wakeful and restless, but also have digestive upsets. So we can try a homeopathic potency of chamomile root for the toothache, and chamomile tea for the stomach. A very experienced nurse recently showed our group how to prepare different teas and compresses. We were amazed to see that one single flower of chamomile immersed in a cup of boiling water, covered and left to stand for three minutes but no more, makes a superb tea with a delicate aroma, and the power to sooth stomach pains.

Then there is my friend the marigold (*Calendula officinalis*). It has come to our rescue many times. At the birth of one child, I had a bad tear. I began to dab it with cotton wool soaked in calendula lotion. Both doctor and midwife were astonished at the speed of healing. Later on, many a cut and graze were helped to heal cleanly and fast with the help of this beautiful sunny flower.

This is not the place to expand at length on home remedies and home nursing. Some further references are given at the end of this chapter, and there is useful material in some of the other contributions. (See especially Wendy Cook on *Feeding the Family*; and Margret Meyerkort on *Sleeping and Waking,* and on *Thinking About Clothes*.) My aim, is simply to show that here, too, there is an opportunity for a schooling prompted by our children's minor illnesses which can be exceptionally fascinating and rewarding.

Towards An Art Of Healing

As Rudolf Steiner gave new impulses for education, so, too, he helped doctors. He valued scientific medicine, but warned of its limitations and blind spots, of what it would leave out. For the health of medicine itself, he hoped that the science could be deepened, widened and extended so as to grow into an *art* of healing (much as he worked for an art of education). Above all, he was concerned that the sick patient should not be viewed as an object separated from everything else in the universe, but rather as a human spirit finding its way amidst a complex of relationships--relationships with nature, with the body, with the people around. Just as a part of a work of art is incomprehensible except in the context of the whole, so is an illness meaningless in isolation. The same notes have different meanings in different melodies, so the meaning of an illness is also to be grasped in the context of an individual's biography and surroundings. Some illnesses, physical handicaps, chronic and degenerative diseases, seem most "hopeless" to the purely scientific eye. But in certain biographies, such as those of Paul and Dibbs, we can perhaps begin to glimpse a deeper and ultimately meaningful music, conditions of destiny in which there is a great schooling and healing for all concerned, reaching far into the future. If we seek for a greater intimacy with such events, and try to "know our hearts in truth", we may gain confidence that "nothing is impossible for us"—including a growing perception that an art of medicine of the future will come to understand each biography as having its origins in earlier lives, and its continuation in future ones.

The actual practice of medicine directly inspired by Steiner's work is mainly developed in continental Europe, although there are doctors and clinics in several other parts of the world. In such work, the healing possibilities are greatly enriched by artistic and other auxiliary therapies: Painting, eurythmy, sculpture, music, as well as nutrition, massage, baths and external applications of herbal oils. This is, in fact, already a highly developed practice of "holistic medicine". That it is so little known is perhaps because it demands more than a repertoire of methods. It can be merely another set of technologies, a little closer to "nature" perhaps, but just as mechanistic in spirit, unless it is accompanied by inner effort, a schooling of the "eye of the heart", so that doctors, nurses and parents can look more intently for the meaning of illness.

What Paracelsus calls the "feel" and the "touch" which enables us to be "in sympathetic communication with the patient's spirits", means developing an ear for the clash of illness in individual lives, and for its musical resolution in the process of healing. In nursing our children, we may come closer to hearing this "music" than anyone else, and can learn to play an artistic, creative and fruitful part in the therapeutic orchestra. I hope this chapter may encourage mothers and fathers to discover themselves as therapeutic musicians, and to accompany with more perceptiveness the melodies of their children's development—which includes the discords of illness.

9.   A SICK CHILD IN HOSPITAL

Stephanie Westphal

A small boy is lying in an oxygen tent. He is two and a half years old. He is joined by intravenous needle to a glass bottle which feeds him a drug successful in changing the course of advanced pneumonia. His mother sits by his bed, a mixture of horror at the hospital situation and relief that her child is being looked after by people who are experts. But something else works inside her, something stronger than the drug in the bottle and purer than the air in the tent, and more instinctive and perceptive than the combined minds of the dedicated medical team. This is her will for the child to live. Her heart beats for him and her lungs breathe for him. The bond between mother and child is stronger than the bond between child and medical staff, and her determination pours through the child's being. In ordinary daily life she must constantly guide her child so that his lively spirit doesn't overwhelm him, and his family. This task of guidance becomes even more important in times of grave illness. The mother's commitment to the child's life and spirit can combine with the efforts of the medical team, but it must not be *weakened* by the knowledge that she is not an expert in medicine.

This commitment can come to expression in a number of practical ways. There are many things the mother can do which will help her child's recovery enormously. Among the essentials for the young child in hospital are that his mother should not, if possible, leave his side;

she should be with him as much as possible, protecting him and being a home for him in the strange hospital world. She needs to be present both physically and spiritually. The mother can still nurse him regardless of how many trained nurses are about. So long as she behaves quietly, calmly and inconspicuously, without upsetting the hospital routine in any way, she can in fact be a help to usually overworked nursing staff.

A small child, as much as an older person, needs close attention. Small things are important. He needs to be refreshed by propped up pillows, dry nappies, and tangled hair must be combed and smoothed. In place of the orange squash or lemonade drinks, a freshly made bottle of real fruit juice mixed with spring water or fresh vegetable juice, can be brought by a friend or another member of the family. When the child begins to eat, then peeled and grated raw apple is a good start. Other fruit, fresh and raw vegetables such as carrots and celery will supplement the usual hospital diet of toast, powdered egg and jelly. Arnica can be put on flesh bruised by needles, again without fuss so that the mother does not give the impression that she thinks she knows more than the nursing staff, and it is essential that this feeling does not grow in her soul. It must be replaced by the thought that the nursing staff are as concerned as she is for the child's well being, although in a different way.

Well meaning but unthinking visitors can be a disturbing influence. The ill child, whether at home with chicken pox or in hospital with acute asthma, should see only the adults of his or her immediate family, without noisy toys or exaggerated good humour. Naturally if the child has a close bond to some other person, a grandparent or a close friend perhaps, a visit can also be a help. But the next-door neighbours, younger children, odd uncles and aunts with unsuitable gifts in a constant demanding stream can drain from the child the strength he needs, and destroy the equilibrium that has been gained so far. We do not normally notice how much strength is taken up by the act of thinking, and how much effort is needed to respond to pointless or thoughtless questions. These can be very difficult indeed for the young child.

Prayers can be said with the child at night, and the usual bedtime songs can be sung very softly. The mother can draw around the child an atmosphere of peace and serenity, even in a hospital ward where the television is clamouring day and night. She can build around the child a wall of love and devotion, regardless of the chaos in the rest of the room. It is particularly important that her visits and all of her activities should be regular and unhurried. Anything unrhythmic or unexpected is a disturbance and may affect the child's recovery. The mother can keep herself calm and strong, as well as the child, with simple prayers and meditations for the child, and experienced doctors too have no doubt that the effect of these can be very real. One meditation in particular, given by Rudolf Steiner, can be especially helpful. In his words, this meditation is for *Friends on Earth, especially for those in danger*, and it can be adapted for the ill child.[1]

> Spirits ever watchful, Guardians of your souls,
> May your pinions carry
> Our souls' petitioning love
> (my soul's)
> To the human beings on Earth committed to your care
> (substitute child's name)
> That, united with your power
> Our prayer may radiate with help
> (my prayer)
> To the souls (soul) whom our (my) love is seeking.

Another beautiful prayer by Adam Bittleston called *Against Fear* can be a source of strength for the mother.

> May the events that seek me
> Come unto me;
> May I receive them
> With a quiet mind
> Through the Father's ground of peace
> On which we walk.
>
> May the people who seek me
> Come unto me;
> May I receive them
> With an understanding heart
> Through the Christ's stream of love
> In which we live.
>
> May the spirits which seek me
> Come unto me;
> May I receive them
> With a clear soul
> Through the healing Spirit's Light
> By which we see.[2]

10. PLAY IN ILLNESS AND HEALTH

Jean Evans

Laurens van der Post relates the story of a Bushman who had to spend some time in prison away from his people because he had been caught killing a protected species of animal. The Prison Governor could not understand why the Bushman showed such signs of physical and psychological deterioration, for he felt the prisoner was being well cared for under his supervision. In a very short time, he felt, this man would die and so he asked the advice of someone who respected and understood the Bushman. The Governor was then told that this man was in such a sad state because "He could no longer hear the stories of his people on the wind."

This story impressed me deeply, and when I look back to the time, nearly thirty years ago, when one of my children had to go into hospital for a few weeks, I can find an interesting link between the Bushman and this young child. Like the Bushman, he was used to hearing his father's stories each night before he went to sleep—during the day he spent his time taking part in the family life, helping to prepare meals, carrying some of the shopping, digging up the vegetables from the garden and playing imaginative games of "Being the coalman" and asking "Where do you want the coal, Missus?", or of emptying my pantry so that he could "Be the shopman". He was always "Being Someone" in his imagination, and when he quietly listened to a story, his whole being would expand and he would even move physically nearer and nearer to the story-teller. Overnight all this changed: he was admitted to hospital, where even his much loved companion, "Pooh-Bear", was taken from him. We, his parents, were told to go home, a card of visiting times was thrust into our hands—"twenty minutes three times a week and no visits the day of an operation". He entered another world; no-one told him stories; instead he was told to sit in front of a television set. No-one answered his questions about why his parents had left him in such a place, no-one encouraged him to play or talk about his home and family, and so, when we were allowed to visit him for the first time, he was in a desperate state. All he could say was, "Tell me a story—read to me—tell me a story". We tried to comfort him, but he just said "Take me home—take me home": and when, after a few weeks, we took him home, his attitude to us had completely changed. He no longer trusted parents who had left him in such a place and didn't come to help him when he came back from the traumatic experience of an operation. He asked, "Why didn't you come?" and when we told him the Doctors and Nurses had said we weren't allowed to, he said "But you are my *parents*."

These words penetrated deeply into me, and worked in such a way that when all my children were busy at school, I became a Play Therapist in the children's ward of our local hospital, because, although parents are now welcomed both day and night in children's wards, very many are not able to come, or don't want to stay with their children, so we use play first and foremost as a link with home. We use simple "puzzles" of houses where windows and doors open, revealing mother, father, grandmother, children, so that the child can feel free to talk about his own home and family: puzzles where shop-fronts lift out, showing people shopping for bread and cakes, fruit and vegetables; a mother and child buying stamps before posting letters in a pillar box. All these simple everyday home experiences, talked about and played out by the child separated from his home environment, have a calming effect and thus are of therapeutic value to the whole child.

It has been interesting for me to observe that while children at home will so often play at being in hospital, being a nurse, being a doctor, children in hospital always play at being at home (the house-corner in the playroom is used more than any other)—being the mother, father, baby, postman, milkman; and through their home play activity they begin to compensate for their loss and come to terms with their temporary exile. One four-year-old boy so much enjoyed his stay in hospital that he only agreed to go home if he could come back "for his holidays next year"!

A child coming back into the Play Room, after some painful or frightening treatment is very often pale, in tears and visibly shaking, so very gently we take the child over to the water-play corner, where the other children are busy washing the dolls, blowing bubbles or making soapy tea. Sitting the child on our lap, we let him (or her) experience the water flowing over his hands while at the same time talking quietly to him. Gradually the colour comes back into his cheeks; his breathing becomes more even and the trembling subsides until eventually he gives a contented sigh, slides off the lap and joins the other children at play. Although this happens frequently, it always fills me with wonder that water can have such a magical effect. At times, when a group of children are playing with water, the room is filled with a musical hum of contentment.

The importance of play as a necessary ingredient to becoming a whole and well-balanced human being was shown to me recently when a Paediatric Consultant asked me to take a three-year-old boy into the Play Room and observe him for signs of mental retardation, as he had been brought to the Hospital because of severe speech problems. His mother had said he only made strange noises. The first question I asked the mother was, "What does he like playing with at home?" "Only guns" was the answer. I pursued the question, "But what else does he like doing?" "Oh, he loves the telly, especially gangster films, he always watches those", she replied. "I hear you are worried about his speech—do you tell him stories or sing nursery rhymes to him?" "Heavens!" she said, "I haven't time for that sort of thing, I go out to work." "But, if you are worried about his speech, how do you think he is going to learn if you don't have time to talk to him?" "Well, he watches the telly, that ought to learn him to talk." She didn't believe me when I explained that it needed one human being to talk to another human being to learn speech.

While she went to have coffee, he moved to the water play, and when I put on his water play overall, I found he had six guns in holsters round his waist! He played very happily with the other children and then settled down at the table to make plasticine worms; At this moment his mother came back and looking at him in amazement, said: "He never sits down at home, he's always tearing round with his guns, I have never seen him play quietly like that". At the end of the day I realised that the sound he was making "D-D-D-DDDDD" was the sound of machine-gun fire he had heard on television, and that he was not mentally retarded, but his environment had caused his lack of speech development and his inability to concentrate and enjoy creative and simple play. This was remedied by sending him to a play group near his home, where his mother would be welcomed and encouraged to play with him.

A few years ago a group of psychologists chose as their theme for a project, "Signs of Deprivation in Children of under Five in Hospital". They spent some time in the children's wards of our hospital, and their findings were that very few signs of deprivation were observed because of the use made of play and because of the lively interest that was created in the play room which was, for the children "a security base".

This objective assessment shows the value of creative play for all children, and underlines the importance of not only giving children imaginative toys but but giving them and attention. In a word, YOURSELF.

11. THINKING ABOUT CLOTHES

Margret Meyerkort

The human being is born without physical protection. So he begins his earthly path in a most vulnerable condition, dependant on the caring concern of others. In nature we see everywhere that enveloping sheaths are needed so that life can unfold: the seed of the plant requires the warm soil, and the bird's egg needs the shell. So the human being too has to be protected from wind and weather and from the pollution of an industrialised world.

For some time and for varying reasons it has been fashionable to expose young children to a lot of light and air and it has been a policy generally to toughen them up at a very early stage in life. Such a practice forgets that the human being has to build up his own warmth organism largely independent of nature. Directly the child raises himself into the upright posture, he lifts himself above the realm of the mineral, plant and animal and follows his own individual path which is no longer that of the species.

In fact, the human being is above all a creature of warmth. His warmth organism is most finely differentiated in that it continuously balances heat and cold. Thus he maintains a definite temperature in spite of the variations of temperature in his surroundings.

In man we find neither excessive cold nor heat, the former with its contracting, the latter with its dissolving tendency, but a middle region of temperature. It is this balance which the human being needs to be active.

The faculty of balancing the opposing forces of heat and cold is acquired gradually during the first years of the child's life. Moreover the balancing of these two forces is an ongoing process—which has to do with the fact that man's body, soul and spirit remain in a continually varying relationship to one another throughout life. When we are not quite "here", we feel cold, at some other moments burning hot. Man has to re-establish his specifically human warmth at each stage in his life if he is to be a happy and healthy person.

So it is important for parents and educators to establish and refine the warmth organism of the growing child. Mostly it is a question of protection. Dr.W.zur Linden deals with it in his book "*A Child is Born*". In addition I offer the following from my experiences with playgroups and kindergarten children.

It seems almost better to err on the side of overdressing than putting too few clothes on the young child. In England the most treacherous times of the year for health generally are spring and autumn. At these times we tend to think a few warm days in May are already summer and a few days of warmth in October are still summer. Those children who right through all the colder days wear woolly tights and in winter a pair of trousers on top and only one jumper seem to me cheerier than the ones wearing two jumpers but little below. It is the lower half, where our inner "kitchen" is situated which needs extra warmth.

I found that out of doors head, hands, and feet need to be covered and kept warm to prevent forces of warmth from streaming out through these five sensitive points. One just must remember that the child's warmth organism is more delicately balanced than the adult's.

We often see little boys especially running around with partly bare backs and tummies. Young children wearing trousers are unable to keep them up because the waist has not yet formed. It begins to develop around the seventh year. The liver and kidney regions, which need warmth most, will have lost warmth before the children pull up their trousers, that is, if they can do it by themselves. Braces or straps on the trousers are preferable to a firm elastic around the waist which impedes the circulation. The tummy will then be kept warm and the child will be more comfortable in his play. The old-fashioned smock had its uses; not least, in that woollies which were beyond repair could be worn underneath.

Nowadays more and more women are recognising the difference between synthetic and organic fibres and yet obtaining the latter becomes increasingly more difficult. At the end of this book you will find a list of sources supplying children's clothes made of natural materials which can be ordered by mail. This may seem very expensive, but mothers who have tried it found most of the things of such quality, that they were prepared to make do with far fewer items and wash them overnight. The skin is a tender organ, the outer boundary of the body: it excretes and breathes. So it continuously creates and re-creates a relationship between the body and its surroundings. When the functions of the skin are curtailed by the inorganic fibre of the clothing that immediately covers it, even a healthy skin may get irritated, and so may the wearer.

This dilemma of not being able to find the kind of clothes needed can lead to an interesting group activity. Mothers get together and the following can happen: One mother enjoys knitting and knits woollen or cotton vests, pants, socks and tights for her friend's children, A second mother can afford a knitting machine; a third mother has a sewing machine and can make new out of old clothes. An exchange of clothes can also be organised and the precious garments thus passed on. In this way both mother and child benefit and the whole scheme can be fun too.

The colour of the child's clothing plays a part when we consider his age and the need to harmonise his temperament and his character traits. Clothing that is chosen because it is fashionable can be impersonal and therefore educationally unhelpful.

People's characters and instincts find expression in their outer acti-vities and behaviour, including their choice of colour. There lies a chal-lenge for parents and educators to try and understand the growing personality of their child. I remember the days when five-year old choleric Jack was dressed in red, and even when he was not wearing his red jumper he proudly showed me his red socks and red pants. He was quieter and adapted more easily to other children than on days when he wore nothing red.

In accordance with the stages of his incarnation, the young sensitive child is more related to the seven colours of the rainbow (red, orange, yellow, green, light blue, dark blue, violet.) and not yet to the heavier and more material shades of grey, brown, and black. A boy of five who had come to the Kindergarten in earthy shades, grew more open and talkative when he was dressed in blues and yellows. The nightmares of a four year old, after weeks of consultation between mother and teacher were found to have been caused by the teacher's black pinafore dress. So often have I heard both boys and girls exclaim; "Pink is my favourite colour. Just as at the beginning of a day pink is the colour of the sky, so the human soul feels pink at the dawn of life. Sometimes children go further and say to the mother and even to the teacher; "I wish you would wear pink."

I have found that a print on a child's clothing matters, too. In fact, when he wears a plain coloured shirt or dress, he tends to be more harmonious within himself and more concentrated: the eye drinks in, as it were, the one colour and does not have to hop about from one small impression to another. Clothes with prints of words or pictures, let alone prints of caricatures on them, always have the effect of a rude awakening of the defenceless soul to the harshness of adult life.

A growing child's clothes need to be rather on the loose side. The skin as a breathing organism can fulfil its functions better, the movements of the limbs will be freer, more agile and so the child can enjoy his activities more, an important point for any parent.

Lastly, "we do not go into battle unarmed", which means that our clothing should suit the occasion. It was only as an adult that I could articulate for myself one of the reasons why Christmas was so especially wonderful throughout my childhood: it was because my mother wore the same long skirt and blouse year after year only on Christmas Eve and Christmas Day. When later as a Kindergarten teacher I wore a long skirt , how protected the little one felt who was unwell and had my skirt wrapped around him; and when at Whitsuntide at our celebrations I wore a white dress, a child whispered into my ear, "I wish you would always wear white."

All these considerations don't make it easier to choose clothes, but it can be immensely satisfying and rewarding to have arrived at a really suitable choice.

12.   BE YOUR OWN TAILOR!

Roswitha Spence

There is a photo of a little three year old Roswitha sitting in a cot, threading a needle to sew yet another garment for the huge teddy bear sitting next to her!—I have often been asked where did I learn to sew, and my answer could be I was born with scissors in my hand. If my parents couldn't find me, they only had to look in my mother's clothes cupboard, and if a play was to be done at school the corrrect side of the scenery was always *behind* it. Cloth in all its jewel bright colours and textures has always been a source of the most intense joy and inspiration to me, and clothes a preoccupation to the point of embarrassment! So the question comes quite naturally: what is clothing really all about?

In everyday life experience, garments are as common as food and drink, and just as the quality of the meal affects our well-being, so too do the garments we wear, affect not only ourselves, but also the well-being of those around us. And each stage in our development, as well as each different aspect of our lives, need the appropriate clothing.

Physical life begins with the new born babe. Up until the moment of birth, the child was tightly secure in the warmth of the mother's womb, when suddenly all that open space and fresh air becomes a terrifying abandonment. So the babe is wrapped secure and warm in the very first garment. I remember so well as a mother this picture of the first tight wrapping, that in the weeks to follow loosened more and more, and how in the growing child I became aware of how that boundary of wrapping became the boundary of cot and playpen, of the house, the garden, the school; and as the physical boundaries widened and the world grew larger, those "walls" were more and more transformed into authority, as security and outer discipline, gradually taken over by the teenager to become their inner discipline, so that as an adult security can develop as an inner reality. Clothing is a little like that too, in the first place provided from outside by the parents, and very definitely taken over from within by the teenager.

So what is most important in the youngest years? My golden key to this period is "goodness", not only in mood and deed, but in clothing. By good clothes I do not mean stylish and pricey, but healthy and practical. A child reaches half his adult height at two years old—what a lot of growing! So pure wools and cottons to let the skin breathe all it needs, and as often as possible in a knitted texture to allow the maximum unhampered activity of limb. We have never been so energetic in our limbs since our babyhood! And colours? It's not for nothing most baby clothes come in light fresh colours (or did anyway) as the baby's consciousness lives still much in the spiritual world of light and colour, that darkness has as yet no place in it. And as our toddler gains confidence, so too should the clothing gain durability for scuffed knees and everlasting washing. At three years old or there about, a personality is very definitely in front of us, with all the determination that promises fun and games for the parents in years to come. What a challenge to find the right "good clothes"! During this time and onwards, a lot of help can be given the child in finding the right colour to suit the temperament: blue for the melancholic, green for the phlegmatic, yellow for the sanguine and red for the choleric—this as general guide. I was very choleric as a child, and being lucky enough to have very wise parents, my fourth birthday was entirely and completely red! Every single gift on the red table cloth of my birthday table was a brilliant rich red: a brush and comb, wellington boots, raincoat and hat, even my doll had a brand new red dress—I cannot begin to describe the joy, the richness that feast gave me, and still today over forty years later I can remember that birthday as though I am at a banquet of an incredible inner experience.

So then our little one reaches school age and near to the time of the change of teeth, and now the golden key for me is: Goodness transformed into "beauty". Little boys love to look smart "like Daddy". and little girls want pretty ribbons in their hair and many frills all over their dresses, and as for that party: "Oh Mummy, I *must* have a new frock!"

Around this time it is good to be a bit more determined about helping the child to learn to care for their clothes. Care altogether could be in danger of becoming old fashioned, and yet to care for one's possessions not only keeps them fresh and beautiful, but in fact even imbues them with our own personality, giving them character and warmth.

Only compare the bright new shiny surface of silver, with the deep inner glow from years of loving use. I remember once having to give evidence in Court and being fascinated by the lawyer's shoes, they were so old, but oh so individual and expressive, and positively glowed through their polished crinkles, giving such a comforting air of dependability.

But back to our seven to eight year old. Another popular trend at this age are the T-shirts with writing on them, perhaps to encourage their reading abilities; but I have to admit to a sadness here, as not only do the slogans become stale, imprinting their staleness on the subconscious of the child, but our attention is continually drawn to the shirt, instead of the beauty of the developing being of the child himself that shines out of his eyes.

Gentle guidance in a mutual choice of clothing can do much to help a future artistic taste, but the accent is on "gentle" as there must be much give and take. I can remember a very beautiful dress that I had when seven years old, and I knew it was beautiful, but I hated it and literally felt ill when made to wear it—my tantrums must have been a sore trial to my parents! In the early school years, clean and pure colours are still of great value and help to the child, the beauty of colour still a very real link with the spiritual world, but pretty prints and varied textures are also good, with attention to cheerfulness and comfort, so that play can be as free and creative as possible. At nine and again possibly at twelve first inner "shadows" gather, and awareness of self can make a child choose darker shades, and this leads to my third golden key: of transforming "goodness and beauty" into "truth".

Here, in their early teens the male and femaleness of our child begins to manifest physically, bringing with it quite a new inner experience of soul. Individuality begins to be felt, a confrontation with self, and with it comes a new loneliness; and suddenly "Unisex" is all important in their clothes, as though the pain of separation from their previous "oneness" is utterly unbearable. The blue jeans: a new safe uniform crying to the world that all humanity are brothers and equal. A desperate search for truth means to grapple with darkness, so blacks and browns and dull dirty between-shades become a need and a hunger. Then suddenly—how uncertain are our moods in those teen years—

a switch to sharp and brilliant crashing colours: "Look at me, I'm here, I AM." And all that was till now outward show, begins to awaken as inward struggle—that warmth body that we helped to develop with all those baby wools, now burns with an inner fire, and they need no pullovers in the biting cold. Those pretty frills on party frocks that made our seven-year-old so feminine—now it's Dad's shirt that makes her sexy. The more uniform is the outer shell, the more the inner individuality has freedom to develop what is concealed behind it. Our youngsters need so much patience, understanding, tolerance, and above all love, at this time of their struggle to grow; above all in support for their choice of clothing, how else are they to express who they think they are, and find out who they really are going to become. It may all sound confusing and contradictory, but what else are those teen years,—do you remember?

And so at last "I" am 21 years old, "I" am an adult, "I" can do as "I" please and wear what "I" like! But the process continues. However, as an "adult", our lives begin to settle a bit more, falling into three patterns of activity, all needing their own wardrobe: there is our "private" life where battered old pants and slippers emphasise our need for *comfort*; then our "social" life, where our clothing takes on a bloom of *elegance*, providing a wide scope for individual expression. And thirdly there is our life "at work" where very often we are even confronted with a *uniform*. But what really is a uniform? It is a garment very much born out of the practical necessity of the job in hand, in its durability and flexibility according to the task; but just like the teenager, the individuality can either hide behind the uniform, or rise to a higher and more objective individuality—how very vulnerable a nurse would be in her own private clothing, a policeman be ignored, a priest without his robes could never stand within his ritual. These last two in their black—black is a colour that draws us into ourselves and helps us to take hold of our ego, hence the colour for mourners; white on the other hand, as in the nurse's uniform, has more "gentle compassion". The road menders' jerkin a red for warning, and so on. . . how devastating, should they all suddenly decide to exchange their garments without exchanging their tasks!

The world of sport too, has in the last decades developed a whole new world of "uniforms", not only in style, but in the invention of quite new fabrics—rubber for water sports, quilting for snow sports, for example—all made to protect the body from outer conditions, and free the body's own inner striving to achieve excellence. It is however a whole world directed to the inner/outer life of the physical body, and very much a picture of the western world of today. What will the picture look like in centuries to come, when the inner/outer needs of the spiritual world seeks to be manifest in our "garments"?

It is very obvious to see that clothing is not just there for the wearer's sake, it really is like the visible skin of my choice: "I" need to not only protect myself from wind and weather, but "I" want to show myself to the world as I want the world to see me, in this or that colour mood. And when "you" see me in blue, it's different from when "you" see me in red, and "we" both act accordingly, without being in any way conscious of it. The same goes for the cared or uncared for "look", and so we have a powerful weapon in our hands in how to influence our fellow humans.

So how can we in adult life, through the continuing process of development into old age, strike a balance between who we are and what the world needs of us, and make this visible in our clothing? Strangely enough this question is easier than you would at first expect, because if you are able to enter fully into your tasks, you take "your-self" with you and become "one" with it. I remember as a young mother how I loved to wear light young colours in crisp cool cottons to run and play with my children in the garden, and in winter by the fire, in my soft warm woollens, the children would love to snuggle up on my skirt and lap for endless stories, secure in the "feel" of Mummy as well as voice and mood. I remember as a child, one of my teachers always wearing drab tans, browns, and greys and being filled with a mood of heavy sadness every time I thought of her. Another time the whole lesson was one of breathless suspense, because the teacher had a hole in his jacket pocket and the keys were hanging out just to the point of falling—but they didn't. . . We did not learn much that lesson! Another teacher, who had quick lively movements, wore simple clean colours in well fitted yet simple styles, and my wellbeing expanded in her presence to a deep sense of love and joy.

If we find ourselves in a simple homely task, or if we stand in a prominent place in the public eye, each situation has a meeting of inner and outer quality that can be silently expressed in our clothing. And as we grow maturer and develop in our inner awareness, so too in the outer world of taste and style awareness is changing and developing, perhaps in this century faster than ever before, so that more and more people are finding their own free style, and "fashion", as decreed by the designers, limited to an even smaller circle.

The world of fashion is altogether a crumbling one, if I am allowed to be that sweeping! But looking through the whole historical evolving of dress, a picture emerges utterly in tune with the whole evolving of consciousness, and just as we are now in the time of individuality struggling for individual freedom, so too do we have need to express that individuality in our garments;—the garments as visible skin of who we are.

Perhaps that is very much the conscious or unconscious theme for those young and middle years of adult life. Health and strength can still be taken for granted, and the world is there to be transformed through thought, love and deed. Then, perhaps during the early or late forties, and for some much later, a new feature enters the dictates of our clothing, namely bodily health. For one it might be a problem with their feet, so goodbye to all those dainty stylish shoes, another might have a very real weight problem, and garments must again hang from the shoulders, as they did in childhood before the waist was formed. The most usual is an ever-increasing sensitivity to temperature that in old age can become a very real problem. Our warmth body expresses itself directly in our sense of well being, and the older we get the more we have to take care of it, so as to be able to continue with those tasks the world asks us to do.

Throughout life, clothing is something that can give, or rob us of, confidence. What a simple tool to make sure that it *gives* confidence to us, as well as to those around us, in its colour to create the right mood, in its texture to give it the right feel, and in its cut and style to allow us freedom in movement and deed. And if the garment, that is to express the "you" truly, is not available in the shops, why not then try to create and sew it for yourself? I promise you, it is a lot of fun!

Sewing is not so much an ability of the hands, as an attitude of mind! We tell ourselves all sorts of extraordinary things of what we can or cannot do, until we have so convinced ourselves that it seems to be true; but this process can also be reversed, and if we are prepared to have some gloriously catastrophic disasters, only progress can ensue. I still have some spectacular disasters every now and then, but have learned to quite enjoy them, as each time a new surprise of self discovery is about to be revealed to me. (Success doesn't seem to have that element attached to it!) Perhaps the first ingredient is interest and joy in the adventure of the process, rather than an economic need for the result. Then try to have a good chunk of uninterrupted time at fairly regular intervals—short spasmodic sessions can prove very discouraging—if you are lucky enough to have a space where you can just shut the door you are already well on the way to success. The next most important detail is to find the tools, especially needles and scissors which feel "right" in your hand, everybody has an individual way of using their hands, and just as a fountain pen becomes "yours" so too do scissors. They should have the weight you like, ease of opening, without falling apart, should cut at first closing and glide happily snipping across the table—in fact your scissors should feel like an extension of your own hand, just like the needle too, in its length and thickness in relation to the particular cloth. Sewing machines are very varied in character and abilities; the most important thing is to feel that you are its master, and it is there to serve *you*! Often the simpler the machine, the easier it is to understand, and work. In fact for years I have taught sewing on the old-fashioned treadles, they were cheapest at the time of purchase, and are so simple to understand and maintain. They are also not so sensitive as to who uses them and are ideal for learning on—they just go on for ever!

Ironing is another great ingredient towards encouragement and success: each time a series of seams have been completed, iron them well, before new seams go across them, and if the bulk or particular corner is awkward, pin the required area to the ironing board so that it cannot slip away. If a damp cloth is needed, the best level of moisture is achieved by wetting and squeezing out only half the cloth, and then rolling the wet half into the dry half and squeezing very tightly again. The steam iron is also possible, but never gives such a good finish, and tends to give the cloth a shiny look. The constant ironing of seams and sewing away of thread ends, keeps the cloth fresh, and gives the whole work a clean feeling.

Sewing a garment is a creative activity where you are taking a two dimensional substance and transforming it into something to envelop a three dimensional body, and it can help enormously towards your whole ability and understanding, if you awaken to what you are becoming involved in, becoming aware of what part of the body you are dealing with at each particular task; this inside sleeve is curved—why? My elbow can only move my lower arm forward, so the back of my sleeve needs more cloth than the front—my shoulder seam is curved because my back is more convex and shoulder front more concave. . . and so forth; and each one of us has individual nuances at each point. If I want to be comfortable and free in my new outfit, then these sort of details have to be attended to.

Finally the finishing off—only the wearer knows what the garment looks like on the inside, the surface that touches the body; if you are making something for a friend, you love and care for the inside is more important than the outside, it is the intimate unseen gesture that reaches to a deeper knowing, a confirmation of a relationship and respect. We can respect our own bodies as well as our workmanship, to take pride in a neat and tidy finish for its own sake. Then the garment can become an outer union of those three golden keys: "goodness, beauty and truth", to help us in the wearing of them, to strive towards living "truth, beauty and goodness" from our innermost being.

There is a saying that "clothes maketh the man". Shakespeare in many of his plays has edged comments about the subject, especially in "Cymbeline" when Cloten says: ". . . knowest me not by my clothes?" Guiderius: "No, nor thy tailor. . . which as it seems, make thee." For me this is a picture of what we are struggling away from, into a transition period of trial and error, from an anonymous fashion to a discovering of who I am becoming, towards a new freedom where I can know myself and know the world.

When confronted by the task of designing the colours and costumes for a stage play, my one golden rule is, that everything created must be there as a framework that reveals and enhances the true inner quality and development of the story, and each individual soul journey within that story. In a similar way our clothes and home environment can be a framework for our own individuality, growth and development, so that we do not become smothered and uniform in fashion but, by finding our own unique "style", we become confident, joyous and free.

APPENDIX I

REFERENCES

I. PARENT'S WAYS

1. *The Meaning of Being a Mother* Margli Matthews

    For more information about *Ariadne* see my biographical note.

2. For example: *Androgyny, Towards a New Theory of Sexuality*, June Singer, Routledge & Kegan Paul, London 1977; *Cosmic Memory: Atlantis and Lemuria*, Rudolf Steiner, Steinerbooks, New York, 1976; *Myth Religion and Mother-Right*, J.J. Bachofen, Princeton University Press, Princeton, 1967; *The Greek Myths*, Vol. 1 & 2, Robert Graves, Penguin Books, 1977 *The Origins and History of Consciousness*, Erich Neuman, Princeton University Press, Princeton, 1973; *The Spirit of the Valley: Androgyny and Chinese Thought*, Sukie Colegrave, Virago, London, 1979: *Mothers and Amazons, The First Feminine History of Culture*, Helen Diner Anchor Press, N.Y., 1973.

3. Since writing this Betty Friedan's new book *The Second Stage*, (Michael Joseph, London, 1982) has been published and I recommend it to all who are interested in a more thorough consideration of the Women's Movement today. She looks at its achievements, its weaknesses, its future possibilities and, if it is to continue to be a significant force for social renewal, its responsibilities. Basically, Betty Friedan calls for the Movement to give new attention to family life and the choice to have children. She calls for women and men to join together, free now of old limits and roles, to work for a new mobility and wholeness of soul for themselves and for society and in the face of the increasing abstraction, materialization and the forces of reaction and fear that would enslave us in old ways and values. She emphasizes the importance of resisting *either/or* choices—for example, that we are either single and independent or married and dependent, that we either have a career or a child, that we either have work or a family.

4. For a fuller picture of how the feminine and masculine polarity works in the physical, psychological and spirit levels of a human being see *The Anthroposophical Review* on "Man and Woman", Vol.2, No.1, Winter 1980 and *Phases: Crisis and and Development in the Individual*, Bernard Lievegoed, Rudolf Steiner Press, London, 1979. For more elaboration of karma and reincarnation in relation to man and woman see: *The Manifestations of Karma*, Lecture 1 Rudolf Steiner, Rudolf Steiner Press, London, 1968 and *Theosophy of the Rosicrucians*, Lecture V, Rudolf Steiner, Rudolf Steiner Press, London, 1981.

5. See, *Our Bodies Ourselves*, The Boston Women's Health Book Collective, British Edition 1978 by Angela Philips and Jill Rakusen, Penguin.

6. For example, *The Wise Wound: Menstruation and Everywoman*, Penelope Shuttle and Peter Redgrove, Victor Gollancz Ltd, 1978.

7. *Embryology and World Evolution*, Dr Karl König, Reprinted from The British Ho-eopathic Journal, Vol. LV111: No.1. Jan 1968; No.2. April 1968; No.3, July 1968; No.4, Oct. 1968; Vol.LV111: No.1, Jan 1969; No.2, April 1969.

8. See, *The Natural Birth Control Book,* ed. Art Rosenblum, Aquarian Research Foundation, Pa. U.S.A. 1976.

9. Two places, out of many,where Rudolf Steiner speaks about heart thinking are: *Ancient Myths, Their Meaning and Connection with Evolution*, Steiner Book Centre, Inc., Canada, 1978, especially Lecture VI and *Results of Spiritual Investigation*, Multimedia Publications, 1973, especially Lecture 4.

10. *Loose Change, The Women of the Sixties*, Sara Davidson, Doubleday & Co., Inc., New York, 1977.

11. For different examples of this same point see *The Second Stage,*, by Betty Friedan.

2. *The Journey of a Mother* : Gudrun Davy

1. R. Steiner, *The Study of Man*, Rudolf Steiner Press, London

2. See Martin Large, *Who's Bringing Them Up? Television and Child Development*, Hawthorn Press, 1980

3. For adult phases of development see B. Lievegoed, *Phases*, Steiner Press, London or G. Sheeby, *Passages*, Bantam N.Y.

4. R. Steiner, *Introduction to Goethe's Scientific Writings*, Chapter 6 (American Edition, *Goethe the Scientist*—at present out of print)

5. R. Steiner, *The Eightfold Path*, referred to in *Guidance in Esoteric Training, Knowledge of the Higher Worlds, The Gospel of St. Luke*. Also Adam Bittleston; *Speech in the Family, The Golden Blade*, 1973, all published by Rudolf Steiner Press.

6. Mercury Vapour from broken puzzle toys is exceedingly noxious when inhaled—such toys should therefore be avoided for young children.

7. R. Steiner, *The Spiritual Foundation of Morality*, Steiner Book Centre North Vancouver, Canada.

5. *Coping Alone as the Father* : Stephen Briault

Rudolf Steiner, The Kingdom of Childhood, Rudolf Steiner Press, London, 1964
Rudolf Steiner, At the Gates of Spiritual Science, R. S. P. London, 1970
Rudolf Steiner, Occult Science—Lecture 6, An Outline R.S.P. London, 1972
Rudolf Steiner, Curative Education, R.S.P. London 1972, Lecture 2

7. *Family Relationships : Bearing and Being* : Signe Schaefer

1. Betty Friedan, *"The Second Stage"*, Abacus, 1983, p. 100

2. Rudolf Steiner, *"Love and its Meaning in the World"*, Rudolf Steiner Press, London, 1972, p. 16

3. Lee Sturgeon Day, *"Reflections on Marriage"*. Ariadne Newsletter, No. 14, 1982, Forest Row, England.

II. FAMILY WAYS

2. *Sleeping and Waking* : Margret Meyerkort

1. Dr W. zur Linden, *A Child is Born*, Rudolf Steiner Press

3. *Family Mealtimes* : Bons Voors

1. Michael Jones, *Prayers & Graces*, Floris Books, Edinburgh

5. *Why Festivals*: John Davy

Easter, Another Birth : Caz Iveson
Quotes from T.S. Eliot's *Journey of the Magi*, and *Boy with a Cart* by Christopher Fry

Advent as a Preparation for Christmas : Elizabeth Sheen

1) "Over Stars is Mary Wandering" in *The Key of the Kingdom*, E. Gmeyner and J. Russell, Rudolf Steiner Press London, 1968

2) R. Steiner, *Signs and Symbols of the Christmas Festival*, Anthroposophic Press New York, 1969

3) Selma Lagerlöf, *Christ Legends*, Floris Books

Laura Ingalls Eilder, *Little House in the Big Woods*, Penguin Alison Uttley,

Alison Uttley, *Little Grey Rabbit's Christmas,* Collins.

Alison Uttley, *The Country Child*, Penguin

Laurie Lee, *As I walked out one Summer Morning*, Penguin

III. CHILDREN'S WAYS

1. *The Temperaments* : Ann Druitt

Rudolf Steiner, *The Four Temperaments*, Rudolf Steiner Press, London

4. *A Key to the Images in Fairy Tales* : Almut Bockemühl

1. R. Steiner, *Theosophy*, Rudolf Steiner Press, London

2. R.Steiner, *A Way to Self Knowledge*, R.S.P. London

3. Padraic Colum, *The King of Ireland's Son*, Floris Books

5. *The Hidden Treasure* in *Fairy Tales* Margret Meyerkort

1. J. Jacobs, *English Fairy Tales*, Dover

2. *Grimms Fairy Tales,* Victor Gollancz

7. *Feeding the Family* : Wendy Cook

Dr. R. Hauschka, *Nutrition*

R. Steiner, *Agriculture*, Rudolf Steiner Press

R. Steiner, *The Effects of Spiritual Development* Rudolf Steiner Press

Dr. zur Linden, *A Child is Born*, Rudolf Steiner Press

Eugen Kolisko, *Nutrition Nos 1–2*, Kolisko Archive Publications, 62 Frederica Road, Bournemouth BH9 2NA

9. *A Sick Child in Hospital* : Stephanie Westphal

1. R. Steiner, *Verses and Meditations*, R.S.P. London

2. A. Bittleston *Meditative Prayers for Today*, Floris Books, Edinburgh

APPENDIX II

RUDOLF STEINER

John Davy

In 1919, in a Germany shattered by the first world war, a Stuttgart factory manager asked Rudolf Steiner to help inaugurate a new school for the children of his work people. It took root in those difficult times, and has proved to be a plant of wonderful vigour. "Waldorf schools" are now sprouting all over the world, and new seeds germinate every year.

Steiner's work, though, was not confined to education. He was born in Austria in 1861, grew up in small villages where his father was station-master, attended the Technical High School in Vienna, made a living as a tutor, was called to Weimar to edit Goethe's scientific works, went on to Berlin to run an avant-garde magazine and teach at a Trade Union school. But all his early life was a search for freedom.

In 1897, he published a book "The Philosophy of Freedom" and sent a copy to a Viennese friend, Rosa Mayreder, one of the greatest pioneers of women's liberation of that time. He hoped with all his heart that she of all his contemporaries would understand it, although his search for freedom was very distinct from hers. Since childhood, his inner life had extended into far-reaching spiritual experiences. They included perceptions of gathering crises, both inner and outer, for the new century. But he was surrounded by an uncomprehending culture. The church was concerned with the defence of faith; science with the manipulation of matter. Neither saw what Steiner was describing, at first only to himself, as the "battle for the human soul".

Today, we have a word for what he meant: Alienation—the experience as separation from oneself, from nature, from one another, from meaningful work. In his book, Steiner recognises alienation as a phase of the human condition, but not the whole of it, as a meeting with limitation in oneself, not in the universe, to be transcended through one's own activity. But freedom to speak of his own deeper insights he found at first only among the theosophists, one of the first Western groups to rediscover Eastern wisdom and teachings.

The last thing Steiner wanted, though, was to be a "spiritual teacher". "I don't want to be believed", he said, "I want to be *understood*". By the outbreak of the first world war, he had parted company with the theosophists, and began to work freely with friends and associates, notably artists seeking new ways in drama, speech, dance, painting, architecture. The anthroposophical movement was taking shape.

Steiner disliked definitions as much as doctrines, and remarked of the word "anthroposophy" that he would have preferred a different word each day. But he did once describe what he meant by it, namely "awareness of one's humanity". The challenge in this definition is that Steiner regarded our awareness and our humanity as very far from complete. We are not nouns, finished objects, but more like verbs. We are emerging, in development—but our development depends very much on us. This is, in fact, our path to freedom. As human beings, we are still cosmically speaking, beginners. Beginners, but not incompetent to help ourselves.

Steiner's own competence must have seemed phenomenal to his contemporaries, and may easily seem unbelievable to us. After the first world war, Steiner was putting forward radical new concepts for social, political and economic reform, and was lecturing to huge audiences throughout Germany. The first Waldorf school was founded. Others were beginning. Special schools for handicapped children were being started. Doctors, farmers, theologians, architects, were asking Steiner for help in renewing their work. Steiner designed and supervised the building of the first Goetheanum, a huge double-domed structure with auditorium and stage, all in wood, on a hill near Basle, Switzerland. An arsonist set fire to it in 1922, and it burned down. Steiner began the design for a new building, this time in concrete, which still stands. He died in 1925, aged 64, unexpectedly early, surrounded by many beginnings. His last years were like a scattering of seeds which have continued to germinate throughout this century, and look to be viable and intensely relevant well on into the next.

The various activities of the anthroposophical movement which are now to be found all over the world, are documented elsewhere. This brief survey is simpy to provide a backdrop for the search for a renewal of family life with which this book in concerned.

People who become interested in Steiner's work quite quickly get used to some far-reaching thoughts. Steiner has a high opinion of what he called "the healthy human intelligence". When people objected to his reports of his own "spiritual research" on the grounds that he was talking about things they hadn't experienced so that they had either to

believe him or ignore him, he responded briskly: we can all think
through such reports, and decide for ourselves whether they are somehow
intelligible. We don't refuse to hear about Tibet from people who have
been there, because we haven't. And in any case, he says, we did know
what he was talking about before we were born, and will know again
after death; indeed we still know a good deal intuitively, but not always
quite consciously.

Perhaps this accounts for the fact that for people who do find Steiner
intelligible some of the time, and interesting most of the time, the
experience is not like believing but more like remembering. So the contributors to this book have felt no need to apologise for exploring quite
familiar experiences against what will sometimes seem a rather extraordinary background.

When Steiner gave a first brief training course to the first teachers of
the first Waldorf school, he spoke to them most earnestly of the vital
necessity for a "new mood" in the classroom, a mood which he described as a sense for "unborness". We can see what he was asking for if
we recognise the force of the familiar assumption that children are products of nature and nurture, determined genetically at conception,
shaped thereafter by their environment. Such an outlook has in any case
no room for a free human spirit. But Steiner was concerned that
teachers should lay aside their conventional spectacles and look afresh
at the mysteries of birth and childhood. Then they might perceive in
their children, and indeed in themselves, not only a physical birth, but a
series of births, new capacities unfolding as a plant unfolds leaves,
flowers, then fruits. Where do these come from? No-one has discovered
thoughts by dissecting brains. So we cannot expect to find in the physical world the origins of the unpredicted and unpredictable adult who
eventually emerges from childhood. One day it will seem very queer
that people assumed that enough knowledge about genes and
environment would explain their friends and their children—much
queerer than the idea that their origins lie before birth.

Imagine, said Steiner to the Waldorf teachers, that you are receiving
your children from a heavenly schooling, a preparation for life far more
profound than anything you can expect to organise in your classrooms.
Their spiritual guardians will accompany them as they grow up. When
you enter your classroom, you are going to meet them as well as the
children. They are concerned—and will help you, if you ask them.

If teachers need a "new mood" like this and a sense for their childrens' spiritual guardians, then surely so do mothers. The idea of "unborness" makes each day a birthday. Even crises can become birth

moments, rites of passage: observant mothers will often notice how their children grow, mature, often resolve some particular difficulties, as they pass through childhood illnesses, mumps, chicken pox, measles. And they will notice how help can come, inwardly as outwardly, seldom expected, but always timely.

Then there is the whole matter of being a woman and a mother. One of the most fundamental unfreedoms of all is to be male or female. But imagine, says Steiner, that you have in fact chosen a female embodiment for this lifetime and may choose to be male in another. The human spirit itself is beyond gender, but gender brings particular possibilities as well as particular limitations. Perhaps we are more aware of this now. The very notion that an individual may seek to develop both masculine and feminine qualities of character, whatever his or her gender, implies the existence of an essential human being who transcends the body it inhabits.

Unbornness implies that we can go on being born all our lives (and perhaps death itself will prove to be another kind of birth). In overcoming disinterest, habit, discouragement, seeing what is familiar afresh, opening our hearts to change, surprising one another, we can reach into those mysteries of what we can become, born a little more, and win small victories in the battle for the soul.

What is now sought in various modern psychologies of human potential and growth was richly described and explored by Steiner at the beginning of this century, in a way which is both practical and profound. In so doing, he was extending the idea of evolution, which he recognised as one of the nineteenth century's most significant contributions to our culture, liberating it from the materialistic framework in which it is caught by Darwin or Marx. So he included in evolution the human soul and spirit as well as all the inwardness of nature (the earth seen not merely as assemblage of matter, but as a community of beings).

So he sought to show a path, a way of living which can lead "the spiritual in the human being to the spirit in the universe". It is a path to be discovered, not by withdrawing into special settings or practices, but in life as it is: "ordinary life" lived so that we begin to awaken to its extraordinariness. It is in this spirit that the contributors to this book venture to share something of their experiences with each other.

APPENDIX III

CONTRIBUTORS

Gudrun Davy, daughter of Dr Wilhelm zur Linden who wrote *"A Child is Born"*, has four children. She has run study groups and workshops for young parents connected with Emerson College and is now training in art therapy.

Bons Voors-Schokking, studied theology in Amsterdam and is taking a doctorate whilst bringing up three children.

Margli Matthews, graduated in English from Berkeley, U.S.A., went to Emerson and has brought up two children. For ten years she has been involved with *Ariadne,* an international women's working group which works out of the spiritual perspective offered by Anthroposophy on questions of women's consciousness.
  There are now Ariadne groups in Detroit, U.S.A. and Holland as well as in England. They have particularly concerned themselves with building an understanding of the working of the feminine and masculine polarity within individuals, throughout the evolution of consciousness and in society today. They have addressed questions of male-female, inner balance, sexuality, conception and contraception, relationships, rhythm, fear and stress, family life and human development. Through the *Ariadne Newsletter* that they edit, through workshops, seminars, lectures and evening courses on these themes they have tried to encourage people to meet together and explore the nature and meaning of their lives, to discover their creative resources and to renew the art of living. They have aimed to foster greater balance within individuals and in society at large.
  She is involved in adult education, counselling and biography work and works at Emerson College.

Welmoed Torenstra, is married with two children. She was a Social Worker and is a member of the Ariadne Group in Holland.

Trudy Derwig, teaches at Michael Hall School, has worked as a secretary, and is bringing up her family. She is interested in counselling.

Stephen Briault, graduated in English from Cambridge and has worked in curative communities within Camphill and now works at the Centre for Social Development at Emerson College.

Barbara/Sim, graduated in the U.S.A. went to Emerson and is raising a family of three with *Robert Sim*, who took his doctorate in the U.S.A. and now teaches at *Übalingen* Waldorf School in West Germany.

Signe Schaefer, lives near Detroit with her husband Chris and two teenage children. She teaches at the Waldorf Institute and at the Centre for Life Studies and was a founder member of Ariadne.

Ernestine Ingenhousz, Dutch, with three grown-up daughters has worked at the Tavistock Institute of Human Relations in London, at *Family Focus* in Chicago, as a social worker and now works in a Waldorf School in the U.S.A.

Joy Mansfield, graduated in English, taught gymnastics and brought up a family of three. She now helps edit the *Anthroposophical Review*.

John Davy, is the Principal of Emerson College. Formerly a zoologist and later science editor for *The Observer*, he finds the birth and death of living things, and especially of human beings, the most mysterious and wondrous phenomena we know.

Margret Meyerkort, trained as a nurse, specialising in children's nursing, She taught Kindergarten at Wynstones School, Gloucestershire, from 1953-1980 and in 1978 founded the first English speaking Waldorf Kindergarten training course there. She lectures widely on Kindergarten work.

Caz Iveson, trained in art and as a teacher, worked in a Camphill curative home and is now bringing up her family of four children.

Marieke Anschutz-Schoorel, Dutch, has four children, was a teacher and is involved in a group working with festivals.

Hannelie Glasl-ten Siethoff, trained in art and physiotherapy and has three teenage children. She is concerned with festivals and runs a travelling marionette theatre with her husband.

Elizabeth Sheen, worked in the arts and drama, has a family of four and hopes to study at Emerson as a mature student.

Almut Bochemühl, lives in Switzerland with her husband and four children. She writes and lectures on fairy tales and literature.

Ann Druitt, was born in the West of England and now lives in Forest Row, Sussex, pursuing her fourth career—as a housewife and mother of four young children. Having started out in life as a personal secretary, she spent four years as a studio manager with the BBC, then decided to go to Art College and study pottery. There followed a period of three years teaching pottery at Emerson College before she married Roger Druitt, who is a priest in The Christian Community.

Cecil Harwood, who died in 1975, was a founder of the first Steiner school in England, Michael Hall. He was a poet, writer, an inspiring teacher, and a profound guide to all the mysteries of childhood.

Joan Marcus, has taught in Waldorf Schools for many years and now teaches Kindergarten at Elmfield School after bringing up her family of four.

Jean Evans, has worked for nearly eighteen years as a play therapist in a hospital near Cardiff and lectures on play questions. She has three children.

Wendy Cook, graduated in illustration and theatre design, sends her two daughters to Michael Hall School and is concerned with nutrition.

Stephanie Westphal, is from New York, has three young children and does Kindergarten work.

Roswitha Spence, worked in theatre as a cutter in the wardrobe department. Now, after raising a family, she teaches colour and form in connection with stage work at Emerson.

Kevin McCarthy, teaches English at a Gloucestershire Secondary School with his wife and will take the Wynstones Waldorf teacher training course.

APPENDIX IV

BIBLIOGRAPHY

E. Frommer   *Journey through Childhood into the Adult World,* 1969, Pergamon Press.

A. C. Harwood   *The Way of a Child,* R. Steiner Press, London.

K. Koenig   *The First Three Years,* Anthroposophical Press, New York.

K. Koenig   *Brothers and Sisters,* Antroposophical Press, New York.

B.C.J. Lievegoed   *Phases, Crises and Developments in the Individual,* R. Steiner Press, London.

G. Sheeby   *Passages,* Bantam, New York.

R. Steiner   *The Four Temperaments,* R. Steiner Press, London.

R. Steiner   *The Education of the Child,* R. Steiner Press, London.

R. Steiner   *A Modern Art of Education,* R. Steiner Press, London.

M. Strauss   *Understanding Children's Drawings,* Steiner Press, London.

D. Turner   *Parenting—A Path through Childhood,* Floris Books, Edinburgh.

CHRISTIANITY AND RELIGION

A. Bittleston   *Meditative Prayers for Today,* Floris Books, Edinburgh

F. Bock   *The Three Years* (The Life of Christ between Baptism and Ascension), Floris Books, Edinburgh.

E. Capel   *The Reappearing of Christ,* Floris Books, Edinburgh.

F. Rittelmeyer   *Meditation (Guidance of the inner life)* Floris Books, Edinburgh

EDUCATION

F. Carlgren   *Education Towards Freedom,* Lanthorn Press, Peredur East Grinstead

L. F. Edmunds   *Rudolf Steiner Education, The Waldorf Schools,* R. Steiner Press, London

A. C. Harwood   *The Recovery of Man in Childhood,* R. Steiner Press, London

A.E. McAllen   *Teaching Children to Write,* R. Steiner Press, London

A. E. McAllen	*The Extra Lesson* (reading and writing problems) Anthroposophical Press, U.S.A.
A. E. McAllen	*Sleep—an unobserved Element in Education, 1982*
R. Steiner	*Free Education,* Lanthorn Press
M. Spock	*Teaching as a Lively Art,* R. Steiner Press, London
E. Gabert	*Punishment & Self Education in the Education of the Child,* Steiner School Schools Fellowship Publication, Michael Hall, Forest Row.
R. Wilkinson	*Questions and Answers on Steiner Education,* R. Steiner Press, London
R. Steiner	*Overcoming Nervousness,* R. Steiner Press, London

FESTIVALS

F. Benesch	*Easter,* Floris Books, Edinburgh
F. Benesch	*Whitsun,* Floris Books, Edinburgh
F. Benesch	*Ascension,* Floris Books, Edinburgh
E. F. Capel	*The Christian Year,* Floris Books, Edinburgh
D. Carey and J. Large	*Festivals, Family and Food,* Hawthorn Press, Stroud, 1982
A. C. Harwood	*Christmas Plays from Oberüfer,* R. Steiner Press, London
S. Lagerlöf	*Christ Legends and other Stories* (Christmas stories) Floris Books, Edinburgh
M. Meyerkort	*Kindergarten Booklets on the Seasons,* Wynstones School, Whaddon, Glos. *Spring, Summer, Autumn, Winter, Spindrift, Gateway;* New Editions with Music, August 1983
S. Schaefer	*Celebrating Easter* *Celebrating Christmas* *Celebrating Michaelmas* Booklets issued by the Waldorf Institute of Mercy College, 23399 Evergreen Road, Southfield, Michigan 48075
G. Sehlin	*Mary's Little Donkey* (Christmas stories) Floris Books, Edinburgh
R. Steiner	*Festivals and their Meaning,* 29 lectures, R. Steiner Press, London

HEALTH AND MEDICINE

V.Bott W. Buhler	*Anthroposophical Medicine, An Extension of the Art of Healing,* R. Steiner Living with your Body,
W. Buhler	*Living with your Body,* R. Steiner Press, London
M. Crawford	*Birth and the Human Soul,* in The Golden Blade 1983, R. Steiner Press, London
K. Köenig	*Illnesses of our Time,* Kolisko Archive Publications, Bournemouth
Dr. C. H. Sharma	*A Manual of Homoepathy and Natural Medicine,* Turnstone Books, London 1975
O. Wolf	*Anthroposophical Orientated Medicine and its Remedies,* Weleda A.G. Arlesheim, Switzerland, 1977
W. zur Lindon	*A Child is Born,* R. Steiner Press, London

310

NUTRITION

M.Jones	*Prayer and Graces,* Floris Books, Edinburgh
H. Koepf, Petterson Schaumann	*Bio-Dynamic Agriculture,* Anthroposophoc Press, New York,1977
R. Steiner	*Agriculture,* R. Steiner Press 1977
G. Schmidt	*The Dynamics of Nutrition,* R. Steiner Press, London

PLAYS, TOYS, GAMES, POEMS AND MUSIC

G. Bittleston	*Healing Art of Glove Puppetry,* Floris Books, Edinburgh
H. Britz-Crecelius	*Children at Play, Preparation for Life,* Floris Books, Edinburgh
F. Jaffke	*Making Soft Toys,* Floris Books, Edinburgh
J. Jacobs	*English Fairy Tales,*The Bodley Head, London
M. Large	*Who's Bringing Them Up? Television and Child Development,* 1980,Hawthorn Press, Stroud
M. Strauss	*Understanding Children's Drawings,* R. Steiner Press, London
W. Buhler	*Living with your Body,* R. Steiner Press, London
Evans Brothers Ltd., London	*Book of 1000 Poems*
Mercury Press, 241 Hungry Hollow Rd, Spring Valley, USA	*Fingerplays*
E. Poulson, Dover Public. Inc. New York	*Fingerplays*
Victor Gollancz, London	*Grimm's Fairy Tales*
Grimm	*Cinderella, a Picture Book for Children,* Steiner Press, London. Pictures by R. Elsoisser
Grimm	*Six Swans Picture Books,* Steiner Press, London. Pictures by A. Koconda-Breus
M. von Heider	*And then Take Hands,* Dawn Leigh Books, Celestial U.S.A.
Oxford University Press	*Oxford Dictionary of Nursery Rhymes*
Waldorf School, Toronto, Canada	*Pentatonic Songbook*
Waldorf School, Toronto, Canada	*Shepherd Songbook*
Glencraig Craigavad, Holywood North Ireland, BTL3 GDB	*Therapeutic Games*

WOMEN'S QUESTIONS

The *Anthroposophical Review* on *"Man and Woman"* Vol 2. No 1, Winter 1980

Bachofen, J.J.	*Myth, Religion and Mother Right*
Boston Woman	*Our Bodies Ourselves,* The Boston Women's Health Book Collective, British Edition 1978 by Angela Philips and Jill Rakusen, Penguin
Boston Woman	*Ourselves and our Children.* The Boston Women's Health Book Collective, 1978
Claremont de Castillego, 1.	*Knowing Woman, A Feminine Psychology* Harper Colophon Books N.Y. 1974
Colegrave, Sukie	*The Spirit of the Valley,* Virago, 1979
Crawford, Mary	*Birth and the Human Soul,* in Golden Blade 1983 R. Steiner Press, London
Diner, Helen	*Mothers and Amazons, The First Feminine History of Culture,* Anchor Press, 1973
Drake, Stanley	*The Path to Birth,* Floris Books, 1979, Edinburgh
Friedan, Betty	*The Second Stage,* Abacus 1982
Graves, Robert	*The Greek Myths,* Vol. 1 & 2 Penguin
Harding, Esther	*The Way of All Women, A Psychological Interpretation,* Rider & Co. London 1975
Howard, Alan	*Sex in the Light of Reincarnation and Freedom,* St. Georges Publications 1980
Koenig, Dr. Karl	*Embryology and World Evolution,* The British Homeopathic Journal No 1-4, 1968
Lievegoed B.	*Phases,* Rudolf Steiner Press, London 1979
Rosenblum, Art.ed.	*The Natural Birth Control Book,* Aquarian Research Foundation, 1976
Shuttle, P and Redgrove, P.	*The Wise Wound: Menstruation and Everywoman,* Victor Gollancz Ltd, 1978
Singer, J.	*Androgyny,* Routledge & Kegan Paul, 1977
Steiner, R.	*Cosmic Memory,* Atlantis and Lemuria, Steinerbooks, 1959
Steiner, R.	*Results of Spiritual Investigation* (especially Lecture 4), Multimedia Publications 1973
Steiner, R.	*The Manifestations of Karma,* R. Steiner Press, London 1968
Steiner, R.	*The Philosophy of Freedom,* R. Steiner Press, London
Steiner, R.	*The Being of Man and his Future Evolution* Rudolf Steiner Press, London 1981

SOURCES OF INFORMATION

COLLEGES

Emerson College, Forest Row RH18 51X, Sussex, England
Waldorf Institute of Mercy College, 23399 Evergreen Rd, Southfield, Michigan 48075 U.S.A.
Rudolf Steiner College, 9200 Fair Oaks Blvd. Fair Oaks, California 95628 U.S.A.

BOOKCENTRES in different English Speaking Countries

Rudolf Steiner Press, 35 Park Road, London NW1 6XT, England
Anthroposophical Press Inc. 258 Hungry Hollow Road, Spring Valley, N.Y. 10977 U.S.A.
St. George Book Service, P.O. Box 225, Spring Valley, N.Y. 10977 U.S.A.
Steiner Book Center, 151 Carisbrooke Crescent, North Vancouver, B.C. Canada
Anthroposophical Books, C.P.O. Box 529 Auckland 1, New Zealand
Raphael Art Centre, 26 Rouwkoop Road, Rondebosch C.P. 7700 South Africa
Rudolf Steiner Bookshop, 722 Darling Street, Rozelle N.S.W. 20399 Australia

ANTHROPOSOPHICAL MEDICINES

Weleda (UK) Ltd, Heanor Road, Ilkeston, Derbyshire DE7 8DR, England
Weleda Inc. 30 South Main Street, Spring Valley N.Y. 10977 U.S.A.
Swiss Herbal Remedies, 181 Don Park Road, Markham, Ontario L3R 1C2 Canada
Weleda S.A. P.O. Box 494 Bergvlei Transvaal, South Africa
Weleda Austrlia 'The Natural Gourmet'. 366 Military Rd, Cremorne 2090, Australia
Weleda N. Zealand Ltd, P.O.Box 132, Havelock North, New Zealand

NATURAL MATERIALS

D.Hess, Wallstrasse 8, 6380 Bad Homburg, West Germany

BOOKS FROM HAWTHORN PRESS

"Who's Bringing Them Up?'—Television and Child Development by Martin Large
The startling fact that many children watch television more than they are in school prompts the question:-
— What effects does viewing **irrespective of programme content**, have on children's developing senses,
— social skills, language, play thought and imagination?
— How does television influence children's behaviour?
— How does the T.V. 'Pied Piper' exert its magic?
— What other activities are being sacrificed for the sake of viewing?
— How can the 'TV Habit' be broken?
Since publication in 1980, **'Who's Bringing Them Up?'** has been reviewed in over thirty publications,
including **'The Guardian'**, **'The Daily Telegraph'**, **'The New Internationlist',** **'The Friend',** **'The Observer'**,
'The Australian', **'The Rand Daily Mail'**, **'SHE'**, **'Here's Health'**, **'New Scientist'**—stimulating much
discussion.
"For anyone with children or interested in the effect of T.V. on the family, particularly now that breakfast
time programmes are due to appear, this book makes extremely interesting and helpful reading"
Family Bulletin (No.3 Winter 1980/81)
"As a drug, television is particularly useful in calming schizophrenic girls. What makes us so sure that it does
not act as a drug on normal children as well? Watching television is a passive, undemanding activity. In small
doses it cannot do any harm to the developing mind and personality. But in large doses it may deprive
children of the will and opportunity to play, deny them all but superficial communication with their
parents, neutralise their senses and leave them illiterate or at least lazy readers".
John Rae, reviewing **'Who's Bringing Them Up?'**, **Times Educational Supplement** 20.2.81

"A clear and accessible book for the concerned parent"
NEW INTERNATIONLIST,
Behind the Screen, Jan. 1983
"An interesting and a provocative Read"—THE GUARDIAN 2.12.1980

ORDERS

£3.95 P.B. ISBN 950706213 U.S.$7-95; $ 9-95 CN; $6-95 AUSTRALIA; $8-45 N.Z.
£5.95 H.B.   09507062 05

Can be obtained from **Hawthorn Press**, 1, Berkeley Villas, Lower Street, Stroud, Gloucestershire, U.K. Please
add £0.50 OR $1-00 for postage.

SOCIAL ECOLOGY

Exploring Post Industrial Society—Martin Large

Social Breakdown or Breakthrough?
As the existing 'social household' or 'social ecology' breaks down—the challenges of personal growth, group work organisational development and taking social initiatves emerge.

Social Ecology: Contents
Social Ecology describes an integral approach to individual, group, organisational and societal development. These originated with the N.P.I.—a Dutch consulting, training and research institute—through work in industry, education and government over the last 25 years.

The book includes sections on:-

* Working with the Process of Development
* Human Life Phases
* Group Work
* Organisational Development
* Societal Development
* Taking Social Initiatives
* Individual and Social Growth
* The Trebor Case

Who is 'Social Ecology' Written For?
It will be of use to those in management, counselling, group work, adult education, training, social development, as well as students studying people in organisations and those interested in social questions.

'Practical Optimism—
"The main strength of the book lies in the combination of a consistent and deeply founded concept of development with experienced—based practical approaches to creating social balances in the various spheres of life: for once we see ideas about individual, group, organisational and social development brought together in an organic way..."
Personnel Executive October 1981

'Recognising Social Ecology'

Social Ecology '........is well written in a readily accessible and lively style, with plenty of references to other contemporary thinkers. Newcomers to this area will find no trouble in getting into this book, and those more familiar with social questions, will find it stimulating and provocative. My guess is that (readers) will find some new insights that directly relate to their own experience.'

Daniel Jones, reviewing in The **Anthroposophical Review** Autumn 1981
The Developmental Perspective
'It throws up much that is likely to be of real interest to readers with a wide range of concerns, including: new horizons in management and organisation; the present state of anthroposophical thought; and, above all, the social initiatives which will open the way for a post-industrial society whose goal is human development.
James Robertson, **Resurgence** Nov/Dec 1981.

ORDERS

ISBN 09507062 21 162 pp £4.95 post free from Hawthorn Press in U.K; U.S.A.$7-95; CANADA$9-95; AUSTRALIA$9.-00; N.Z.$11.00 plus$1-00 post & packing

LIFEWAYS

LIFEWAYS : ORDERS
Copies of Lifeways may be ordered direct from Hawthorn Press if you have difficulty obtaining it from local bookshops.

Single Orders: £4.95 per copy plus £0.50 p&p (U.K.)
U.S.$9-95 per copy plu $ 1.00 p&p.
CANADA 11-95; $11-45 AUSTRALIA $ 12-95 N.Z; ($1.00 p&p).

PAYMENT
Sterling cheques preferred, to 'Hawthorn Press', but dollar cheques are acceptable if $1.00 bank service charge is included. Books can be sent to separate addresses.

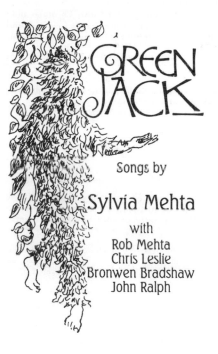

Songs by

Sylvia Mehta

with
Rob Mehta
Chris Leslie
Bronwen Bradshaw
John Ralph

SONGS BY SYLVIA MEHTA

Sylvia Mehta's latest cassette includes
The Fosterer as well as Green Jack . People of the Earth, Corridors of Time, December, Je me demande, Shooting Stars, Blue Whale, The River-Man, Make my Peace and five other songs.

She has sung for several years at the Festival for the Mind, Body & Spirit, at Conferences, at Schools and at Folk Clubs — touching many with her vivid and haunting songs. 'The Fosterer' alone is unforgettable.
(57 mins playing time/15 songs).

ORDERS: Cassette with accompanying notes:
£4.95/ post free from Hawthorn Press (U.K.)
US $9.95; CN $12-00; AUSTRALIA $11-00;
NZ $14.50 post free.
(Also available is the 'Rob amd Sylvia Mehta' cassette (1981) with Song Hunt, The Juggler, Arthur the King & Lament for the Trees—13 songs in all. Prices as above).

FESTIVAL, FAMILY & FOOD

Diana Carey & Judy Large

8" x 10": Full Colour Cover Paperback.

£5-95 U.K: U.S. $11.95 Overseas: 216 p.p.

1982. ISBN 0950 7062 3X

"Packed full of ideas on things to do, food to make, songs to sing and games to play, it's an invaluable resources book designed to help you and your family celebrate the various feast days scattered round the year."

The Observer 27 March 1983

"A lovely book, Festivals recalled for me many of the delights I remembered from childhood...The book, which I feel every young couple should read—gives a round-the-year evocation of all the traditional feasts and customs which used to play such a large part in filling the home with pleasure and fund.."

The Daily Mail 10 March 1983

"We always remember before we go to bed to put out a drink and mince pie for Father Christmas and a carrot or two for the Reindeer, and possibly some hay in the fireplace. In the morning the food and drink are gone, only the tops of the carrots are left." This charming disappearing act comes from Festivals, Family and Food.

Guardian Women 22 December 1982

A REAL FEAST
"This is the book I have been looking for....Festivals is a big book, beautifully illustrated and produced....
I don't think I have ever seen a book which deals with its subject so comprehensively."

Church of England Newspaper II March 1983

"An attractive book which will have year round usefulness"

Stroud News & Journal 16 December 1982

"A delightful book about celebrating the festivals of the year."

Festivals
This is a resource book for exploring the festivals—those 'feast days' scattered round the year which children love celebrating. It was written in response to children and busy parents asking, 'What can we do at Easter and Christmas? What games can we play? What can we make? How can we prepare for the festivals as centres of stability in our family life?'

Festivals, Family & Food is written with families, and especially children, very much in mind—for children can remind us of the wonders we might otherwise forget. The underlying theme is a simple but bold suggestion:-that if celebrating festivals was formerly the focus of community life, then rediscovered in the modern context, such seasonal activities may enrich family life.
Even though Christmas comes but once a year, there are at least eighteen other festivals to celebrate! Each festival, such as Candlemas,Whitsun or Midsummer, has its own chapter. There are songs to sing, games for fun, food to make, stories, poems and things to do with over 200 illustrations. The festivals are grouped into the four main seasons. There are also sections on Birthdays, Hungry Teatimes, Rainy Days. Convalescence, Extra Touches, a Birthday Calendar—and space for your own ideas. You will discover that once tried out, these festive suggestions will soon enter the family repertoire of activities. It is hoped Festivals, Family & Food will encourage a close relationship with the natural rhythms of the seasons—and will be enjoyed.

RATES FOR ORDERS

U.K: Single Orders: £5.95 per copy plus £1.00 p&p. U.S.$11-95 plus$1-00 p&p
Sterling cheques preferred, to *Hawthorn Press,* but dollar cheques are acceptable if a $1.00 bank service charge is included. Books can be sent to separate addresses as gifts. (Prices subject to revision over long term.)